1852932287

The Greening of Rural Policy

The Greening of Rural Policy
International perspectives

Edited by
SARAH HARPER

Belhaven Press
London and New York
Co-published in the Americas by Halsted Press,
an imprint of John Wiley & Sons, Inc.

Belhaven Press
(a division of Pinter Publishers)
25 Floral Street, Covent Garden, London, WC2E 9DS, United Kingdom

First published in 1993

Co-published in the Americas by Halsted Press, an imprint of John Wiley & Sons, Inc., 605 Third Avenue, New York, NY 10158-0012

British Library Cataloguing in Publication Data
A CIP catalogue record for this book is available from the British Library

ISBN 1 85293 228 7

Library of Congress Cataloging-in-Publication Data
A CIP catalog record for this book is available from the Library of Congress

ISBN 0 47021 931 9 (in the Americas only)

Typeset by Florencetype Ltd, Kewstoke, Avon
Printed and bound in Great Britain by
Biddles Ltd., Guildford and King's Lynn

Contents

List of figures

List of tables

The contributors

Neil Adger is a Senior Research Associate at the Centre for Social and Economic Research on the Global Environment (CSERGE), at the University of East Anglia.

Theresa Bristow is a member of the Geography Department, Royal Holloway, University of London.

Frederick Buttel is Professor of Rural Sociology, University of Wisconsin.

Paul Cloke is a Reader in Geography, University of Bristol.

Lori Cramer is an Assistant Professor, Department of Sociology, Utah State University.

Gärd Folkesdotter is a Research Fellow in the Urban and Regional Research Division of the National Swedish Institute for Building Research, Gavle.

Charles Geisler is an Associate Professor in the Department of Rural Sociology, Cornell University.

Mark Goodwin is a Lecturer in Geography at St David's University College, University of Wales.

Sarah Harper is a Lecturer in the Geography Department, Royal Holloway, University of London.

Harvey Jacobs holds Associate Professorships in the Department of Urban and Regional Planning, and at the Institute of Environmental Studies, University of Wisconsin.

Richard Krannich holds the position of Associate Professor in the Department of Sociology and Department of Forest Resources at Utah State University.

Gareth Lewis is a Senior Lecturer in the Department of Geography, University of Leicester.

Tom Lyson is an Associate Professor in the Department of Rural Sociology, Cornell University.

Olle Pettersson holds the position of Professor of Agricultural Sciences, at The Swedish University of Agricultural Sciences, Uppsala.

Ken Sherwood is a Senior Lecturer at Nene College, Northampton.

Louis Swanson is an Associate Professor in the Department of Sociology, University of Kentucky.

Martin Whitby is a Reader in Rural Resource Development, Department of Agricultural Economics, and the Director of the UK Economic and Social Research Council's Countryside Change Unit, both at the University of Newcastle upon Tyne.

PART I
Environmentalization and Greening

1

The greening of rural discourse

Sarah Harper

Introduction: the case of Hindhead Common

In June 1992 the Department of Transport announced that it was 'minded' to construct a section of the A3 London-Portsmouth dual carriageway through Hindhead Common, in south-west Surrey, the 'New Alternative Route'. The threatened site comprises 1,500 acres of National Trust Land[1] of which 72 acres would be taken for the road, and many more acres destroyed in its construction. It is a Site of Special Scientific Interest and an Area of Outstanding Natural Beauty under UK legislation, and a proposed Special Protection Area of the European Community under the Birds Directive. That they were minded to adopt this route has a complex history. However, the *public* reason presented by the government department during the consultation period was that the 'Previous Alternative Route' was 'of higher importance environmentally than had been previously thought' (DOT Public Consultation document, June 1992). In fact the 'Previous Alternative Route' took only one-third of an acre of ancient woodland, compared with the tens of acres of lowland heath destroyed by the 'New Alternative Route'.

The official stance of the Department of Transport, and the subsequent public reaction are of interest. The 'Previous Alternative Route' ran through a large urban area of several acres; however in the public exercise which announced the rejection of this route, the Department chose instead to highlight the *environmental* significance of a small area of woodland – which was inaccessible to the general public and of value for some rare mosses and lichens.

The public consultation occurred in the wake of the Rio Conference which had increased public awareness of the consequences of deafforestation. The one-third of an acre of ancient woodland (presented by the Department of Transport as one acre) caught the public imagination. It was widely felt immediately after the first public exhibition that the woodland must be protected. The 'New Alternative Route' threatened tens of acres of lowland heath of H2b status (category: very rare) recognized as an internationally endangered habitat, and protected under the 1984 Berne Convention. Yet in the initial public perception after the Department's exhibition of the two routes, it was seen as 'scrubland' and of little or no environmental value. We may be becoming 'green' but at what cost to our environment? Interestingly, one of the campaigning groups fighting against the adoption of the 'New Alternative Route' used the metaphor 'Lowland Heath is Britain's Rainforest'. It took several weeks of campaigning for local environmental groups to re-educate public perception.

A second process is also of interest, namely aspects of the response from informed local residents and conservationists. The 'New Alternative Route' ran through a local authority estate of some thirty houses adjacent to the Common, destroying a dozen homes and severely affecting the remainder. The residents of these houses joined with the middle class owner-occupiers who lived in the area, but not in the vicinity of the route, in forcefully opposing the route. Meetings and social gatherings took place which crossed the traditional income/class based relationships of the area, and cut across party-political lines. A sense of 'community' was achieved among those who had formerly barely spoken to each other. Members of the opposition groups admitted that they became 'green' in other aspects of their lives. Those who had occasionally used the Commons for recreation became avid walkers, bird watchers, and conservationists. In protecting the 'rural idyll', they had created, at least in their minds, the 'idyll of the community'.

The greening of western society

The case of Hindhead Common highlights many aspects of the following collection. The parallel examples of the Department of Transport's official output and the subsequent public reaction reflect the dual concepts of 'environmentalization' and 'greening', (after Buttel, Chapter 2). The following chapters thus address both the environmentalization of the institutions of rural policy, the public bodies and their servants, and also the 'greening' of rural policy – whereby the very social discourse within which society conceives and expresses itself has subtly become green. The terms in which western society perceives its world underwent substantial changes in the late 1980s. 'Traffic taming', 'traffic calming', 'environmentally-friendly', 'wilderness gardens', 'bottle-bank', 'recycling', 'biodegradeable', 'lead-free petrol', 'ozone-friendly', 'deafforestation': these phrases have entered common, daily English speech. The penetration of 'green' thought, language, action and ideas has led to the internalization of environmental symbols in many aspects of life. It is now politically and socially acceptable to be 'green', indeed almost unacceptable not to be seen to be so. Furthermore the state and its institutions of power are beginning to recognize this.

Several key themes are identifiable in the greening of late 20th-century western society: the place of the green movement within the recent emergence of 'new social movements'; the relationship between the greening of the public and the environmentalization of the state and its institutions; and the societal implications of the symbolic interweaving of mythology and environmental concerns in the late 20th-century quest for the 'idyll'.

THE GREEN MOVEMENT

It is argued by many (including contributors to this collection) that the green movement can only be understood in relation to the emergence of 'new social movements', which transcend former alliances of power and class (Scott, 1990). It is from this very eclectivity that such movements gain their power base: based on 'the public good' rather than on self-interested class ideals, their appeal is directly to concepts of human justice. In relation to rural policy, the green movement can be seen nationally to define public consensus, and locally to unite locality based members around a common theme.

The green movement, along with other such new social movements, thus threatens the legitimacy of capitalist, paternalist society by cross-cutting the social divisions which allow these institutional forms to exist. It questions the accepted frameworks established by these institutions, presented as unquestionable, indeed beyond question, by these ideological forms. In other words, it redefines the framework within which traditional social, political and economic allegiances have been bred, and by displaying the vulnerability of economic capitalism in its many variants, opens these to attack. These movements thus reject the epistemological frameworks from whence emerged late 20th-century social forms, revealing the possibility of new cultural and social alliances which emerge outside the direct expression of economic phenomena. They are beyond economic/capitalist structures, both in coherency, alliance and content. Indeed, it is this lack of economic coherence that may eventually be their downfall. It should, however, be noted that some (including contributors to this collection) would argue that the green movement, while providing the external structure for a non-economic movement, is riddled with economic interests. Clearly the requirement to interface with other political and economic bodies questions the post-materialist stance of the green movement at the institutional level.

THE GREENING OF THE PUBLIC AND THE ENVIRONMENTALIZATION OF
THE STATE

Like other ideologies, environmentalism is socially-constructed, but it is an especially indeterminate, malleable ideological form (Buttel, 1991:19).

This relationship attracts analysis from many of the contributors to the collection, forming an underlying theme to the remaining chapters in Part One. Sufficient, then, to highlight here the multi-facets of the green movement, and the consequent potential for manipulating and emphasising those elements which are likely to produce appropriate political support at particular times and places.

THE QUEST FOR THE IDYLL

Cultural analysts of the greening of society cannot ignore the role of mythology in defining and sustaining images of, and subsequent reflexive behaviour towards, the 'rural'. We all seek the idyll. Yet late 20th-century westernism provides a tension in this quest. Modern media transmission of information has led to an insatiable quest for knowledge, experience, stimulation – quite incompatible with the simplistic holism of the idyll.

The myth of the idyll is complex and beyond full discussion here. Existing at many levels and in many forms, the green movement particularly impacts upon the powerful symbolic messages of 'the rural' and 'the community'. Fundamental to the former is the agrarian myth, in which agriculture is seen as natural, of the earth and thus in sympathetic co-existence with the earth, and as such without environmental implications. The symbol is further empowered through the addition of the myth of community. Here it is represented by the family farm – a body of like-minded people working in harmony with their environment; benevolent and guileless, the antithesis of the scientific conglomerate. The symbolic narrative is concluded by the nostalgic reconstruction of the rural community – based inevitably on the family farm in sympathetic harmony with the earth . . .

The implications for the green movement as a cultural force are at least two-fold. In pragmatic terms there is little public perception of agriculture as both a polluter and an environmental hazard, exploiting and destroying the environment in its attempt to respond to the demands of urban modern life – which it sustains. Many who are environmentally concerned about the urban/industrial destruction and contamination of the environment often appear oblivious to the potential for pollution of modern farming practices.

On a different level, those in search of nature and who in some sense reject modernity and its urban child, turn to the green movement in an attempt to sustain and recreate the idyll. As Berman has written:

> contradictory forces and needs . . . inspire and torment us: our desire to be rooted in a stable and coherent personal and social past, and our desire for growth – not merely for economic growth but for growth in experience, in pleasure, in knowledge, in sensibility – growth that destroys both the physical and social landscapes of our past, and our emotional links with those lost worlds (Berman, 1982:35).

This then is the tension that at one level sustains the green movement: our desire for the idyll of our other places, our other times contradicts with our need to translate this into new thought, new stimulation, new experience. The recognition that in attaining the latter, we destroy that which we need to transport us into the idyllic time we seek, has led to a belief in active conservation, preservation, communal action against the urban destroyer. In the very preservation of the idyll, we create a new form of idyll. We become green in our thoughts, images and action, and thus reflect through our behaviour the very times and places, the social forms that we are seeking to preserve. The tension is temporarily satisfied.

In saving the Common we protect the *rural idyll*; we create warm communal structures that support our cause, that cut across our normal class-based social relationships, the *idyll of the community*. In preserving the past, we behave as a community of the past. We are green – we have been 'greened'.

The collection

As Buttel (Chapter 2) states, while it is now widely acknowledged that environmentalization is one of the most important contemporary social forces, it is generally regarded in terms of environmental problems *per se*, to the neglect of the consideration of the social antecedents and likely consequences of the movement itself. It is aspects of these latter considerations that this collection addresses in relation to the internalization of environmental symbols, concepts and beliefs and their, sometimes subconscious, reproduction in rural policy. Many of the chapters overtly discuss issues of greening and environmentalization, but an almost equal number have taken on board themes of the movement and present these in an implicit manner. Yet while these contributors may not overtly discuss environmental issues, it is evident throughout that the paradigms within which they operate are 'green'.

Summary of Chapters

Part I directly addresses environmentalization and greening, introducing terms, concepts, antecedents and implications. Nowhere is this more apparent than in Chapter 2. Here Buttel discusses the rise of the environmental movement, through an analysis of the reciprocal relationship between the ideological force itself and the changing twentieth century social structures within which such ideology is located. Drawing on the theoretical discourse surrounding new social movements, Buttel highlights the distinction between the culturalist/expressive dimension of NSM, reflected in the concept of greening, and the instrumentalist aspect, as seen in environmentalization. Taking ecology to be the master NSM issue, he argues that as environmentalism is an intrinsically indeterminate ideological form it has no natural constituency. Indeed opposition to environmentalism on grounds of threatened material interests is actually easier to explain than environmental advocacy. It is thus transient in nature, with several varied forms. The chapter concludes by examining three emergent problems arising from the eclectic formation of the ecology movement: its relation to issues of social justice, its contribution to the scientization of social movements, and its vulnerability to superficiality and trivialization.

The expressive/instrumentalist – greening/environmentalization dichotomy is further explored by Cloke and Goodwin in Chapter 3, within the framework of regulation theory. Using Harvey's (1985) notion of structured coherence they present the configuration of the mode of regulation and societalization (the process of regulation at societal level) as an 'ensemble of multifaceted relations and institutions, which are applicable at particular places and at particular times'. These are then discussed in relation to the role of the state in the emergence of new rural coherences, and the environmentalization of rural politics.

The themes from these two chapters are then applied in a case study of environmental awareness by Bristow (Chapter 4). Discussing the contemporary rise of environmentalism, she examines the greening of British social discourse, in the context of the growing environmentalization of British (and American) political institutions, and their reciprocal relationship as mediated by the media.

In Part II the analysis turns to the application of environmentalism to aspects of land use and agricultural policy. An overview of UK land use in relation to the global commons (Chapter 5), is followed by discussion of particular issues: the negotiation between economic, political and environmental factions in the recent development of Scandinavian agriculture (Chapter 6); agroenvironmentalism and US soil conservation policy (Chapter 7); and environmental debut of agricultural biotechnology in the US (Chapter 8).

The theme throughout this section is the internalization of environmentally related symbols into the debate, both in actuality and in expert discourse. As Whitby and Adger state in Chapter 5, the past two decades have seen a broadening of the land use debate, encouraging the inclusion of environmental agendas. Highlighting the impact both of global warming on agricultural production and conversely of variable land use on the emission of greenhouse gases, they examine the environmental implications of the conversion of agricultural land to forestry under the British Farm Woodlands Scheme, part of the Alternative Land Use and Rural Enterprise Package. Arguing for the inclusion of *environmental costs and benefits* in any aggregate assessment, they stress that the environment is a stock of natural capital, which like societal capital can be added to or depleted by economic activity. Only when environmental externalities, such as nitrate pollution and carbon dioxide emissions, are added into the equation, can policy makers be presented with the true aggregates of land use policy.

This analysis of the potential environmental pollution through the creation of large tracts of re-afforested land is complemented by Pettersson's analysis of Scandinavian agricultural practices. As he states, environmental impact is an unavoidable secondary effect of cultivation. Examining the *paradise myth* in which agriculture is perceived to be in natural harmony with nature and without environmental implications, Pettersson explores the implications of the displacement of the natural ecosystem, based on survival and competition, with an agricultural system based on regulated specialization and the provision of surplus.

The following chapters examine environmental issues in relation to particular farming practices. Discussing the recent changes in US public policy towards agroenvironmental issues, Swanson (Chapter 7) highlights the tension between the cultural and environmental imperative embedded in public perceptions of the American family farm. The American agrarian myth, he argues, assumed both a unity between conservation practices and family farming, and the dominance of such farms within the US farm structure. Assessing the greening of agroenvironmental policy, in relation to soil conservation, Swanson highlights the role of the farm financial crisis in the early 1980s in pushing agroenvironmental issues to the fore, and tarnishing the agrarian myth.

The discussion is extended by Geisler and Lyson (Chapter 8) with reference to the introduction of agro-biotechnology. Examining the range of social and environmental effects likely to accrue if bovine growth hormone (bGH) is commercialized in the US they contrast the two major systems of dairy production – small scale heterogeneous family-farms and large-scale, highly specialized industrialized dairy factories. Mass adoption of bGH will, they argue, lead to the increasing dominance of the latter over the former with widespread environmental implications from spatial over-specialization to increased pollution of ground and surface water, and methane emission.

Taken together these two chapters highlight the inherent tension between environmental protection and scales of production within the American farming system. As indicated earlier, the mythology enveloping small craft-based farmers publicly absolves them from conservation practices. Large, corporate agribusinesses are required to follow rigid environmental procedures, although ultimately those defined by the state.

In Part III the discussion turns to settlement and society. All three countries under consideration are facing changes in their population structure. While the USA sees a return to the former 20th-century pattern of rural depopulation, both the UK and Sweden are still experiencing population drifts into rural areas, though different in type and degree. In particular all three countries face pressure on the rural-urban fringe.

The section is introduced through an analysis of the changing nature of US settlement planning (Chapter 9). Case study work on the emergence of boom towns as a result of energy development in the American West (Chapter 10), the planned development of local rural housing in Britain (Chapter 11) and the growth of rural settlement in central Sweden (Chapter 12) all strongly illustrate the growing importance of environmental considerations in the development and evaluation of new settlement.

Reflecting the rise of new social movements highlighted by Buttel, and the new rural consensus of Cloke and Goodwin, Jacobs discusses the impact of the *populist citizen movement*. Linking with the environmental movement, the populist citizen movement has highlighted the failure of private property ownership to serve the public interest and now demands the redefinition of US property rights. Under this banner agricultural land is perceived not as a *private* but a *public* resource, with implications for environmental space and equity. Drawing on the citizen movement for growth management in Lancaster County, settled by the Amish community, Jacobs argues that future US policy will need to perceive settlement planning as a process of generating alternatives, whereby the costs and benefits of the economic, environmental and social impacts of alternative land schemes are presented for informed public discourse.

The impact of rapid population growth in remote rural communities of the American West forms the focus of Krannich and Cramer's analysis. As a result of large-scale energy resource developments in this area, some small rural communities experienced a two- or even three-fold increase in their population in a matter of two or three years. Along with the environmental consequences of such rapid growth sit various social consequences. Owing to the failure to implement advance planning programmes to absorb the increased demands on housing, public services and local infrastructure, many of these early 'boom towns' experienced severe social disruption. Drawing on two case studies, Evanston, Wyoming, and Delta, Utah, Krannich and Cramer illustrate how recent developments have been successfully integrated into existing communities through the use of impact mitigation programmes. Development of sound infrastructure and housing in line with the population growth enabled Delta, for example, to remain both environmentally and socially similar to 'the predominantly Mormon agricultural village that had persisted for most of the twentieth century', despite a tripling of the population between 1980 and 1984.

Slower, but equally potentially disruptive, population growth is highlighted by Sherwood and Lewis in their examination of the recent planning of rural settlements in the UK. Drawing on a case study of Northamptonshire, they highlight that environmental considerations are now firmly on the agenda along with social, economic and political constraints. In addition, they too perceive the growing importance of local public consensus as the basis for formulating policies targeted on a demonstrable need.

The final contribution to the collection, an examination of the settlement of central Sweden by Folkesdotter, also highlights the influence of environmental concerns both in current policy-making and in individual decisions behind the increasing move to rural zones. However, she concludes that despite the greening of the Swedish people and their institutions, a range of social, economic and political factors are combining to threaten this greening of Swedish rural policy.

Conclusion

The debate over Hindhead Common continues. Environmental groups are currently (August 1992) introducing the scheme of an 'on-line' improvement to the existing road, rather than a new road *per se*. Given the complex physical terrain through which the existing A3 traverses (the geomorphological sap-spring hollow of the Devil's Punch Bowl), this would require considerable 'traffic taming' in order to attain safety standards, including a speed limit of 40 or 50 mph (70–80 kph). This would cause considerable traffic flow restriction in an otherwise almost exclusively 70 mph (120 kph) road from London to Portsmouth.

There is, however, growing recognition that the agenda which was set in the 1970s for fast, 70-mph roads does not necessarily lie comfortably with the new environmental climate of the 1990s. Proposals put forward by Hindhead Common protection groups to the Department of Transport argue for Britain's first 'environmentally-safe-road' – a road lined with Department of Transport signs informing drivers that they are required to slow down owing to the extreme environmental importance of the area they are crossing.

This has strong support from local and national environmental groups, local residents (and thus road users) are moving behind it. It is unclear whether the Department of Transport will be persuaded that the time is right for a fundamental review of road schemes, or that the public is now sufficiently green that they will accept such restrictions. If they are, then Hindhead Common will set a new agenda for the environmentalization of road construction of the 21st century, and will publicly display the greening of the British people.

Notes and references

1. The National Trust for Places of Historic Interest or Natural Beauty is an independent charitable organization funded primarily by public subscription which looks after countryside and buildings in England, Wales and Northern Ireland.

Berman, M. (1982) *All That is Solid Melts into Air*, Simon and Schuster, NY.

Buttel, F. (1991) Presidential Address to the AGM of the Rural Sociological Society, Columbus, Ohio, August 1991.

Harvey, D. (1985) *The Urbanisation of Capital*, Blackwell, Oxford.

Scott, A. (1990) *Ideology and New Social Movements*, Unwin Hyman, London.

2

Environmentalization and greening: origins, processes and implications*

Frederick Buttel

Introduction

It is apparent to most sociologists that environmentalization – or 'greening', as it is often called – is one of the most important social forces of our time. But most social scientists tend to take greening to be a mostly *sui generis* phenomenon, deriving more or less from the growing recognition of the severity of local, regional and international environmental problems and the need to address them. In other words, we tend to take greening as being an exogenous force or factor and to give little attention to the social antecedents and likely consequences of the modern phase of environmentalization in which we currently find ourselves.

While the notions of greening and environmentalization are very closely related, leading me at times to use them more or less synonymously, they are not, strictly speaking, identical. By greening, I mean the process by which modern environmentally-related symbols have become increasingly prominent in social discourse. By environmentalization, I mean the greening of institutions and institutional practices – or, in other words, the trend towards environmental considerations being increasingly brought to bear in political and economic decisions, in educational and scientific research institutions, in geopolitics, and so on.

In this chapter I take the phenomena of greening and environmentalization and set forth some observations on their origins and implications. I will consider greening and environmentalization in the context of theory on 'new social movements' (NSMs). One prominent strand of NSM theorizing stresses their 'culturalist' or 'expressive' (meaning, self-identification) dimension, while other perspectives on NSMs see them in an instrumental way (i.e., as neo-parties or pressure groups seeking to influence public policy and institutional practices). My distinction between greening and environmentalization thus parallels, respectively, the culturalist and instru-

Adapted from the Presidential address delivered to the annual meeting of the Rural Sociological Society, Columbus, Ohio, 18 August 1991. A fuller version of this speech is published in *Rural Sociology* 1992.

mental themes of the NSM literature to some extent. I will utilize a number of rural-related examples – mainly agricultural sustainability in the West, and the environmental symbolization of rural spaces. I will develop two basic arguments. The first is that while greening is, in substantial measure, an ideological or symbolic phenomenon and a response to environmental destruction (or more specifically to the institutionalized rationalities and the practices of centralized bureaucracies of state and economy that lead to technological, health and environmental risks), the rise of green must be located in the larger currents of social change in the late twentieth century. We must not reduce greening to these social changes, or see greening as being a mere epiphenomenon of large-scale social structural change. Instead, we must take into account the reciprocal interactions between this ideological force and the social structures within which it is located. Second, growing out of this social structural assessment of greening, I will attempt to show how and why greening's parallel process – the environmentalization of our institutions – has both promise and limitations for achieving this and other goals.

Greening and twentieth-century structural change

From social democracy to neo-conservatism

Despite the many differences among the classical sociological theorists, we can note that they were in agreement on one fundamental premise: the nature of modern market societies – given their extensive divisions of labour and growing technological complexity, along with the anarchic tendencies of full blown market forces – is such that the notion of a self-regulating market system is a social and practical nonsense. Thus, we find that Marx's theoretical system stressed the notion of superstructure – that is, the state, law, ideology, and so on – as essential to the reproduction of the capitalist mode of production. Durkheim's core concepts, such as organic solidarity, moral individualism, and the state as a guarantor of moral individualism and as an agent of collective reaffirmation, were integral to his critique of utilitarianism and to his notion of economic life as a regulated moral order. Weber essentially theorized capitalism in terms of its ethos (the spirit of capitalism), the social origins of its characteristic forms of rationality (instrumental rationality, rational capital accounting), and the nature of the modern state (legal-rational domination).

In sum, there is a long tradition within Western sociological thought of conceptualizing matters of modern economy and society in terms of their relationship being one of *regulation* of the latter by the former. The mid-century sociological tradition that followed was to identify what were thought to be a number of 'natural' – and thus presumably irreversible – institutional forms that were said to accompany the transition to mature market economies and democratic polities. These institutions included new forms of social organization (e.g. trade unions, collective bargaining, intermediary or occupational groups), new state structures (the 'regulatory state,' modern political parties, corporatism, the welfare state), and new cultural forms (the elaboration of a civic culture in which attenuating the effects of the market was seen to be a proper role of the state). This ensemble of an advanced division of labour, a mature market economy, and institutions of social regulation of economic life was itself taken to be a logical, developmentally-immanent trajectory of large-scale social change.

In the early 1990s, however, neither social life nor social theory bears much resemblance to those of the mid-century. The massive, and largely unanticipated, changes in the social structures of the advanced countries since the late 1960s have led many sociologists to recognize that many of these forms of social regulation of the economy have not continued their inexorable elaboration. Accordingly, the major shift in social theory since the mid-century has been the growing recognition that the institutions of the post-war West must be understood more in terms of discontinuity, divergence and contingency than of continuity, convergence, and 'evolution'. Trade unions and their influence in industrial relations and national politics have declined, the welfare state and the 'social wage' are being selectively rolled back, economic inequality is increasing, political parties have declined relative to special interest groups and social movements, corporations and market transactions have become increasingly transnational in scope (and thus less amenable to nationally-ordered regulation), and political cultures have shifted from an emphasis on mitigating the impacts of private accumulation to ensuring the sanctity of entrepreneurship. There has, in sum, been a shift towards neo-conservative regimes that feed from and bolster the new civic culture in most of the Western world.

Coincident with these structural changes has been a marked shift in the economic performance of the advanced industrial economies. Their rates of growth are far slower and more unstable than those of the heyday of modern industrial civilization in the post-World War II period. For the bulk of their labour forces – that is, for the majority that works in non-supervisory occupations – hourly earnings have declined in real terms. Large cities, which were integral to post-war growth as combined sites of worker residence and industrial production, have become increasingly crisis-ridden and ghettoized, as capital has shifted to the suburbs and low-wage non-metro zones in the advanced countries or the Third World, and as municipal fiscal crises have ensued (Gottdiener and Komninos, 1989). Whereas post-war accumulation was based on the linkage between rising real wages and the growth of mass consumption industries, accumulation since the early 1970s now appears to be based on a rather different kind of linkage: between growth in middle-class incomes, on one hand, and the growing role of 'flexible' industrial production of goods to targeted affluent sections of the consuming population, on the other.

Further, there has been a substantial shift in international patterns of industrial, monetary and financial hegemony. Whereas the post-World War II period was defined in substantial measure by American industrial and geopolitical dominance, the American role in regulating global society through the international monetary order, world trade and foreign aid has slowly but surely declined. The growing multipolarity of the global economy is reflected most ominously in the international monetary sphere, in which the US, which once dominated and regulated international payments systems, is still dominant but can no longer regulate (Bellon and Niosi, 1988:206).

These transitions have led to many attempts to theorize their origins and significance. These include, most prominently, various strands of so-called French regulation theory, in which the concepts of Fordism and post-Fordism were originally elaborated (Aglietta, 1979; Lipietz, 1987), the resurrection of long-wave theory à la Kondratieff and Wallerstein (Gordon et al., 1982; Wallerstein, 1984), international relations and international political economy theories of the rise and decline of global hegemonic stability (Gilpin, 1987; Keohane, 1984), theories of the new international division of labour (Frobel et al., 1979), and theories of modernity and post-modernity (Turner, 1990). Instead of evaluating each of these theories, I will want to draw on their overall insights and present a composite view of the transitions of the past two decades and their relevance to greening and environmentalization. Most of the important features of these transitions are summarized in Table 2.1, adapted from Roobeek (1987). This should be interpreted with caution in several respects. Not only are the structural features of post-Fordism or neo-conservatism unclear at this point, but it is very likely that there will be as much, if not more, institutional diversity among the advanced countries in the new regulatory regimes than was the case during the Fordist or social-democratic phase. Thus, it should be recognized that the social-democratic era witnessed considerable variation in several respects – for example, in 'welfare-state development' (Esping-Andersen and Korpi, 1984) and in incidence of corporatist vs. 'pluralist' state forms (Goldthorpe, 1984).

In the necessarily highly schematic treatment that follows I will rely particularly heavily on Lash and Urry (1987), since their work, on the transition from what they call 'organized' to 'disorganized' capitalism, draws together more elements of the story that needs to be told about greening than any other treatment. I will use the expression 'social-democratic,' in a general way, to pertain to a cluster of institutions through which subordinate classes tangibly affected and benefited from changes in industrial relations and politics in the roughly three decades following World War II, and the expression 'neo-conservativism,' to pertain to the transitions since that time.

First, not only did most post-War (macro) social theories implicitly view institutions such as the welfare state and collective bargaining as logical concomitants of the transition to a mature market economy and an advanced division of labour, but they essentially took national societies as their unit of

Table 2.1 Differences between Fordism (social-democratic society) and post-Fordism (neo-conservative society)

Characteristics	Fordism	Post-Fordism
Core technology	Electronics, chemicals, plastics, petroleum, car industry	Microelectronics, biotechnology, new materials
Production concept	International mass production	CIM (Computer integrated manufacturing); 'Hollow factory'; hyperindustrialization
Consumption pattern	Mass consumption	Highly-differentiated consumer styles
Market	World market	'Triad' markets (N. America, EEC, Pacific Rim)
Employment	Full employment; homogenous mass workers	Job-losing growth; structural unemployment; individual decentralized workers
Labour relations	Mass trade unions; collective bargaining	Company and individual agreements; basic income
Government policies	Keynesian socioeconomic policies; welfare state; social democracy	Deregulation; state intervention in technology policy; self-servicing society; neo-conservatism

Source: After Roobeek (1987:150).

analysis and tended to see social change as immanent within national social structures. We must now recognize, however, that to account theoretically for twentieth-century social change we will need to resort to social theories that are more situational or contextual in their logic, more encompassing or global in the concepts they bring to bear, and more historical in their methods (see e.g., McMichael, 1990).

Second, and related to the first, we can now see in retrospect that the core institutions of social-democratic society began to undergo a decline due to their internal dynamics and on account of historically-contingent factors. For example, the very logic of social-democratic industrial relations – the corporate/trade union bargain of wage increases in tandem with productivity increase, which along with low unemployment levels and the social wage guarantee in effect put a floor under wages – led to rapid automation and eventually to more active corporate efforts to resist unionization. Ultimately, the industrial working class declined in both its share of the labour force and in its political potency. The decline of the industrial working class – from about 50 per cent in Belgium (Przeworski, 1985:23) and several other countries in the late 1940s and early 1950s (Singelmann, 1978) to less than 20 per cent today in most OECD countries – in turn led to erosion of the strength of social-democratic parties, and thus in general to a decline in party politics and its analogues such as corporatism. As a consequence of the fiscal demands of the welfare-warfare state and of social Keynesianism as economic policy, state fiscal commitments eventually came to be well in excess of the ability of the American government to satisfy through taxation. There was, in other words, a tendency to endemic and deepening fiscal crisis (as O'Connor, 1973, predicted well before its onset).

Situational factors played a parallel role. For example, the severe balance of payments problems experienced by the US as a result of the Vietnam War and the 1973–74 Arab Oil Embargo led the US state to undertake controlled currency devaluations and promote foreign direct investment in order to solve these problems (Block, 1977). Gilpin (1975) noted early on that state promotion of direct foreign investment involves 'exporting or trading away its comparative advantages (technological, technical know-how, and management) and potential productivity gains in exchange for future foreign exchange earnings. . . . The United States . . . is converting itself into the type of *rentier economy*, that is, one which lives off investment income, that Great Britain became in the latter part of the 19th century' (1975:198). As Foster (1989:105) would note nearly a decade and a half later, 'In short, the US economy was following a path of hegemonic decline analagous to the one that Britain had proceeded down in the final decades of the 19th and the opening decades of the 20th centuries.' Owing in part to declining fiscal capacity, to the transnational expansion of industrial capital during the social-democratic period, and to the liberalization of world trade achieved through American influence in the 1960s and especially the 1970s, states have decreased ability to regulate capital. In particular, states have far less leverage in extracting tax revenues from private firms, given slow growth, profit squeezes, and the declining barriers to the mobility of industrial and especially financial capital. Private profit squeezes, the decline of working class power, and the growing opportunities of (and imperative for) capital mobility have combined to undermine the welfare state, the social wage, and ultimately the real wages of non-supervisory workers. Social-democratic industrialization contributed to severe environmental problems and to movements against many of the industries and production processes that lay at the heart of the post-War economy.

Most observers of the demise of what I call social-democratic society remain tentative, and some even bewildered, about the ultimate path that post-industrialism or post-modernity will take. I believe there are historical precedents for guessing that neo-conservatism will be a cornerstone of the types of social structures that will emerge in the future. The economic slowdown of the 1920s and the Great Depression of the 1930s ushered in most of the components of what I have referred to earlier as social-democratic society. The same process with respect to neo-conservatism may very well be occurring during the long slump, which began at about the time of the 1973–74 Arab Oil Embargo and continues today.

Neo-conservative society may prove to have two defining features. Structurally, it will have a highly differentiated or pluralistic class structure, consisting of the remnants of the post-War class structure – the industrial working class and the white-collar managerial strata – plus the 'new service class,' informal sector workers, and the urban and rural underclasses in which racial and ethnic minorities are over-represented. The differentiation of these subordinate class groupings will militate against their being a singular force, as was the case with the trade union/social-democratic party linkage after World War II. Ideologically, neo-conservatism acquires its name from an emerging consensus that the proper role of the state is not to mitigate market forces, but rather to augment them.

The rise of new social movements

From the late 1960s, American sociologists increasingly began to understand modern social movements from a 'resource mobilization' perspective (McCarthy and Zald, 1973). Shortly thereafter the European literature on social movements would depart substantially from that of North America as European scholars came to stress the notion of 'new social movements' (NSMs) (Touraine, 1971; Castells, 1978; Offe, 1985a, b). Since that time, American scholarship has begun to shift to the European position, having found resource mobilization theory inadequate for the 'expressive' side of social movement mobilization.

While there are a good many rival definitions of and perspectives on NSMs (Scott, 1990; Kriese, 1989), most scholars have defined these movements in terms of a rejection of the institutional practices of the modern state and economy. Most agree that their main bases of support are professionals, social and cultural service workers, and public service and administrative employees, and more generally among young, well-educated persons who are employed outside of corporate milieus.

Most observers take the environmental, anti-nuclear, peace and feminist movements to be the core of the NSM ensemble. On one hand, each movement has an 'expressive dimension', involving motivations such as the quest for 'identity', 'meaning' and 'autonomy from statist technocracy'. On the other, NSMs emerged and/or blossomed during the period when the transition from social-democratic to neo-conservative society was underway. Some treatments of NSMs draw a clear connection between the rise of these movements and the decline of social-democratic society. Scott (1990:25), for example, has noted that

> the politically integrative function of the new social movements suggests that their development can be seen, in part at least, in more conventionally political terms, namely, as a consequence of the failure of social democratic parties to undergo a

process of political renewal. Particularly within the European ecology movements the criticism is often made that social democratic parties have either stuck too closely to the major historical interest they represent, or they have adopted 'statist' strategies through which they hope to win wider appeal as effective managers of the Welfare State and mixed economy (for example, in West Germany).

Many NSM theorists stress that the distinctiveness or significance of these movements lies in their being 'expressive', identity-oriented, anti-technocratic, autonomy-seeking, post-materialist, and decentralist in their thrust. Others argue their significance lies in their being a potent force of political opposition to neo-conservative regimes, apart from and often in overt opposition to existing left or working-class parties. My own view, similar to that expressed by Scott (1990) is that both components are essential in understanding what is new and social about NSMs: these movements are alternative modes of expression and political mobilization to trade unions and labour and working class parties of social-democratic society.

There has thus been an upwelling of NSMs to fill the void of social-democratic party decline. These movements take many forms, including the local, 'expressive' groups and, more importantly in my view, groups, typi-fied by the modern *environmental movement*, for which achieving particular policy goals are their *raison d'être*. Their influence is being felt not only in the advanced countries, but increasingly in geopolitics and the Third World as well. There has emerged an increasingly dense network of non-governmental organizations (NGOs) that now contests almost all issues of international relations: GATT, the World Bank, international development policy, international environmental treaties. Some have even suggested that NGOs are assuming a level of power and influence that was previously thought to be possible only for states and large multinational firms. NGOs are able to do so through their mobilizational capacity, and through filling the vacuum created by the lost-legitimacy of national states and the inter-national regimes they have fostered.

Some general implications of new social movements and greening

Given the apparent significance of NSMs, one of the major issues is whether these movements are destined to be the historical bearer of transformative social forces equivalent to that of the working class during the first two-thirds or so of the twentieth century. Such a claim involves several major arguments: first, industrial workers' organizations and traditional social democratic parties are structurally and ideologically incapable of being a significant transformative force, creating a political vacuum; second, the size of the 'new class' is destined to increase even further as the modern post-industrial division of labour proceeds; and third, neo-conservative policies will inevitably generate intense opposition among the growing 'new class'. Furthermore, the support base of NSMs is articulate, politically-skilled, and able to exercise influence disproportionate to its numbers, and NSMs are structurally flexible and can take a variety of forms depending upon the context. In some places, for example Germany and possibly several of the Nordic countries, NSM and ecology mobilization has been focused around Green Parties. Elsewhere, particularly in the US and other countries with plurality voting systems in which viable third parties are essentially precluded, NSMs and ecology take the form of multiple, overlapping local grassroots organizations, lobbying groups, think tanks and NGOs.

There are both strengths and weaknesses in the emerging NSM mode of political mobilization. On one hand, I suspect that NSMs will become a predominant, and perhaps the most broad-based, mode of opposition to neo-conservatism. Furthermore, NSM claims will have the advantage of being based on 'public interest' arguments, rather than on only material self-interest, potentially enhancing their legitimacy. On the other, I suspect there are likely to be major limits to the political potency of the new class and NSMs. In so far as this class is based heavily in public and other non-corporate employment, fiscal crisis will limit public payrolls and the size of the new class. Also, in so far as neo-conservatism is likely to engender even more income inequality, NSM issues will likely not attract much interest from the growing ranks of the urban underclass, the rural poor and the working poor. NSM concerns, when expressed in the political arena, essentially involve either pursuing public goods (e.g., environmental integrity) or consumptionist goals (reducing health risks by limiting nuclear power or nuclear weaponry); in other words, these concerns are not buttressed by the encompassing material interests of the type that were integral to labour movement mobilization during the social-democratic epoch. The expansion of NSM concerns will likely impel further fragmentation of political parties, which have historically been the most efficacious form of interest aggregation in parliamentary democracies. Finally, each of the NSM issues can, at least in principle, be resolved in a way that is moderately reformist at best, and quite consistent with neo-conservatism at worst. In other words, NSM issues have potential for state and corporate elites to take a particular NSM issue as their own and to embrace it in a superficial way. Some NSM positions will even be embraced by parties of the right – for example the endorsement by all six of the seven neo-conservative G7 governments, save for the US, of the creation of an international treaty to address global warming at their July 1991 meeting.

Environmentalism as a collective action problem

There is a growing sense that the political centre of gravity of NSMs will likely lie, if it does not already, in its green or ecology component. Oloffson (1988:15), for example, has argued that 'the most likely centre for a possible coalescence of a multitude of NSMs into a major social movement, if not in the class formative sense, is the societally-basic relationship, nature-society.' I am inclined to agree, and for the remainder of this chapter I will take ecology to be the master NSM issue.

It is useful to begin an analysis of modern greening by recognizing that environmentalism, involves a more complex collective action puzzle than is often realized. While some environmental issues may be directly or indirectly construed in ways such that immediate material interests are involved and in which particular social categories are obvious proponents of a particular environmental initiative, most environmental issues are of a quite different character. Environmentalism is intrinsically indeterminate as an ideological form because, unlike most 'old' or even 'new' social movements, such as the women's movement, the civil rights movement, it has no 'natural constituency' or 'bearers.' *Opposition* to environmentalism, on grounds of threatened material interests or aversion to state intervention, is actually easier to explain than environmental advocacy. For most environmental issues, those who act to protect or 'save' the environment can expect to receive no personal material benefits. There are, of course, exceptions, such as the 'no-growth' politics of suburban communities that will tend to bolster property values (Logan and Molotch, 1986) or mobilizations against toxic wastes based on immediate health concerns. A high-quality environment tends to be a public good, which when achieved cannot be denied to others, even to those who resist environmental reforms. Because of the situational and transitory nature of environmental mobilization, environmentalism can and does take many forms: 'environmentalisms' of left, right and centre. These will tend to be constituted, respectively, as a critique of industrial capitalism, as a squeeze on consumption levels to facilitate accumulation, and as a managerialist or lifestyle politics (Buttel and Larson, 1980). NSM environmentalism has a general tendency to be a centre-left hybrid, albeit with considerable variation by country (for example the relatively left version as represented by the European Green Parties, and the more centrist version in the US).

There have been several predominant tendencies in environmental ideology formation since the decline of social-democratic society began. The first is the tendency to 'package' the need for implementing a lengthy agenda of environmental goals within a comprehensive, compelling framework. The second is to accede to the well-institutionalized instrumental-scientific rationality of the modern world (see, for example, Aronowitz, 1988: Chapter 1; Offe, 1985a) by transforming scientific concepts into value or ethical claims – or, in other words, into ideology – which are in turn legitimated by the authority of science. The third is to invoke alarmism in order to dramatize the fact of the environment as an imperative public good. These tendencies are revealed in three of the major recent phases of twentieth century environmentalism: the 'population bombism' of Paul Ehrlich and Garrett Hardin during the late 1960s; the 'limits to growthism' of Meadows *et al.* (1972) during the mid 1970s; and the global environmental and climate change framework that has been promulgated over the past half dozen or so years (Buttel *et al.*, 1990).

Rural social change in an era of greening

Thus far I have made very few connections between my analysis of greening and environmentalization on one hand, and rural societies and social structures on the other. Nonetheless, I believe that greening has had, and will continue to have, many crucial relationships to rural social structures. I will stress three such relationships here, each of which represents the tradeoff of NSMs and greening becoming the most persuasive and broad-based underpinning of social transformation. First, greening, in the context of the decline of social-democratic society and the rise of neo-conservative society, has been crucial in leading to the substitution of environmental for social justice discourse. Yet I suspect that greening and environmentalization will probably need to be tied to social justice in order to be enduring. Second, greening is contributing to the 'scientization' of social conflicts and policy formation. The scientization of social movements confers legitimacy but often serves to limit issues to those that can be handled in a technocratic framework. Third, greening involves breadth of appeal, but this very breadth can lend itself to superficiality and trivialization. I will explore each of these dilemmas by commenting briefly on two issues involving rural society and the environment: sustainable agriculture in the West, and the growing ecological symbolization of rural spaces across the globe.

Sustainable agriculture

Agricultural sustainability is a post-social justice formulation, having been the successor to the 'family farmism' that was the main preoccupation of agrarian activists in the 1970s. It represents a substitution of environmental for social justice discourse in a milieu in which social justice claims have increasingly lost their standing. Sustainable agriculture is at root a scientific notion and involves claims in which scientific data and the authority of experimental natural science are employed to confront the data and scientific knowledge claims of advocates of agricultural chemicals, monocultural practices, and so on.

The agricultural sustainability movement lacks a centralized international environmental bureaucracy. It is free-wheeling in its structure, and grass-roots in its impetus.

The base of sustainable agriculture is wide, but it faces several problems in becoming a major force for change in rural America. First and foremost is the threat that it will fail on technical-agronomic grounds – that is, it will not deliver the goods in farmers' fields. One possible ground for failure is that it is difficult to fine-tune integrated systems of crops, livestock and other biota quickly so that these systems can compete effectively with the engineering-type models of traditional agronomy. The major prototype of sustainable systems, that of traditional agriculture in the Third World, is based on long experience ('indigenous knowledge') and on the biological processes of co-evolution that are difficult to mimic in experiment station time-frames. Another problem is that many of the barriers to production systems that use fewer chemicals are to be found in federal policies. For example a number of other federal policies, particularly the structure of commodity programs, provide disincentives to adopting nonchemical production systems. Prior to the 1980s American environmental groups' interest in agriculture was mainly confined to pesticides and, to a lesser degree, to soil erosion. Over the past decade they have begun to substantially increase their emphasis on the agricultural environment and to focus considerable lobbying efforts on the farm bill and other federal agriculturally-related legislation. They have achieved some federal legislative successes, such as the conservation reserve and cross-compliance provisions of the 1985 farm bill, but these were made possible primarily by the fact that these ostensible environmental measures were also disguised supply control measures at a time of a major overproduction-induced farm crisis. In addition, the scientific and activist groups that are the strongest supporters of sustainable agriculture tend to be ones that want research results and practical information tomorrow, if not sooner. There is, in other words, not much of a constituency within contemporary sustainable agriculture doctrine for basic, long-term agroecological research, upon which a more environmentally-benign agriculture twenty years hence will need to be built.

A second problem facing sustainable agriculture is that by its nature sustainable agriculture must depend primarily on public funding. With federal agricultural research funding being tilted increasingly toward basic research in biotechnology and state funding declining precipitously, sustainable agriculture research has been heavily dependent on 'special appropriations' (the federal LISA programme and related state programmes) that must be fought for in each farm bill and state budget period. A third dilemma concerns sustainable agriculture's very breadth. Even chemical companies, for example, have little difficulty making claims that chemical agriculture is sustainable, since these chemicals are profitable and integral to sustaining farms financially. Finally, sustainable agriculture may prove to be more variegated in social justice terms than many imagine. It is an article of faith among most sustainable agriculture proponents that the spread of sustainable practices will bolster the role of family farms and impede the spread of corporate-industrial agriculture. I am suspicious about this assumption, and in fact there are some grounds for suggesting it could prove to be wrong. To the degree that diversification, involving many crop and livestock enterprises, crop rotations, and tighter recycling of wastes, is a cornerstone of sustainable practices, those who farm large acreages will be in the best position to utilize efficiently the multiple lines of machinery and the capital investments that will be required for enterprise diversification.

Environmental symbolism of rural spaces

For decades there has been a debate within rural sociology about whether the 'rural' or 'rurality' is to be understood mainly in structural or ideational terms. From the Sorokin years to the 1960s, rurality was thought to be mainly a cultural or ideational phenomenon. Over the past twenty years rural sociology has shifted, seeing rurality more as a structural phenomenon, mainly in spatial division of labour terms. Most recently, a number of scholars, particularly from the French tradition of cultural sociology, have resurrected culturalist notions of rural society. Mormont (1990:36) has claimed that 'rurality is not a thing or a territorial unit, but derives from the social production of a set of meanings'. While I am inclined to think that non-metro spaces are implicated in both a concrete division of labour and cultural meaning, I believe this new French tradition has a strong element of truth. In particular, I cannot help but wonder whether greening and environmentalization might over time lead to a fundamental shift in how rural spaces are symbolized, and accordingly how we define and deal with rural problems.

While the rural tradition in the US clearly has long had environmental–symbolic elements (Burch, 1971), the strongest and more enduring cultural connotation is one that has seen rural communities and households tending to be underprivileged and worthy of assistance. The establishment and institutionalization of land-grant universities and the priority given to rural places and people in the 1960s war on poverty are excellent cases in point. Many of the positive things we have been able to accomplish in rural America have been premised on this symbolism. What, then, will be the future of rural America if it becomes defined in strong symbolic terms as forest sites or prospective forest acreage needed to curb the greenhouse effect, as pristine ecosystems to ensure clean water for urban use, and as more desirable to the degree that fewer people are there to pollute, disrupt natural habitats, and the like? Will we, in other words, witness a further erosion of commitment to improving the livelihoods of the rural poor and to rural development?

Discussion

In this chapter I have sought to move beyond the *sui generis* conception of greening and environmentalization that has tended to prevail in most quarters of the social sciences. I believe the rise of green must be located in the discontinuity from post-War social-democratic/industrial society to neo-conservative post-industrialism. Further, I believe the long-term social and ecological significance of greening, new social movements, and the 'new class' will lie in the alignment of these forces of greening with the two others – neo-conservative state and corporate elites and the increasingly differentiated, fragmented groupings of low-wage service sector employees, informal sector workers, the urban and rural underclasses, and the working poor – that will in all likelihood define the future epoch of neoconservatism.

Rural sociology has long had something of an identity crisis because its subject matters seemed increasingly residual to the major social changes of twentieth-century social change. We should recognize, however, that environmentalization portends a decisive reversal of the inconsequentiality of matters rural and non-metro. Much of the green agenda brings rural societies and their environments centre stage. In so far as the green agenda is malleable, there will be much research and outreach work to do to ensure that environmentalization is as meaningful as it can be and adds to rather than detracts from the quest of the majority of the world's population to earn an adequate livelihood, have economic security, and live in dignity.

References

Aglietta, M. (1979) *A Theory of Capitalist Regulation*, London: New Left Books.

Aronowitz, S. (1988) *Science as Power*, Minneapolis: University of Minnesota Press.

Bellon, B., and J. Niosi (1988) *The Decline of the American Economy*, Montreal: Black Rose Books.

Block, F. (1977) *The Origins of International Economic Disorder*, Berkeley: University of California Press.

Burch, W.R., Jr. (1971) *Daydreams and Nightmares*, New York: Harper & Row.

Buttel, F.H., A. Hawkins and A.G. Power (1990) 'From limits to growth to global change: contrasts and contradictions in the evolution of environmental science and ideology', *Global Environmental Change* 1:57–66.

Buttel, F.H., and O.W. Larson III (1980) 'Whither environmentalism? The future political path of the environmental movement', *Natural Resources Journal* 20: 323–344.

Castells, M. (1978) *City, Class and Power*, New York: St. Martin's Press.

Esping-Andersen, G., and W. Korpi (1984) 'Social policy as class politics in post-war capitalism: Scandinavia, Austria, and Germany', pp. 179–208 in J.H. Goldthorpe (ed.), *Order and Conflict in Contemporary Capitalism*, Oxford: Clarendon Press.

Foster, J.B. (1989) 'The uncoupling of the world order: a survey of global crisis theories', pp. 99–122 in M. Gottdiener and N. Komninos (eds), *Capitalist Development and Crisis Theory*, London: Macmillan.

Frobel, F., G. Heinrichs, and O. Kreye (1979) The New International Division of Labour. Cambridge: Cambridge University Press.

Gilpin, R. (1975) *U.S. Power and the Multinational Corporation*, New York: Basic Books.

Gilpin, R. (1987) *The Political Economy of International Relations*, Princeton: Princeton University Press.

Goldthorpe, J.H. (1984) 'The end of convergence: corporatist and dualist tendencies in modern western societies', pp. 315–343 in J.H. Goldthorpe (ed.), *Order and Conflict in Contemporary Capitalism*, Oxford: Clarendon Press.

Gordon, D.M., R. Edwards, and M. Reich (1982) *Segmented Work, Divided Workers*, New York: Cambridge University Press.

Gottdiener, M., and N. Komninos (eds) (1989) *Capitalist Development and Crisis Theory*, London: Macmillan.

Keohane, R.O. (1984) 'The world political economy and the crisis of embedded liberalism', pp. 15–38 in J.H. Goldthorpe (ed.), *Order and Conflict in Contemporary Capitalism*, Oxford: Clarendon Press.

Kriese, H. (1989) 'New social movements and the new class in the Netherlands', *American Journal of Sociology* 94:1078–1116.

Lash, S., and J. Urry (1987) *The End of Organized Capitalism*, Madison: University of Wisconsin Press.

Lipietz, A. (1987) *Mirages and Miracles*, London: Verso.

Logan, J.R., and H. Molotch (1987) *Urban Fortunes*, Berkeley: University of California Press.

McCarthy, J., and M.N. Zald (1973) *The Trend of Social Movements in America*, Morriston, NJ: General Learning Press.

McMichael, P. (1990) 'Incorporating comparison within a world-historical perspective: an alternative comparative method', *American Sociological Review*, 55:385–97.

Meadows, D.H. et al. (1982) *The Limits to Growth*, New York: Universe.

Mormont, M. (1990) 'Who is rural? or, how to be rural: towards a sociology of the rural', pp. 21–44 in T. Marsden et al. (eds), *Rural Restructuring*, London: David Fulton.

O'Connor, J. (1973) *The Fiscal Crisis of the State*, New York: St. Martin's Press.

Offe, C. (1985a) *Disorganized Capitalism*, Cambridge, MA: MIT Press.

Offe, C. (1985b) 'New social movements: challenging the boundaries of institutional politics', *Social Research*, 52:817–868.

Oloffson, G. (1988) 'After the working-class movement? an essay on what's 'new' and what's 'social' in new social movements.' *Acta Sociologica* 31:15–34.

Przeworski, A. (1985) *Capitalism and Social Democracy*, New York: Cambridge University Press.

Redclift, M. (1987) *Sustainable Development*, London: Methuen.

Roobeek, A.J.M. (1987) 'The crisis in fordism and the rise of a new technological paradigm', *Futures* 19: 129–154.

Scott, A. (1990) *Ideology and the New Social Movements*, London: Unwin Hyman.

Singelmann, J. (1978) *From Agriculture to Services*, Beverly Hills, CA: Sage.

Touraine, A. (1971) *The Post-Industrial Society*, New York: Random House.

Turner, B.S. (ed.) (1990) *Theories of Modernity and Postmodernity*, London: Sage.

Wallerstein, I. (1984) *The Politics of the World-Economy*, Cambridge: Cambridge University Press.

3

Regulation, green politics and the rural

Paul Cloke and Mark Goodwin

Introduction

We live in an era when the 'rural' is becoming increasingly commodified. As we engage in more serious and frequent reflexive monitoring of the locales and environments in which we live, work and play, so seemingly there has been a need to give more precise expression to rurality, countryside and environment whether as habitat or as backcloth. Such expression, however, has long been a complex issue. When Thomas Hardy wrote his Wessex novels, he used identifiable places (Dorchester, Shaftesbury, Bournemouth) as settings, but imposed deliberate distortions and omissions on these landscapes so as to focus on the psychological journeys being travelled through them. However, in the Preface which he wrote for later editions of *Far from the Madding Crowd* (see Tindall, 1991) he recognizes that his Wessex was being attributed a far more concrete shape and purpose than he intended:

> Since then the appellation which I had thought to reserve to the horizons and landscapes of a partly-real, partly dream-country, has become more and more popular as a practical provincial definition; and the dream-country has, by degrees, solidified into a utilitarian region which people can go to, take a house in, and write to the papers from.

As with Wessex, so with many rural areas in contemporary Britain. The 'psychological journeys', or idylls, of a rural landscape which offers natural beauty, health, a fulfilling life and a problem-free existence, and a rural community which offers a friendly, close-knit and secure living-place are being made more concrete and marketed as commodities to be exploited in the new politics of the marketplace.

In this chapter we want to suggest some interconnections between the wider changes of economy and politics with the more localized characteristics of commodifying rural areas. 'Rural politics' as such may be seen as a complex modality of power, contest and participation, reflecting change both in the wider political economy and in localized social relations; change both in the wider colonization of the politics of a commodified environment and in the localized politics of those who have colonized a slice of that environment. At the outset we briefly outline some conceptual ideas from the regulationist literature which act as a framework for understanding rural change. Then we trace some interconnections between a regulationist view of rural change and the specific circumstances of rural politics, focusing on two links: first, the political policy-making arising from state involvement at various levels in *enabling* new forms of coherence in rural areas; and, second, the environmentalization and greening of politics in the context of a commodifying rural environment.

Changing regulation and new coherences

The social recomposition and economic restructuring recently witnessed in rural Britain needs to be seen in the context of wider changes which have swept through the economies and societies of the western world. Observers now speak of the 'sea-changes' (Harvey, 1989, p. 189) which have occurred in the nature of capitalism since the mid 1970s, and talk of the rise of post-Fordist economies, post-industrial societies, or post-modern cultures. In each case, the prefix seems to state with certainty that society has moved beyond its old forms of organisation. In the broad field of urban and regional studies researchers have increasingly turned to regulation theory to provide a theoretical framework for analysing a host of recent developments in economy, society and politics (see for instance Chouinard, 1990; Florida and Feldman, 1988; Harvey and Scott, 1988; Schoenberger, 1989). Those concentrating on rural issues have also begun to use the regulation literature, especially in an attempt to analyse recent change in the agricultural sector (Kenney *et al.*, 1989; Marsden and Murdoch, 1990; Sauer, 1990).

A key notion within this literature, which all these authors draw on, is the idea that the expanded social reproduction of capitalism is never guaranteed, but has to be continually secured through a range of social norms, mechanisms and institutions. Together these help to stabilize relations between production and consumption within a particular regime of accumulation, and it is claimed that the dramatic changes we are now witnessing arise as we move from a Fordist to a post-Fordist regime. One of the strengths of the regulation literature is that it allows us to link and relate changes in the economy to those in society and politics through an examination of the changes experienced in these social norms, mechanisms and institutions.

We have argued elsewhere (Cloke and Goodwin, 1991) that while there is considerable potential for using parts of the regulationist literature in rural studies, some caution should also be employed in the wholesale adoption of that literature in the rural arena. The broad concerns of new times post-Fordism and post-modernism may have become increasingly important in contemporary social science, but in our eagerness to be part of this conceptual stream rural researchers are in danger of borrowing inappropriate ideas and overarching theories in an unwise manner. Current interest in the new times is understandable, but we would want to suggest that what appears to be a sea change, resulting in a new epoch might rather be seen as the latest in a series of constant revolutions, each inextricably linked into previous eras. Thus the search for a post-Fordist 'rural' to replace the previously conceived Fordist 'rural' seems premature.

In order to avoid the obvious danger of gross overcategorization of change in rural areas, we feel that it is more appropriate to use key *middle ground* concepts from regulation theory which appear useful in the context of understanding rural change, and which in particular allow us to conceptualize the links which exist between economic, social, political and cultural change. Using these concepts we can outline a framework from the regulationist literature through which we can begin to interpret changes not only in rural production and consumption, but also in living and thinking and feeling life (Gramsci 1971) in rural areas. Briefly, the three middle ground concepts are mode of regulation, societalization and structured coherence.

It is important to adopt the key concern of regulation theory for the ways in which the tensions and contradictions of capitalism are overcome, or regulated. The idea of the *mode of regulation* focuses on what Lipietz (1988) has referred to as an ensemble of institutional forms, networks, and norms which ensure the compatibility of behaviours within any period of stability between production and consumption (that is, within a regime of accumulation). Thus, any changes in the mode of regulation occurring in rural areas will be crucial in an understanding of changing rural life. The overcoming of contradictions and tensions within capitalism can occur by establishing social norms which are reflected in individual behaviour, often with the aid of state activity (for example, in the area of welfare state). Changing regulation, whether by state intervention or by means of struggle and opposition, will lead to changes in the experience of rural places and lifestyles of rural people. Mode of regulation, then, appears to be a crucial concept in the grasping of contemporary rural politics.

Another key concern of the regulationist literature has been to link changes in the political economy with those affecting other parts of Lipietz's ensemble of relations. *Societalization* refers to the process of regulation at a *societal* level via a complex grouping of social practices which are usually mediated by the institutions of the time. A focus on societalization will shift the emphasis from economic regulation to social regulation wherein social practices operate and integrate diverse social structures, and to secure some form of cohesion amongst competing forces. When societalization achieves a temporary form of stability, it is theorised that two social blocs are created:

- *a historic bloc*, which Gramsci (1971) describes as a historically constituted and socially reproduced structural correspondence between the economic base and the political and ideological superstructure of a social formation; and
- *a hegemonic bloc*, which refers to 'a durable alliance of class forces . . . able to exercise political, intellectual and moral leadership' (Jessop, 1990, 179).

The emergence of new historic and hegemonic blocs in rural society and politics helps us to interpret rural change, although *cultural* leadership is also important here, since much current rural change has involved the appropriation of cultural values and images from a previous historic and hegemonic bloc in order to promote the very commodification of rural areas which underpins the emergence of new blocs.

We can attempt to ground these ideas about the varying practices of regulation by linking them to Harvey's notion of *structured coherence* (1985, p. 139). In using this concept we can present the configuration of mode of regulation and societalization as an ensemble of multifaceted relations and institutions which are applicable *at particular places* and at *particular times*. Sometimes this will take on the form of a localized coherence, structured not only by the prevailing form of production but also by

> standard of living, the qualities and style of life, work satisfaction (or lack thereof), social hierarchies, and a whole set of sociological and psychological attitudes towards working, living, enjoying, entertaining and the like. (p. 140)

Thus the construction of a temporary and often partial coherence in particular places will be linked with particular modes of regulation and strategies of societalization being pursued by recognizable historic and hegemonic blocs which dominate specific areas. Far from representing a thinly-veiled form of grand overarching theory, the notion of structured coherence allows us some sensitivity in characterizing the specificity of particular places and people without divorcing them from wider sets of changing relations.

We therefore contend that appropriate use of these three middle-ground concepts will begin to suggest new ways of theorizing rural change:

> we should look to understand rural change as a whole series of movements between the differing practices and procedures of various strategies of regulation operating at overlapping scales. When successful in achieving partial or contested stability, these help to form a particular structured coherence. This allows us to see rural regions undergoing a series of diverse and contested changes and developments, all socially constructed, rather than leaping from one ideal-typical stage to another. (Cloke and Goodwin, 1991)

New coherences: the role of the state

These concepts of changing economic and social regulation leading to potential coherences in particular time-spaces will allow illustrations of the localized impact of new ensembles of relations in particular locales (see Cloke and Goodwin, 1991). The interrelations between the geography of regulation and rural politics are by no means restricted to the *outcome* of new coherences in rural localities. As we have stressed earlier in this chapter, the political machinery of the state is integrally involved in enabling changes in regulation at various scales, and hence in attempting to form new coherences around these. An understanding of new coherences in rural areas will therefore depend not only on how attractive the area is to capital accumulation under contemporary modes of regulation, not only on how attractive the area is to those seeking a rural 'experience' but also on the extent to which state intervention occurs in an attempt to facilitate these changes. In order to understand changing rural politics it must be stressed that a changing mode of production does reflect shifting relations between state and capital. These formed around a common desire to see new social conditions introduced to suit, and to some extent facilitate, changing economic circumstances. This state activity occurs through different institutions using different programmes at different scales, but at the very least we should differentiate between the levels of governmental action which are currently significant in rural areas.

The local state

Local governments and regional development agencies have been extremely active in different rural areas (see Cloke, 1988; 1989). Part of their function has been to control or zone the development of housing and industry in particular areas, and there is an important link to be made here with the shifting nature of local political control and the resultant sectional interests that have been pursued in different rural areas. The societalization which is expressed through local development planning can be a crucial factor in whether certain areas are preserved as affluent museum pieces (for the purposes of certain class fractions who wish to live in them and others who wish to see this part of their 'national heritage' maintained) or whether some flexibility is available for capital investment in housing, industry or servicing facilities. Changing local social relations will alter, sometimes albeit in a subtle way, the nature of local political objectives and action in rural development planning. Perhaps more often, however, changing social relations at a national scale will cause a shift in central-local relations resulting in conflict between central and local states, for example, in the clash between central support of capital fractions connected with housebuilding in the form of flexibility over the location of new development, and local political action to prevent new housing growth in their back yard. Deregulatory programmes have diluted the strength of development control planning in some rural areas, and localized contesting of development has therefore become even more important.

State action for 'positive' development in rural areas is often channelled through regional agencies. Here again a changing mode of regulation has signalled different approaches by regional agencies than those employed, say, fifteen years ago. At that time, these agencies tended towards a *top-down* approach which consisted of designating boundaries of areas to be developed, implementing subsidies for incoming enterprises including

making land and factory buildings available in key central locations, and
striving to attract new economic enterprises into these new subsidized
facilities. More recently, the deregulatory ideologies of central government
have forced a switch in these tactics. The emphasis is less on subsidy and
more on developing an 'entrepreneurial culture' which involves a seemingly
bottom-up (but actually market-led) strategy of fostering local development
based on localised resources and enterprise. The major role of such agencies
is becoming one of marketing, training and advice rather than producing
subsidized means of production.

State activity at these local levels is highly variegated. The artificially
drawn boundaries of development areas increasingly serve to delineate the
repositories of rural action. Outside these areas much depends on the
resources of local authorities (which have largely suffered in the shifting
central-local relations of the 1980s) or on the degree to which community
self-help can be activated towards rural development objectives. When
added to the rather complex circumstances which dictate whether a rural
place is attractive to capital and/or to an incoming service class, these
structures of state intervention serve to stress the localized nature of particular structured coherences in rural areas.

The nation state

Central governments are obviously an essential mechanism for establishing,
maintaining and if necessary changing modes of regulation. Again, it would
be facile in this limited space to attempt to describe the multi-faceted nature
of radical periods of government such as that of the Thatcher administration
in the 1980s. It is, however, important to stress the ways in which shifting
modes of regulation have been closely linked with creation of new 'cultures'
which have impacted on previous structured coherences in the countryside.
Two examples illustrate this point. First, programmes of privatization and
deregulation are linked with the culture of 'anti-planning'; allowing much
more leeway to capital fractions interested in exploiting certain rural areas:

> The changes in governmental relations have led to significant limitations on the
> ability of planning authorities and other state agencies to intervene in the develop-
> ment of infrastructure and facilities in rural localities. The deregulation of plan-
> ning has begun to offer new opportunities for private sector development in rural
> places, and the signs are that there will be strong incentives for interested capital
> fractions to find new ways to exploit the resources vested in the countryside.
> (Cloke, 1992)

The second illustration would suggest that new modes of regulation, in
tandem with the centralized promotion of an 'enterprise' or 'entrepreneurial'
culture have been directly linked to new forms of commodification in
rural areas. The emphasis on 'diversification' and 'training', alongside the

deregulatory procedures discussed above represent a directed policy of cultural change, which have given rise to

> new markets for countryside commodities: the countryside as an exclusive place to be lived in; rural communities as a context to be bought and sold; rural lifestyles which can be colonised . . . and so on. (Cloke, 1992)

Clearly, action by nation states can radically alter the structured coherences in rural areas. By revising the social contracts inherent in a welfare state; by reducing the power and financial independence of local and regional state authorities; by changing the way in which industry is regulated; by tinkering with development control planning; by prioritizing the needs of particular industrial or class fractions through subsidy, the state has a clear role in the intersection of mode of regulation and societalization – one which helps to provide the foundations for new structured coherences.

The European state

With the arrival of 1992, the institutions revolving around government in the European Community must now be regarded as an integral third tier of state action with clear jurisdiction over rural areas. Until recently European state action in rural areas seemed to be synonymous with agricultural policy. In political and budgetary terms, the Common Agricultural Policy has dominated the way in which rural areas have been discussed and the way in which policies have been delivered. With the decline in the Community's agricultural population, and with the obvious necessity to reform expensive and wasteful agricultural support policies, the prioritization of agriculture is beginning to change. This change should not be overstated. It seems certain that agriculture will continue to play a significant role in the future development of Europe's rural areas in both the economic and political arenas. This is especially true of the Mediterranean regions where the bulk of Europe's agricultural population will reside in the future. Nevertheless, EC documents, for example *Europe 2000* published in 1991, stress that the future economic development of rural areas is becoming increasingly dependent on non-agricultural sectors, and, with the likelihood that GATT negotiations will lead to reductions in subsidies to farmers, this economic trend seems set to continue.

The reform of EC structural funds reflects the growing importance of non-farm economic development in rural areas. The European Council agreed in 1988 to double the expenditure on structural programmes in real terms by 1993. Moreover, five development objectives were accepted which are likely to have important spatial and socio-cultural impacts in rural areas. Of these five, Objectives 3 and 4 deal with combating long-term unemployment and promoting the occupational integration of young people, and

Objective 2 focuses on declining industrial regions. Objectives 1 and 5, however, are crucial to future European state action in rural areas. *Objective 1* is concerned with the future development and structural adjustment required in what are seen as the least developed rural regions where per capita Gross Domestic Product is less than 75 per cent of the average for the Community. *Objective 5* deals with both the adjustment of agricultural structures (5a) *and* with sponsoring locally targeted schemes for integrated rural development (5b).

The drawing of boundaries to establish which rural areas are eligible for funding under Objectives 1 and 5b has therefore become a crucial parameter in the future shape of European state action. Areas eligible for funds under Objective 5b, for example, will depend on

> the degree to which they are rural in nature, the number of persons occupied in agriculture, their level of economic and agricultural development, the extent to which they are peripheral, and their sensitivity to changes in the agricultural sector, especially in the context of the reform of the common agricultural policy (European Commission, 1988, Regulation 2052/88).

In Britain, the Highlands and Islands of Scotland have effectively lost Objective 1 status. Substantial parts of Scotland and Wales, but only limited areas in the south-west of England have qualified for Objective 5b status. These areas will have received some 350 million ECU from the Objective 5b budget by 1993. As rural development grants are now tending to be allocated increasingly at the level of the European and not the nation states, these regulations are having the effect that certain of the more spatially peripheral rural areas are attracting most of the available subsidies and the areas of need which fall outside of these mega-boundaries are unlikely to receive equivalent state support. These European-scale initiatives therefore present opportunities for state-sponsored changes to localized structured coherences *within fixed boundaries*, and by the same token deny state involvement in other rural places which might be seen by many as having equivalent status in economic restructuring and socio-cultural recomposition.

It will be evident from this account that there continue to be contradictions and conflicts in the political relations affecting rural areas. These are most evident at present in the very different directions being taken by intra-national and international state agencies in their policies relating to rural areas. While the central state in Britain is dominating its local counterpart with strategies of fiscal restraint, privatization and anti-planning, the international state in Europe continues to follow a pathway of interventionist politics with prescriptive policies which discriminate between designated rural areas and others. With increasing European integration, such tensions seem likely to increase and the conservative alliances of politics at national and local level will thus become more remote from the seat of policy-making in any contest over particular rural strategies.

Green politics and the rural

It may at first sight seem inappropriate to equate green politics with the 'rural'. Although the discourse of greening finds obvious parallels with popular images of the green and pleasant land of the countryside, there are many key environmental issues – global warming, ozone depletion, the greenhouse effect and the like – which transcend intra- and international boundaries, both cartographic and more obviously socially constructed. Yet the inexorable rise in the profile of environmentalism in British politics has in several ways exhibited connections with the economic restructuring and social recomposition occurring in rural areas. In the following account we trace the ways in which green issues have been adopted in different ways by different parties, and in particular how the government's green response is linked with the emergent coherences described above.

As discussed by Bristow in the following chapter, all political parties have consciously highlighted the environment as an electoral issue over recent years. (Dobson, 1990; Porritt and Winner, 1988). The Liberal party has traditionally been the party to which those with ecological and environmental concerns have clung. Simon Hughes MP, in a speech to the Young Liberals in 1988, outlines a philosophy which underlies the emotions, if not the policies, of many within the Liberal Democrats:

> My politics is therefore about working with all creation, holistically, respectfully, to do all that I can to ensure that every living creature has the best possible quality of life. My daily concern must be to lead people away from the distraction of believing that, apart from the basics of food, shelter, housing, clothing and health, other materialistic possessions are fundamentally important, or necessary to true happiness, self-discovery, or self- fulfilment.

Hughes' views (if not those of the more pragmatic policy-makers in his party) find strong parallels in the emergent Green Party. Despite electoral disappointment – in the 1992 General Election they polled only 0.5 per cent of the votes – the Green Party has sought to establish itself as the principal 'defender of the environmental faith', acting as if it were the fundamental yardstick against which the environmental policies of other parties are to be measured. As Porritt and Winner (1988, p. 78) point out in a typical Green message, the time-frame for this project is a long-term generational one:

> Either the basic green analysis is *right* (in which case the progressive deterioration of our life-support systems and people's real quality of life will in turn progressively deepen people's responsiveness to the green alternative), or it is *wrong* (in which case, sit back and enjoy the health food and organic wines with the best of them).

If the Liberal Democrats and the Greens seem to have made claims to the ideological politics of the environment as well as to the pragmatics of green electoral politics, then other parties have been quick to highlight their own environmental concerns and thereby raise the prominence of green political debate. The Labour Party may often have given the impression during the 1960s and 1970s that environmental issues were not an area of priority in their political vision. In fact, there have always been key individuals within the party (more recently personified by the likes of David Blunkett, Robin Cook and Ken Livingstone) who have sought to introduce radical environmentalism into Labour political philosophy, and during the 1980s conditions were right for the adoption of a higher-profile stand on the environment. In 1985 the party launched its *Charter for the Environment* which emphasized not only the need for a series of interventions to protect the environment and control pollution (with the welcome result of the creation of a whole new range of jobs in the British economy), but also the need for local environmental action in all kinds of localities in Britain.

What then of the Conservative party, whose period of office since 1979 has coincided with many of the regulatory changes discussed earlier in this chapter? As Bristow discusses in Chapter 4, for the first eight years of the Thatcher governments, the Prime Minister neither presented a speech on environmental matters nor visited an environmental project (see also O'Riordan, 1992). Environment ministers were steered towards the reform of local government rather than the protection of the environment, and environmentalism was in a crucial sense portrayed as apolitical in that it could be pursued alongside whatever series of political economic precepts was held by an individual or a party.

From 1987 onwards, however, the Thatcher administration played the environmental card very strongly. The surrender of jurisdiction over environmental matters to the European Commission, the exhaustive media coverage of environmental issues, the growth in the political influence of pressure groups such as Friends of the Earth and Greenpeace, and the welter of scientific predictions (especially relating to global warming), appear to have necessitated a greening of politics in all quarters.

We want to suggest, however, that there are more direct links between this apparent realignment of politics and the changing geography of regulation. For example, the Thatcher government's commitment to a privatization of infrastructural services brought in its wake a series of *post hoc* legitimations which could then be claimed as major environmental initiatives. Thus privatization of the water industry not only led to the establishment of the National Rivers Authority, but it also prompted the argument that denationalization had been carried out *so that* investment could be made available for significant upgrading of sewage disposal and other anti-pollution technologies. Similarly, privatization of the electricity generation industry led to the long overdue acknowledgement that nuclear power generation was an uneconomic process. Suddenly the previous emphasis on the 'cleanness' of nuclear power was switched to some speculative expectations that private sector investment would clean up emissions from conventional generating stations. In these instances, then, the privatization programme provided subsidiary political gain in the environmental arena with the consequence of an apparent greening of policy.

As important as these obvious regulatory changes, however, was a rediscovery by conservative ideologies that a form of environmental awareness was indeed compatible with more deep-seated Tory values relating to rural lifestyles and the countryside. We mentioned earlier in the chapter that some changes in the ensemble of economic, social, political and cultural relations in Britain have been the result of *persuasion* rather than *force*. In particular, recent change in rural areas has been associated with a commodification of rural idylls and lifestyles and with promoting the countryside as a new theatre of consumption. It seems likely that the 'greening' of the Tories has much more to do with their wish to persuade people of a series of countryside values, and in particular their wish to commodify that countryside, than with a sudden awakening to global environmental crises. Thus beneath the rhetoric of international environmental awareness we would emphasize the reinforcement both of Conservative party values, and appeasement of voters in Conservative party constituencies.

One very revealing insight into Conservative environmentalism is Andrew Sullivan's (1985) paper for the Centre for Policy Studies entitled *Greening the Tories*. Sullivan was, amongst other roles, a leader writer for the *Daily Telegraph*, and he used this paper to spell out what is, and what is not, a vital environmental issue for 'ordinary people':

> They care less about levels of sulphur dioxide than about their property; they worry less about dumping in the Atlantic Ocean than about a tangible threat to their part of the green belt; they lose less sleep over the future of the Amazonian rain forest than over what is being done to the character and beauty of their own country and neighbourhood (p. 18).

So far as Sullivan is concerned, it is property ownership that is the most rational defence of environmental balance:

> The extension of property-ownership is the best way to combine human nature with environmental protection, to create proper and enduring links between people and their surroundings and to protect our towns and countryside . . . (p. 20).

Here, then, is the acceptable face of environmentalism so far as a Conservative government is concerned; a natural extension of looking after Tory territory.

After all, this territory had been well cared for in the early 1980s. Blowers (1987), in his account of environmental policy under Thatcher, concluded that such policy had been 'narrowly focused and selective, designed to appeal to partisan interests mainly located in southern, suburban and rural England' (p. 291) – a territory experiencing social recomposition, in which new 'coherences' were becoming evident. But *many* of those wishing to live in or visit the late 20th-century countryside as part of this recomposition remained ultimately concerned with the personal environments of property, view and neighbourhood landscape. And although they were increasingly likely to present a *public* image that problems with personal environments were somehow linked to wider green issues, the Tory philosophy of property-ownership, conservation and private privilege was well placed to link with a high profile 'greenness' which was required to retain their political allegiance.

Even the National Front recognized this change. Porritt and Winner (1988, p. 59) quote from an article in *The Times* (20th October 1984) to illustrate the National Front's new concerns:

> The National Front is moving into 'green' politics: organising vigorously in rural areas, joining protests against acid rain, seal culls and straw-burning . . . The Front's change in focus, described as a 'deliberate policy' of concentrating on the countryside, has been developed over the past year . . . Mr Phil Andrew, a member of the Front's national directorate . . . added . . . 'We were too concerned with urban problems. But the cities are dying and the country towns are thriving. Ideologically, we have developed somewhat.' . . . Successful new membership drives claimed by the Front include Suffolk, where numbers are said to have quadrupled, the West Country, Wales and the Border country, rural Scotland and Hertfordshire.

Environmental idealism can thus be seen in this context as a legitimation for far more earthy concerns: to secure or retain power in the light of subtly changing cultural relations relating to the role of the environment in the reflexive monitoring of both rural and peri-rural people and those living elsewhere for whom the rural idyll remained important. The threat to the Tories was not the National Front but the other opposition parties seeking to move into their territory. Andrew Sullivan's (1985) warning did not go unheeded.

> Charting a 'green' course both within the Department of the Environment and throughout all government policy-making bodies would be worth votes. Both the Alliance and Labour parties realise this and are formulating strategies to reshape the DOE and seize the green initiative. In vulnerable, marginal Alliance-threatened suburbia, the image of a property-developing, polluting government is likely to prove disastrous in an election. Green-belt destruction, countryside exploitation and an attitude reminiscent of General Motors to any sensitive environmental issue are huge electoral liabilities. The green issue will not go away. The correct and healthy Tory reaction to it is to expropriate it. (p. 44).

One part of the persuasion of the late 1980s, then, was to *commodify* environmentalism, both by reinforcing the importance of property and land ownership in a pay-as-you-enter countryside, and by establishing the link between broader environmental concern (replete with T-shirts, OXFAM souvenirs and the cultural competence of environmental group membership) and the more sectoral and self-centred concerns of the personal environment – that highly prized and forcefully protected commodity of the rural house and the rural back yard.

A second significant part of the persuasion of the late 1980s has been the spatializing of treasured environmental territory in Britain. Just as Hardy's psychological journeys through fictional Wessex became solidified, and reduced, to a recognizable utilitarian region, so green consciousness in Britain has been at least temporarily expropriated, and made solid, and certainly reduced, to the political territory of parts of the English countryside.

Conclusion

Mrs Thatcher's conversion to the cause of Green politics in 1988 has been compared to that of St Paul on the road to Damascus, but in spite of appearances, it was not quite as sudden. As we have pointed out above, it represented a measured ideological response to a host of related social, economic and cultural changes which had been taking place in the British countryside. Unlike St Paul there was no blinding light, but instead a highly considered political attempt to appropriate and mould the concerns of a changing rural population.

It is our contention that the rise of green politics in the countryside over the past few years is an attempt to respond to, and shape, these changes. But it remains an attempt fraught with danger. The emergence of new historic and hegemonic blocs in rural society and politics is still partial and contested. All political parties, not least the Conservative government, have to balance their green concerns on a knife-edge between those interests favouring conservation (of property, house-prices, and scenic outlook) and those whose concern lies in opening up the countryside for extended commodification and development. This tension, and the political response to it, has arisen as new rural coherences are actively being shaped and forged in the light of changing economic, social and cultural circumstances. We need to account for these, as they are expressed through changing modes of regulation and societalization, if we are to fully appreciate the growing green concerns of pressure groups, political parties and governments operating at local, national and international levels.

Acknowledgement

An earlier version of part of this chapter was included in a paper presented to the workshop on 'The changing function and position of rural areas in

Europe', University of Utrecht, September 1991. That original paper is to be published in the Netherlands Geographical Studies series.

References

Blowers, A. (1987) 'Transition or transformation? – environmental policy under Thatcher', *Public Administration* 65, 277–294.

Chouinard, V. (1990) 'The uneven development of capitalist states: 1. Theoretical proposals and an analysis of postwar changes in Canada's assisted housing programmes', *Environment and Planning A* 22, 10, 1291–1308.

Cloke, P. (ed.) (1988) *Policies And Plans For Rural People*, Unwin Hyman, London.

Cloke, P. (ed.) (1989) *Rural Land Use Planning In Developed Nations* Unwin Hyman, London.

Cloke, P. (1990) 'Community development and political leadership in rural Britain', *Sociologia Ruralis* 31, 305–322.

Cloke, P. (1992) 'The countryside: development, conservation and an increasingly marketable commodity' in Cloke, P. (ed.) *Policy and Change in Thatcher's Britain* Pergamon Press, Oxford.

Cloke, P. and Goodwin, M. (1991) 'Conceptualising countryside change: from post-Fordism to rural structured coherence', paper presented to the annual conference of the Association of American Geographers, Miami.

Cloke, P. and Thrift, N. (1987) 'Intra-class conflict in rural areas' *Journal of Rural Studies* 3, 321–334.

Cloke, P. and Thrift N. (1990) 'Class change and conflict in rural areas', in Marsden, T., Lowe, P. and Whatmore, S. (eds) *Rural Restructuring*, David Fulton, London.

Dobson, A. (1990) *Green Political Thought*, Unwin Hyman, London.

European Commission (1988) *Europe 2000*, EC, Brussels.

Florida, R. and Feldman, M. (1988) 'Housing in US Fordism: the class accord and postwar spatial organisation', *International Journal of Urban and Regional Research* 12,187–210.

Gramsci, A. (1971) *Selection from the Prison Notebooks*, Lawrence and Wishart, London.

Harvey, D. (1985) *The Urbanisation of Capital*, Blackwell, Oxford.

Harvey, D. (1989) *The Condition of Postmodernity*, Blackwell, London.

Harvey, D. and Scott, A. (1988) 'The practice of human geography: theory and specificity in the transition from Fordism to flexible accumulation', in MacMillan, W. (ed.) *Remodelling Geography*, Blackwell, London.

Jessop, B. (1990) 'Regulation theories in retrospect and prospect' *Economy and Society* 19, 153–216.

Johnston, R.J. (1987) 'The rural milieu and voting in Britain' *Journal of Rural Studies* 3, 95–103.

Kenney, M., Latao, L., Curry, J. and Goe, R. (1989) 'Midwestern agriculture in US Fordism. From New Deal to economic restructuring', *Sociologia Ruralis* 29, 131–148.

Lipietz, A. (1988) 'Reflections on a tale: the Marxist foundations of the concepts of regulation and accumulation', *Studies in Political Economy* 26, 7–36.

Lowe, P. and Flynn, A. (1989) 'Environmental politics and policy in the 1980s' in Mohan, J. (ed.) *The Political Geography of Contemporary Britain*, Macmillan, Basingstoke.

Marsden, T. and Murdoch, J. (1990) *Restructuring Rurality: Key Areas For Development In Assessing Rural Change*, ESRC Countryside Change Initiative, Working Paper 4.

O'Riordan, T. (1992) 'The environment', in Cloke P. (ed.) *Policy And Change In Thatcher's Britain*, Pergamon Press, Oxford.

Porritt, J. and Winner, D. (1988) *The Coming Of The Greens*, Fontana, London.

Sauer, M. (1990) 'Fordist modernization of German agriculture and the future of family farms', *Sociologia Ruralis* 30, 260–279.

Schoenberger, E. (1989) 'Thinking about flexibility: a response to Gertler', *Transactions IBG* 14, 98–108.

Sullivan, A. (1985) *Greening The Tories: New Policies On The Environment*, Centre for Policy Studies, London.

Tindall, G. (1991) *Countries Of The Mind: The Meaning Of Place to Writers*, Hogarth Press, London.

4

Environmental awareness and societal change in the UK

Theresa Bristow

Introduction

Throughout the last two decades concern for the environment has developed not only into a tool used for political advantage, but also into an issue with increasing influence within global and domestic 'talking shops'. The Earth, which was once seen as an infinite source of resources, to be used and discarded, is now recognized as finite, and capable of suffering irrevocable damage. Despite considerable neglect of environmental issues in the early years of her leadership, Prime Minister Margaret Thatcher chose to use her speech to the Royal Society in September 1988 to raise the environment to the forefront of the political agenda, and thus 'conferred establishment legitimacy on the whole of the environmental movement' (McCarthy, 1989). As Lowe and Flynn (1989) point out, the government became aware of the increased lobbying of environmental groups, particularly in the European Parliament, which threatened outside interference if they themselves did not act. Furthermore the environment was becoming a 'popular movement' and the Conservatives saw this as an opportune time to join the green band-wagon. The effect was short lived, after the publication of the British government's White Paper *This Common Inheritance* (1990) the environment once more shifted within party politics, shunted to one side by more 'pressing' domestic and global issues.

The environment has not only fluctuated in importance within the political agenda, but public perception of, and sympathy for, environmental issues have also followed a cyclical pattern, oscillating from complete commitment by a growing proportion of the public to disillusionment and subsequent apathy. One needs only to look at the recent downturn of the Green Party to observe this process. With the environment topping the political agenda, the elections for the European Parliament on 15 June 1989 enabled the Green Party to win 15 per cent of the votes cast, increasing its membership to more than 18,000. Since then, membership of the Green Party has fallen by more than 6,000 (Goodwin, 1991), taking just over 0.5 per cent of the votes cast in the 1992 general election.

The role of the media

Even before Margaret Thatcher's 'green speech' to the Royal Society, environmental disasters had forced environmental concerns to the forefront of British minds. In December 1984, methylisocyanate gas escaped from the Union Carbide pesticide plant at Bhopal, India, immediately killing an estimated 2,500 people, and affecting a further 200,000 (McCormick, 1989, p. 161). The attention drawn towards Bhopal overshadowed another serious incident only the month before: the death of more than five hundred people in Ixhuatepec, Mexico, when a liquefied petroleum gas store exploded (McCormick, 1989). It was not only dramatic catastrophes, illustrating the vulnerability of the environment to human and technological error, which caught the public eye; a more insidious disaster was about to be highlighted. In 1985 the British Antarctic Survey discovered the 'hole' in the ozone layer above the Antarctic and related it to the breakdown of chlorofluorocarbons (CFCs) in the atmosphere. Subsequent public concern was such that Friends of the Earth (FOE) launched a campaign in 1986 to phase out the use of CFCs and by the end of 1989 'ninety per cent of aerosols' were 'CFC-free' as Porritt (1989) stated – a timely illustration of the rising and influential power of the consumer. On 26 April 1986 the Chernobyl nuclear power reactor exploded, releasing a radioactive plume into the atmosphere which deposited radioactive fallout throughout the European continent before slowly dispersing over the Norwegian Sea.

The disasters were to continue: February 1989 saw the *Exxon Valdez* run aground in Alaska, depositing thousands of tonnes of oil into Prince William Sound. The inheritance of the 1980s flowed across the divide into the next decade: in January 1991 contaminated water from Chernobyl seeped through a broken dam into the Dnieper River, the water supply for the city of Kiev; in October, Chernobyl's second reactor was reported to have escaped by metres a fire which lasted for over two hours, destroying an adjacent equipment area. Such is the scenario of the recurring 'Chernobyl nightmare' (Viets, 1991). The burning oil wells of Kuwait dominated television screens for much of the mid months of 1991, and late 1991 leading into 1992 saw wide reports of the fragility of the former Soviet arsenal (Godwin, 1991; Lucas, 1991; *The Independent*, February 1992; *The Times*, February 1992).

Environmentalization

Politicians have not been slow to grasp the importance of environmental concerns as a political tool. As early as 1970 President Nixon adopted the 'environmental issue' as his own in his State of the Union message. That year had witnessed the ecological outburst of the Earth Day, with Nixon stating that 'the 1970s absolutely must be the years when America pays its debt to the past by reclaiming the purity of its air, its waters and our living environment' (*The Times*, 1970, p. 5; the *Guardian*, 1970, p. 2). In his 1971 message he declared that environmental quality would be the 'third great goal' of what he called the 'New American Revolution'. Within the year, however, Nixon had made, 'complete reappraisal of his environmental policies', telling an audience of auto industry executives that he would not permit environmental concern 'to be used sometimes falsely and sometimes in a demagogic way to destroy the system' (Commoner, 1990, p. 125). As in Britain, it was the late 1980s which again saw the overt use of the environmental message for political gain. The US's 1988 presidential campaign witnessed George Bush, the Republican candidate, attacking Michael Dukakis, the Democratic nominee, for the deplorable environmental condition of Boston Harbour. Small mention was made of (Republican) President Reagan's fiscal policies, which created the condition in the first place (Commoner, 1990). As previously mentioned, in the UK Margaret Thatcher was able to legitimize the environmental movement as a whole with her speech to the Royal Society in 1988. Encouraged by her success, Prime Minister John Major, in his first speech on the environment, attempted to pull the environment back from temporary political neglect and reinstate it into the mainstream of political agenda, through the announcement in July 1991 of a new independent and 'electorally attractive' environmental agency. As North (1991) has observed, 'the environment is an issue that gives politicians a chance to show that they have a wider vision and care. And yet making the right noises costs very little' (1991, p. 2.2).

The 'greening' of the British public: a case study

Increased public awareness would, said David Gee, the then Director Designate of FOE, 'keep environmental concern in the mainstream of agenda' (Gee, 1990). Alternatively, however, there is evidence to suggest that the environmental movement is following Anthony Downs' 'issue attention cycle' (1972). This suggests that as the environmental movement becomes part of the mainstream political arena, the number of people involved declines, owing to discouragement, boredom, alarm or the emergence of a new, more attractive, issue. Such a fear – which has been raised by environmentalists and politicians alike – illustrates why the environmental movement has often been described as a 'passing fad' or a 'clever marketing ploy', and may explain its recent decline in the opinion polls. Indeed, despite the mass media, and the vote-conscious politicians, grasping that the environment can be highly emotive, the majority of the general public appear yet to become motivated, interested or subsequently concerned enough to consciously adopt pro-environmental activities. The varied and differential public support for the environment has been widely explored. In particular, regard has been given to sociodemographic characteristics, political ideology and social beliefs (Samdahl and Robertson, 1989, pp. 58–61). A case study of three localities in Britain attempted to examine some of the variables.

Three contrasting areas of Britain were selected: Nottingham, a city situated within the East Midlands and influenced by the decline in heavy industry; Aberaeron, a small remote coastal town located along the west coast of Wales; and Winchester, the county town of Hampshire located within the 'affluent' South-East. These three sites correspond well to Lowe and Flynn's environmental localities (1989).

The first location they describe is that of a traditional industrial town, where the decline of heavy industry has left areas of dereliction and land contamination. Here, they argue that if environmental controls are too tight, new and established industries will be discouraged from the area. Nottingham was chosen as an example of this, for it was thought that with the privatization of electricity and the need to reduce emissions of sulphur in Britain by 60 per cent between 1980 and 2003 (Schoon, 1991a, p. 6), as well as the additional environmental effects of coal production and combustion, there would perhaps be an environmental backlash in a 'dirty' coal-producing area such as Nottingham which would affect how people respond to environmental concern. In Nottinghamshire, 'the coal industry, together with textiles, has traditionally dominated the industrial economy, particularly as a source of male employment' (NCC 1990). Although Nottinghamshire is generally regarded as one of the 'most prosperous and long-term coalfields in the country it has lost more than 26,000 jobs since 1980, with the closure of 15 collieries, 12 being closed after 1984'. Furthermore, with the industry's drive towards increased productivity and mechanization, 'since 1984 over 40% of the total job losses have been in collieries that have remained open' (NCC 1990). Compounding this, more than '70% of the Nottinghamshire produced deep mined coal is burned in power stations in the Trent Valley'; the loss of this market, even in the short term, due to the purchase of cheaper and 'cleaner' coal to reduce sulphur and carbon dioxide emissions, will lead to the closure, it is feared, of several marginal producers in the county.

Here three villages were selected, all situated to the north of Nottingham and within easy access of the M1 motorway: Annesley, a colliery village with an 'active' mine; Newstead, a colliery village situated 1.5 miles away from Annesley, but where the mine was closed in 1987; and Ravenshead, a village linked to Newstead through parliamentary constituency, but consisting of commuter homes and containing no council or colliery property.

The second location Lowe and Flynn describe as smaller settlements and the countryside, experiencing 'diffuse development pressures as well as threats to the landscape from agricultural intensification and afforestation'; an area having mineral, forestry and agricultural interests in conflict with 'national pressure groups and statutory agencies promoting recreation and conservation' (Lowe and Flynn 1989, p. 260). To represent this type of area Aberaeron was selected. Aberaeron has a population of about 1,450 and is under increasing pressure, along with New Quay three miles along the coast, as 'the foundation of the tourist economy'. It is situated along the Ceredigion coastline, and described in *Ceredigion Coast: A Management*

Study (1989, p. 1) as 'a much valued and sensitive resource which needs to be protected as a landscape, amenity and cultural heritage . . . With improved communications to the South of the country, (Wales) will fuel further population changes and create new pressures on our coast and countryside' (Ceredigion District Council, 1989, p. 4).

The third type of location is the South-East, an area of lowland countryside, characterized by 'anti-development, preservationist opinion, expressed by mainly the middle-class who are orientated towards the protection of amenity' (Lowe and Flynn, 1989, p. 259). Winchester is an area influenced by the South-East Regional Planning Conference, (SERPLAN), which envisaged the movement 'from London of both people and jobs to a number of regional growth areas', while mid-Hampshire has been identified as a 're-straint area' in recognition of its agricultural and landscape qualities. Winchester therefore corresponds to their third area. Three contrasting housing areas within the City of Winchester were selected: a long-term owner occupied estate, built in the early 1960s (Teg Down), a council estate built in the late 1940s/early 1950s (Stanmore), and a relatively new owner-occupied estate, catering for both the first-time buyer and for the 'well established family home' buyer (Badgers Farm).

The three research areas were chosen from Lowe and Flynn's criteria primarily to reduce any locational bias within the research and, secondly, because the place of residence is a sociodemographic variable often cited in the literature as an important indicator of environmental concern. However, as it is not a uniform variable, the use of these three contrasting sites would, it was hoped, enable a more satisfactory investigation to be undertaken into why environmental concern is so varied.

The variables selected for investigation

The aim of this research was to examine the concept of environmental concern and the extent to which one can characterize the environmental movement, so that policy orientated proposals can be formulated. Accordingly, the following variables were studied within the three locations.

a) *Age*: investigating whether those who express concern with the environment are more likely to be in their youth, or whether it is in fact inversely related to age, because the young are more concerned about 'the livability of their environment in later life' (Dillman and Christenson, 1972, p. 251).
b) *Social class*: examining whether there is a positive correlation with upper and middle-class social characteristics and environmental concern.
c) *Place of residence*: discovering whether the site of residence is an indicator of the extent and type of environmental concern.
d) *Mobility*: discovering whether growth in mobility has enabled individuals to experience the countryside and other areas under threat which

would not have been possible before, and as a result reduced the urban and rural bias towards conservation and environmental concern (Harry *et al.*, 1969, p. 247).

e) *Other sociodemographic variables*: variables which may positively effect environmental concern, such as gender, suggested by McEnvoy III (1972), monetary and personal incentives, recreational experiences.

f) *Political ideology*: ideological differences towards business and government would differentiate liberals from conservatives in their support for environmental issues (Costantini and Hanf, 1972; Dunlap and Gale, 1972). However, research has indicated that environmental concern crosses these 'left-right cleavages' (Bowman, 1977; Buttel and Flinn, 1978).

g) *Influence of the mass media*: investigating whether, as research has suggested, it has been effective in increasing environmental concern, or in fact it has produced non involvement within society, due to complacency and misinterpretation (Parlour and Schazow, 1975). Coverage of environmental events by the media is a relatively recent occurrence in Britain; it will be interesting to discover (perhaps at a later date) what factor(s) were influential in causing the media to regard the environment as a 'newsworthy' one rather than rather a tedious issue.

The results

AGE

There is considerable evidence that those expressing environmental concern are more likely to be in their youth (McEnvoy III, 1972; Tognacci *et al.*, 1972; Hornback, 1974). Buttel (1979) for example argues that age has been the variable most constantly and consistently related to attitudinal indicators of environmental concern. Describing this as a 'generation-based movement', he explains how age has been the basis of social differentiation in all historical societies, with the bulk of the 'privileges going to the middle and older age groups' (1979, p. 238). Similarly, Hornback (1974) argues that the young, because of their generally low commitment to the dominant value system and existing institutions, and the fact that many regard the activities of corporations as the major cause of environmental problems, are not afraid of joining a movement that singles out these institutions for reform. Ryder illustrates this point well, when he states that the

potential for change is concentrated in the cohorts of the young adults who are old enough to participate in a movement impelled by change, but are not old enough to have become committed to an occupation, a residence, a family or procreation, or way of life (Ryder, 1965, p. 848).

Buttel (1979) argues that on growing old, the environmentally committed youth of the 1960s and 1970s will replace their anti-environmental elders in positions of power and authority, thus enabling institutions to express more environmental concern and awareness (1979, p. 251). Alternatively, Ryder (1965) suggests that they will lose their pro-environmental stance as they age.

Of particular interest are the large section of the currently young British population who have grown up with a Conservative government. These people have not known what it is like to be governed by anything other than 'Thatcher ideology'. Life for this segment of the population has revolved around and been maintained by those very institutions and corporations that the young of the sixties fought so hard to reform. These could provide a key control group in the examination of the relationship between youth and environmental concern.

As a completely independent variable, age did not seem to lead either to a typical 'environmental' response within the three locations, or within the whole survey. The literature had suggested that age could be a factor influencing environmental concern, but upon investigation the responses indicated that it was not a variable that could be analysed on its own. Investigation of the influence of age on the sample indicated that the variables selected could not be analysed without bringing into context the interrelationship of all the other variables. Thus the effect of age will be discussed as it becomes a factor within the following discussion of the influence of socioeconomic variables on environmental concern.

SOCIAL CLASS

Social class is another sociodemographic variable often positively linked to environmental concern (Faich and Gale, 1971; Lowe, 1975; Bowman, 1977 and Van Liere and Dunlap 1981). Lowe and Goyder (1983) argue that 'a major criticism of environmental groups has been that their members are predominantly middle- or upper middle-class, and that their values are unrepresentative of lower-class interests' (1983, p. 10). They question whether the fact that membership of environmental groups is predominantly middle-class indicates that the environment is basically a middle-class concern, or whether it is simply that environmental groups display that 'characteristic of voluntary organisations in general – that they tend to be formed and supported by the middle class' (Lowe and Goyder, 1983, p. 11). Either way, key concern remains the attraction of non-middle-class people to membership of the environmentally attentive public. In addition Cohen perceives that as education provides people with information, those people with more information will be more environmentally concerned (1973, p. 8). O'Riordan suggests that, with more information, people will realize the link between people and pollution, and so become more willing to pay for pollution control rather than to pay to clean up a site once it has been polluted (1971). Clearly the link here between education and class is crucial;

there is a significant positive relationship between education and environmental concern.

THE FIVE MAJOR CLASS GROUPINGS

Both Aberaeron and Winchester had a higher percentage of individuals within the Professional/Managerial occupational bracket than Nottingham, with its high percentage of Unskilled Manual workers (Table 4.1). If one follows the arguments of Faich and Gale (1971); Lowe (1975); Bowman (1977) and Van Liere and Dunlap (1981) that environmental concern is often linked positively to the upper and middle-class social characteristics, this large proportion of professional/managerial occupations within the samples may affect the proportion of who express 'concern' about the environment. At the beginning of the interviews the subjects were asked what they saw as their greatest worry. This was asked primarily to reduce interviewer/subject cross-reference and secondly to discover whether the subject actually saw the environment or environmental issues as their greatest worry in day-to-day life, or whether in fact it was another issue which was more important. As one chemical scientist explained,

> It's a complex problem, it goes a long way back . . . Lead free is a start, but putting stickers on cars is not going to solve any problems. As a conservationist I drive a car . . . what can I say?

If a comparison can be made between Table 4.1 and Table 4.2, the proportion within the three sites who expressed a concern with the environment, it is interesting to note that Aberaeron and Winchester, locations with the highest proportion of upper to middle class individuals, also show the greatest concern for the environment.

Goodchild argues that the working class are primarily concerned with 'such essential goals as avoiding danger, making a living and obtaining a home with adequate space and standards of physical comfort' (1974, p. 159). One respondent gave a description of what he thought were some of his neighbours' problems:

> They pay no rates, no sewage or water rates, if they get an electricity bill it goes straight to the social . . . some even have no interior doors as they've chopped them up for firewood.

Thus Goodchild suggests that those people who may have 'resolved more of their personal concerns and consequently are better able to devote their spare energies to larger, less personal matters such as the environmental movement' (1974) will probably be those in managerial and professional occupations, the middle class.

Table 4.1 Occupation of head of the household throughout the sample

Class groupings	AB Managerial and professional	C1 Technical and clerical	C2 Skilled manual	DE Unskilled manual	19 Unknown	Total
Nottingham	68	18	33	86	15	220
%	30.9	8.2	15.0	39.1	6.8	
Aberaeron	106	6	40	24	6	183
%	57.9	3.3	21.9	13.1	3.3	
Winchester	104	16	26	20	15	177
%	58.8	9.0	14.7	11.3	8.5	

Table 4.2 Proportion of those who expressed concern over the environment

	Environ. 'worry'	Non-environ. 'worry'	Total
Nottingham	38	182	220
%	17.3	82.7	
Aberaeron	99	84	183
%	54.1	45.9	
Winchester	121	56	177
%	68.4	31.6	

PLACE OF RESIDENCE

Place of residence is another sociodemographic variable often cited in the literature as an important indicator of environmental concern; however, as mentioned earlier, it is not a uniform variable, and so was studied in relation to the three contrasting sites.

When studying this residential effect the increased mobility of the public must also be taken into consideration, combined with the increasing recreation and leisure time spent in the countryside. With the growth of mobility, it has become easier for individuals to experience the countryside and other areas under threat which would not have been possible to visit before. Even so, it should be noted here that not everyone has been subjected to this growth in mobility – as one resident of Newstead explained,

'. . . a 42 year old man met us when we first moved here, he hadn't gone further away from here than the institute, the mine and other people's houses'.

There is evidence to suggest that the reason some people have become more concerned with the environment in recent years is because of this growth in mobility (Means, 1972; Hall, 1976; Moore, 1979). With increasing mobility the place of residence and site of employment may no longer be the same, so reducing the influence of residence on environmental support.

Jackson has argued that with the decline in values associated with 'materialism and unqualified economic growth' and the increasing emphasis placed on concepts such as the quality of life, a relationship has developed between values and attitudes towards the environment and outdoor recreation participation (1986, p. 4). Involvement in outdoor recreation, he argued, was an activity that would create an awareness of an environmental problem by exposing the people to instances of environmental deterioration (1986, p. 6). As a result recreational activity, and its location, may become increasingly important when trying to relate the indicators of environmental concern to residential location.

MOBILITY AND ITS RELATIONSHIP WITH AGE

In the case of Aberaeron, a large proportion of the population is retired. In addition, the majority of those respondents who are retired are also 'new' to the area. Over 41 per cent of the retired sample have lived in Aberaeron for less than twenty years, and 28 per cent for less than ten years. When asked why they had moved here, some of the respondents said that they had either returned to their place of birth, having lived away for the majority of their lives, or decided to retire to a location they had visited on holiday.

If one extracts the retired within Aberaeron as a subset of the sample (the retired being defined throughout the whole of this research as those individuals, independent of gender who are fifty-six years or over, irrespective of employment status) a number of interesting observations occur. To begin with, 66 per cent of the retired can be classified within the Professional/ Managerial social class, compared to 4 per cent within the Technical/Clerical social class, 17 per cent within the Skilled manual social class, and 10 per cent within the Unskilled manual social class, using Johnston et al.'s definition of class (1986, p. 54). Using the assumptions obtained from the comparisons between tables 4.1 and 4.2, one can argue that because there is a high frequency of individuals within the Professional/Managerial professions throughout the retired subset, the proportion of retired expressing environmental concern should equally be high. However, only 43.25 per cent of the retired sample when asked expressed concern over the environment. This could be a result of the differing amounts of 'mobility' found within the retired sample. The discussion earlier suggested that the length of residence and the site of employment of an individual could differ over time, and as a result influence how much individuals could support the environment. If a person had resided in a location all their life, the site of their employment could either be the same as their residence, in this case Aberaeron, or be situated close enough to their residence to still make it economical for daily travel. Within the retired sample only 19 per cent have lived in Aberaeron for all their lives. If the shorter the length of residence in a location causes the least amount of influence of this location on their perception, one can argue that a large proportion of Aberaeron's retired sample must have been influenced by this 'mobility'. This may perhaps reduce the influence of living in Aberaeron on environmental support, for the greater the actual length of residence of an Aberaeron resident the more important the local issues affecting that person's immediate surroundings may become.

Taking the investigation a step further, a comparison can be made between Table 4.3 and Figure 4.1. They show that those individuals with different occupational status have lived in Aberaeron for contrasting lengths of time. Figure 4.1 illustrates this factor well, for as the length of residence increases the frequency of individuals within the upper-middle classes decreases (AB). The majority of individuals found within the Professional/Managerial social class have lived in Aberaeron for ten years or less (30.8 per cent) whereas the majority within the Unskilled/Manual social class have lived in Aberaeron for all of their lives (50 per cent).

Table 4.3 Occupation and length of residence within the Aberaeron sample

| | Length of residence | | | | | | | |
	0–10	11–20	21–30	31–40	41–50	51–60	60+	ALL
AB	33	25	20	14	3	4	8	16
% SUM AB	30.8	23.4	18.7	13.1	2.8	3.7	7.5	15.0
C1	1	1	2	0	0	1	1	1
% SUM C1	16.7	16.7	33.3	0.0	0.0	16.7	16.7	16.7
C2	11	6	9	4	4	1	5	10
% SUM C2	27.5	15.0	22.5	10.0	10.0	2.5	12.5	25.0
DE	4	5	3	2	2	2	6	12
% SUM DE	16.7	20.8	12.5	8.3	8.3	8.3	25.0	50.0
19	3	2	0	0	1	0	0	1
% SUM 19	50.0	33.3	0.0	0.0	16.7	0.0	0.0	16.7

Taking into account the affect of this 'mobility' on environmental support, those who have lived in Aberaeron for the least amount of time should show contrasting amounts of environmental support for varying issues when compared to an individual who has lived in Aberaeron for all their life. Thus, with the influence of social class, the results should show a greater swing towards certain types of environmental support as these factors start to work in conjunction with each other.

Specific issues

ANTI-CONSERVATIONIST VERSUS THE CONSERVATIONIST: IS THERE A NORM?

It is evident from this short discussion that sociodemographic variables are difficult to interpret accurately because of their highly interrelated character. Van Liere and Dunlap (1981) argue that this is the reason why research

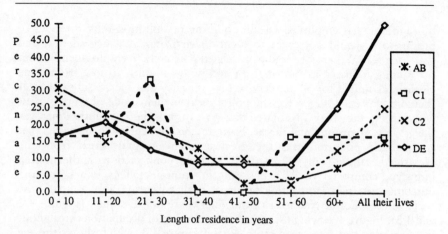

Figure 4.1   Length of residence and social class within the Aberaeron sample

concentrating on these variables has had little success in providing answers as to why there is different support for the environment. Their research, and that of others, was undertaken predominantly in the United States. Whether this will make a difference to the results of this research will, it is hoped, become apparent.

Evidence in the literature indicates that those individuals that are 'anticonservationist' are also rurally based. Harry *et al.* describe those who are 'conservationist' as those people who have an 'appreciative use of natural resources' (1969, p. 247). By this definition, they describe a conservationist as an individual who advocates 'minimal alteration and prefers enjoyment of the resource in its natural state'. Those persons who primarily have an appreciative attitude towards nature, they argue, are those who do not have to earn a living from it. Hence they predict that they usually live and work in urban areas and see the countryside as a place for recreation and enjoyment. Thus Harry perceives agrarianism as running contrary to the principles of conservationism. However, this relationship does not only lie within Harry's 'agrarianism': a number of respondents in both Annesley and Newstead, colliery villages situated to the north of Nottingham, expressed a growing concern with their job and the 'green issue'. As one miner explained,

> When I first started mining the 'green issue' was a few years away . . . now I just hope that the scientists can make this gas flue de-sulphur thing that takes the bad stuff out of the coal, otherwise my job's gone, and I'm stuck here.

It is interesting to note that, even though this conflict between the mining industry and the 'green issue' was expressed by those people with the most to lose from it, those same people did still perceive it as an 'environmental threat' and a problem. This is surprising, as one may have thought that those with the most to lose from growing environmental awareness, those individuals employed within polluting or pollution-related modes of production, would not want to mention environmental degradation and issues for fear of their jobs. Subjects related positively to employment within the mining industry in Nottingham and with the most to lose from mine closure accounted for 50 per cent of the Annesley and Newstead sample. If they did express concern for the pollution that their mode of employment was causing, they may have stated that it was atmospheric pollution that was the greatest environmental threat. From the respondents who answered that atmospheric pollution was the greatest environmental threat from the Newstead sample, only 29.98 per cent were connected with the mining industry, compared to 92.8 per cent in Annesley. This is a surprising outcome, for apart from the location of both villages (1.5 miles apart) the social and economic character of the villages are not dissimilar (Figures 4.2 and 4.3). Figure 4.2, which shows the distribution of occupation throughout the Annesley and Newstead samples, and Figure 4.3, which shows the age distribution between the two villages, serves to illustrate the similarity of the social and economic characteristics between Annesley and Newstead. The two villages have a similar proportion of respondents in each occupation and age group apart from the distribution within the 31–40 and 46–50 age bands. This difference in frequency between Annesley and Newstead may have produced a significant difference in the percentage mentioning atmospheric pollution as a threat.

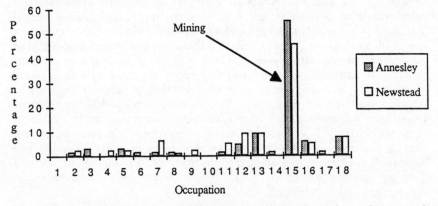

Figure 4.2 Distribution of occupation throughout the Annesley and Newstead samples

On the other hand, it may have been caused by the fact that the two villages are presided over by two different Borough Councils, Ashfield and Gedling. Annesley is within Ashfield and Newstead within Gedling Borough Council boundaries. The significance of this is that Ashfield district council decreed that Annesley be made a 'smoke-free zone' in September 1990. The villagers of Newstead, throughout the period of this

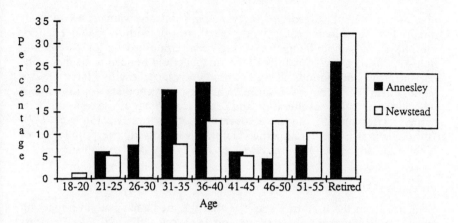

Figure 4.3 Distribution of age throughout the Annesley and Newstead samples

research, were still able to use coal as their main source of heating, for this cheap and convenient fuel was both delivered and heavily subsidized by the National Coal Board and its use was not forbidden.

While the research was being undertaken the difference in air quality between these two villages, just 1.5 miles apart, was astonishing. The weather which was the norm during this period was either fresh and bright or dank and drizzly. There was never much wind, consequently, and because Annesley was within a smokeless zone, the air in this village was noticeably clear and fresh. In Newstead, however, smoke and soot could be seen regularly billowing out from the majority of the houses. This inevitably resulted in partially stagnant sooty smog, which appeared to descend slowly from the chimneys only to swirl and spiral as every car, lorry or bus disturbed it. This site came to be characterized by this sooty, pungent, and cheerless atmosphere where, should it rain, the researcher was often covered in precipitation saturated with sooty black particles. The question to be asked, therefore, is whether the amount of pollution within a location (the air quality in this case) has a direct effect on the perceptions of individuals. One Newstead resident had this to say:

> It's a hideous place this, the smoke rises up from the chimneys, goes straight up and then back down again. It's just so dense . . . You can see it here, in Birmingham you could just taste it. It's more worrying as you can see it.

The Annesley respondents were living in a noticeably cleaner environment than those of Newstead. This perhaps made the Annesley people more 'concerned' about their air quality, especially when they could see a visible difference between a 'smokeless zone' and a non 'smokeless zone'. On the other hand the respondents from Newstead may not have been aware of the bad air quality and in addition, because of the obvious saving that they were obtaining from subsidized coal, they perhaps did not want to mention air quality for fear of losing this subsidy. Furthermore, with over 46 per cent of the Newstead sample being, or having been, employed within the mining industry, using the coal as their domestic fuel could be seen to be maintaining their own livelihoods. This example corresponds with Harry et al.'s 'agrarianism' and 'conservationism' where conservationists are individuals who advocate 'minimal alteration and prefer enjoyment of the resource in its natural state' and do not have to earn a living from it (1969, p. 247). Although it is evident that other factors are involved, the population of Newstead can be seen to fulfil Harry et al.'s theory of 'agrarianism'.

GLOBAL VERSUS LOCAL ISSUES

Evidence from the literature suggests that the media has had an impact on environmental perception (Parlour and Schazow, 1975); the limited discussion at the beginning of this chapter was able to illustrate this. Within the local and national scale the effect of media coverage on environmental awareness is still unknown, however; because of the fortunate/unfortunate time of the field work an indication of the effect of media coverage can be seen, for whilst the research was underway the 'Gulf War' began.

Research in Nottingham took place over twenty-two days from the 18th of February 1991 until the 28th, and from the 10th of March 1991 until the 20th. During this first period the 'allied' ground offensive began into Kuwait and Iraq (Gulf War) and during the second, the cease-fire between the 'allies' and Iraq was called. In addition, throughout this period of research there was enormous mass media coverage of both 'Saddam's Oil Slicks' – "Oil slick damage a 'disaster area' " (The Independent 05/02/91, p. 2), and Saddam's threatened 'Scorched Earth Policy' – "Iraqis 'start oil well inferno' " (the Guardian 23/02/91, p. 1) and its ultimate estimated and actual catastrophic effects on both the regional and global environment. If the media do influence environmental awareness, the considerable amount of coverage produced at this time should, if the effect is significant, lead to an observable pattern within the responses.

Using the twenty-two major groupings of 'worries' and 'environmental threats' mentioned earlier, it is clearly evident from Figure 4.4, which illustrates the range of environmental threats expressed by the respondents within the three locations, that there is a locational difference between the perceived threats and the locations.

The respondents within Aberaeron, the Welsh coastal town, have, not surprisingly, mentioned the state of the seas and the rivers as an 'environmental threat' with more frequency than the rest of the sample. A respondent in Aberaeron was 18.6 per cent more likely to reply thus, compared to 4.96 per cent within the Nottingham and 6.21 per cent within the Winchester sample. In Winchester, the respondents were 13.59 per cent more likely to perceive that 'the ozone' or 'global warming' was their greatest 'environmental threat', compared to just over 3 per cent in both

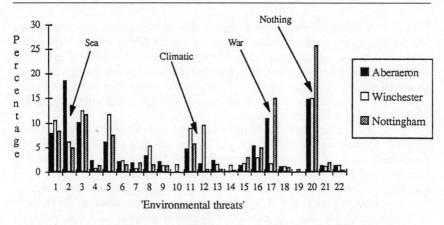

Figure 4.4   Range of 'environmental threats' perceived within the three locations

Aberaeron and Nottingham. From Figure 4.4 it is evident that those who mentioned 'war' as their greatest 'environmental threat' were not respondents from just one sample location, as both Aberaeron and Nottingham have a high proportion of the sample who replied 'war', compared to the Winchester sample. It can be thus deduced from Figure 4.4 that another factor, perhaps that of the media, is influencing what the respondents expressed as their greatest 'environmental threat'.

Using the results obtained from the interviews gathered in 1990 (Figure 4.5) prior to the Iraqi invasion of Kuwait on the 2nd of August 1990 as a 'control', it is evident that the range of 'war-like' or 'Iraqi' responses and the percentage of those subjects who expressed such concerns throughout the whole investigation have increased considerably.

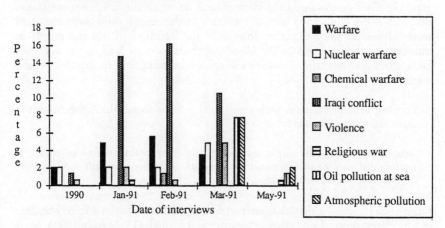

Figure 4.5   Date of interviews and range of 'War' responses

Before the Iraqi invasion of Kuwait, the Middle East was not such a 'media hot-spot', except for an occasional newsworthy event, such as the seizure of the so-called Iraqi 'supergun', or Farzad Bazoft's, a journalist from *The Observer*, execution in Iraq for alleged spying in March 1990. Consequently, a small percentage of the sample mentioned the Middle East as an area for concern, perhaps foreseeing the growing influence of the Middle East on world stability.

Hostilities came to a peak within this region on 2 August 1990, when Iraq invaded Kuwait and again on 16 January when the conflict in the Gulf developed into an air bombardment by the 'allies' on locations within Kuwait and Iraq. This phase of hostilities coincided with a period of interviews carried out in Aberaeron from the 12–19 January 1991. Figure 4.5, which shows the range of 'warlike' responses obtained from the respondents, indicates that the percentage of those who expressed a concern over the Iraqi conflict in January 1991 increased considerably compared to concern for overall world or regional warfare. Perhaps this illustrates what the media thought was the most newsworthy event at this time.

As mentioned previously, the Nottingham research was carried out between 18–28 February and 10–20 March 1991, within which both the 'allied' ground offensive began, and the cease-fire with Iraq was called. It follows that the obvious bombardment of coverage within the mass media may have to some extent influenced the subjects' expressed 'environmental threat'.

While the interviews were being carried out in Nottingham the media coverage changed from one of impending doom, because of the forecasted environmental destruction, to knowledge that now that the war was in progress the environmental catastrophe would not be a global, but a short-term regional disaster – something that would harm the people of Kuwait and Iraq and its neighbouring countries, but not something that would harm 'us'. It is interesting to note that those respondents who expressed a concern with the Gulf conflict and the harm it was doing to the environment stated that they were concerned over the welfare of the animals and birds they had seen helpless in the oil, rather than over the hundreds if not thousands of innocent civilian victims of the allied bombardment of Iraq, who were not gaining media coverage. Two typical responses obtained during this period were:

The death of those animals makes me upset . . . The sooner the Americans get in there and flatten him the better.

When I saw those birds it upset me, more than when we saw the injured babies. It weren't real, not the war. We said when we saw it that we wouldn't mind packing our sleeping bags now and helping them.

Figure 4.5 illustrates this change in concern, and its relationship to the date of the interviews. Once the cease-fire was called (13 March 1991), it is evident that concern moves from the Iraqi conflict itself towards the environmental costs of the war, the oil pollution at sea, and the immense atmospheric pollution caused by the numerous oil-well fires. It should be noted here that the data illustrated in Figure 4.5 represent those interviews where oil in the Gulf and atmospheric pollution in Kuwait was actually mentioned as a concern, and not just air and sea pollution. Whilst the final interview period was being undertaken in Aberaeron (4–11 May 1991), evidence from Figure 4.5 suggests (if one can argue that coverage of the 'Iraqi Conflict' in the media has influenced the subjects' response), that coverage of the Gulf conflict and its environmental repercussions declined considerably during this period. If this is an indication of the influence of the media on environmental awareness, one can infer that although a positive relationship between coverage in the mass media and the environment cannot be made, its obvious influence on whether the subject expresses a concern for local, national or global environmental concerns is clear.

Conclusion

It is evident that support for environmental issues develops because of, and due to, the varied and interrelating relationships of these different variables illustrated throughout this chapter. An individual's sociodemographic status, political ideology and broader social beliefs, as well as other variables such as monetary and personal incentives and the varied influence of the media must be acknowledged if a broader understanding of why there is such varied support for environmental concern is to be achieved.

It is clear that little is known about why there is such varied support for environmental concerns: why two individuals from essentially similar backgrounds can react so differently to environmental information. We should acknowledge not only the change in the way in which we perceive the environment and try to understand it, but also the shift in the way we perceive places themselves, due to changing historical and/or cultural perspectives (Gibson, 1978). For example, an industrial town with factories and smoke stacks may have once been seen as the centre of progress and production, but now because of the awakening of the environmental consciousness it may be seen as a place at the centre of pollution and ecological destruction. It is hoped that people are generally concerned for the environment wherever their place of residence, unless their mode of employment and livelihood is in jeopardy. As a consequence, the main problem in contemporary planning and conservation is the difficulty in combining the landscape ideas of, for example, 'city dwellers' who often use the rural landscape for leisure activities, and tend to have an extreme sensitivity to anything that is perceived to damage the countryside, to the livelihoods of some of the inhabitants of such rural landscapes (Cosgrove, 1984). What is needed is a thorough understanding of what causes the variations in environmental concern described here, so that ultimately livelihood and environmental concern can be associated with a 'rich' and stable society, where the good of the environment is not seen as detrimental to the livelihoods of the majority of the population.

Undertaking research in three contrasting locations in the country, in conjunction with information gathered from the media, it was hoped that both the extent to which the media influences behaviour and the effect of other interrelating variables could be established. What has become evident from this brief discussion is that although the long-term influence of media exposure on an individual's perception and corresponding behaviour is not clear, the short-term influence of such exposure cannot be underrated. It is apparent, therefore, that further analysis is required to establish whether there is a relationship between threats to a local community and the stimulation of the community's residents into pro-environmental action (Manzo and Weinstein, 1987), whether stimulus is obtained from media events, or that the media in fact produce a tendency to view an issue or a problem such as pollution as a general problem, external to one's own community and thus not inspiring pro-environmental behaviour.

Only then, through discovering what may cause an individual to react positively to an environmental issue, whether local, national or global, can we hope to leave the environment in a condition which we would find suitable for our future generations. Because, as the *Global 2000 Report To The President*, commissioned by President Jimmy Carter in 1977, said:

> if present trends continue, the world in 2000 will be more crowded, more polluted, less stable ecologically, more vulnerable to disruption than the world we live in now (*Global 2000 Report*, 1980, p. 1).

> The solution to ecological disaster does not lie in technological approaches, but rather in the alteration of human behavior (Maloney and Ward, 1973, p. 583).

This behaviour has to be 'altered' now, through a better understanding of why there is such varied support for environmental concern, so that we stand a better chance of succeeding; after all, 'the turn of the century is no further in front of us than 1980 is behind' (McKibben, 1990, p. 7).

Bibliography

Bowman, J.S. (1977) 'Public opinion and the environment: post-Earth Day attitudes among college students', in *Environment and Behavior*, 9(3) 385–416.
Breach, I. (1990) 'Green vote effect', in *The Listener*, 8 November, pp. 4–5.
Brittain, V. (1991) *Guardian* 20 September, p. 28.
Brown, L.R. (1990) (ed.) *State Of The World: A Worldwatch Institute Report on Progress Toward a Sustainable Society*, London: Unwin.
Buttel, F.H. (1979) 'Age and environmental concern: a multivariate analysis', in *Youth and Society* 10(3) 237–256.

Buttel, F.H. (1990) *From Limits To Growth To Global Change: Constraints And Contradictions In The Evolution Of Environmental Science And Ideology.* Paper given at the Manconochie lecture, University College London, 8 February 1990.

Buttel, F.H. and Flinn, W.L. (1978), 'The politics of environmental concern: the impacts of party identification and political ideology on environmental attitudes', in *Environment and Behavior* 10(1) 17–36.

Ceredigion District Council (1988) *Aberaeron and New Quay Draft Local Plan.*

Ceredigion District Council (1989) *Ceredigion Coast: A Management Study.*

Cohen, M.R. (1973) 'Environmental information versus environmental attitudes', in *Journal of Environmental Education*, 5(2) 5–8.

Commoner, B. (1990) *Making Peace With The Planet*, London: Victor Gollancz Ltd.

Cosgrove, D.E. (1984) *Social Formation And Symbolic Landscapes*, London: Croom Helm.

Costantini, E. and Hanf, K. (1972) 'Environmental concern and Lake Tahoe: A study of elite perceptions, backgrounds and attitudes', in *Environment and Behavior* 4 209–242.

Dillman, D.A. and Christenson, J.A. (1972) 'The public value for pollution control', Paper 12, 237–256, in Burch, W.R., Cheek, N.H. and Taylor, L., *Social behavior, natural resources and the environment*, New York: Harper and Row.

Downs, A. (1972) 'Up and down with ecology – the issue attention cycle', in *Public Interest*, 28 38–50.

Dunlap, R.E. and Gale, R.P. (1972) 'Politics and ecology: political profile of student eco-activists', in *Youth and Society* 379–397.

Elkington, J. (1989) *The Green Capitalists*, London: Victor Gollancz Ltd.

Faich, R.G. and Gale, R.P. (1971) 'The environmental movement: from recreation to politics', in *Sociological Perspectives*, 14 (July) 270–287.

Gee, David, speech given to Surrey Friends of the Earth at University of Surrey, 9 February 1990.

Gibson, E. (1978) 'Understanding the subjective meaning of places', in Ley, D. and Samuels, M.S. (eds), *The Human Experience Of Space And Place*, London: Croom Helm.

Godwin, P. (1991) the *Guardian* 4 October, p. 27.

Goodchild, B. (1974) 'Class differences in environmental perception: an explanatory study', *Urban Studies*, 11 157–169.

Goodwin, S. (1991) *The Independent*, 19 September, p. 6.

Hall, I.M. (1976) 'Community action versus pollution: A study of a residents group in a Welsh urban area', in *Social Science Monograph 2*, UN Board of Celtic Studies, Cardiff.

Hampshire County Council (1987) *Hampshire: Adopted County Strategy 1991–2001*. Background paper.

Harry, J., Gale, R. and Hendee, J. (1969) 'Conservation: an upper-middle class social movement', in *Journal of Leisure Research*, 1 246–254.

Hornback, K.E. (1974) *Orbits of Opinion: The Role of Age in the Environmental Movement's Attentive public*, unpublished Ph.D., Michigan State University.

Jackson, E.L. (1986) 'Outdoor recreation participation and attitude to the environment', in *Leisure Studies*, 5(1) 1–23.

Johnston, R.J., Gregory, D. and Smith, D.M. (1986), *Dictionary of Human Geography*, Oxford: Basil Blackwell.

Lowe, P.D. (1975) 'Science and government: The case of pollution', in *Public Administration*, 54 287–298.

Lowe, P.D., and Flynn, A. (1989) 'Environmental politics and policy in the 1980s', in Mohan, J (ed.) *The Political Geography of Contemporary Britain*, London: Macmillan.

Lowe, P. and Goyder, J. (1983) *Environmental Groups In Politics*, London: George Allen and Unwin.

Lucas, E. (1991) *The Independent*, 22 October, p. 12.

McCarthy, M. (1989) *The Times*, 5 June.

McCormick, J. (1989) *The Global Environmental Movement: Reclaiming Paradise*, London: Belhaven Press.

McEnvoy III, J. (1972) 'The American concern with environment', pp. 214–236 in Burch, W.R., Cheek, N.H. and Taylor, L. (eds) *Social Behavior, Natural Resources and The Environment*, New York: Harper and Row.

McKibben, B. (1990) *The End Of Nature*, London: Viking.

Major, J. (1991) Text of speech on 'The Global Environment', at the *Sunday Times* Environment Exhibition held at Olympia on Monday 8 July.

Maloney, W.P. and Ward, M.P. (1973) 'Ecology: let's hear from the people: an objective scale for the measurement of ecological attitudes and knowledge', in *American Psychologist*, pp. 787–790.

Manzo, L.C. and Weinstein, N.D. (1987) 'Behavioral commitment to environmental protection: A study of active and nonactive members of the Sierra Club', in *Environment and Behavior* 19(6) Nov. 673–694.

Means, R.L. (1972) 'Public opinion and planned changes in social behavior: The ecological crisis', pp. 203–213 in Burch, W.R., Cheek, N.H. and Taylor, L. (eds) *Social Behavior, Natural Resources and The Environment*, New York: Harper and Row.

Moore, G.T. (1979) 'Knowing about knowing: The current state of theory and research on environmental cognition', in *Environment and Behavior* 11(1) 33–70.

North, R. (1991) *The Sunday Times* 14 July, p. 2.2.

Nottinghamshire Coal (1990) Nottinghamshire Coal 1988/89.

Nottingham County Council (1990) *Profile*, September, 'Planning And Transportation'.

O'Riordan, T. (1971) 'Public opinion and environmental quality: A reappraisal', in *Environment and Behavior* 3 191–214.

Parlour, J.W. and Schazow, S. (1975), 'The mass media and public concern for environmental problems in Canada, 1960–1972', in *International Journal Of Environmental Studies* 13, 9–71.

Patterson, W.C. (1990) *The Energy Alternative*, London: Macdonald Optima.

Porritt, J. and Winner, D. (1988) *The Coming of The Greens*, London: Fontana.

Porritt, J. (1989) *The Times*, 5 June.

Ryder, N.B. (1965) 'The cohort as a concept in the study of social change', in *American Sociological Review*, 30, 843–861.

Samdahl, D.M. and Robertson, R. (1989) 'Social determinants of environmental concern: Specification and test of the model', in *Environment and Behavior* 21(1) Jan 57–81.

Schoon, N. (1991a) *The Independent* 30 September, p. 6.

Schoon, N. (1991b) *The Independent On Sunday* 20 October, p. 16.

The Global 2000 Report to the President (1980) Vol.1: The Summary Report. New York: Pergamon.

Guardian (1970) 2 January, p. 2.

The Independent (1992) 'Election 92: The full results', 11 April, I–IV.

The Times (1970) 2 January, p. 5.

This Common Inheritance (1990) Britain's Environmental Strategy. Government White Paper, September, London: HMSO.

Tognacci, L.N., Weigel, R.H., Widen, M.F. and Vernon, D.T.A. (1972) 'Environmental quality: How universal is public concern?', in *Environmental Behavior*, 4, 73–86.

Van Liere, K.D. and Dunlap, R.E. (1981) 'Environmental concern: Does it make a difference how it's measured?', in *Environment and Behavior* 13(6) 651–676.

Viets, S. (1991) *The Independent On Sunday*, 13 October, p. 11.

Weiner, J. (1990) *The Next One Hundred Years*, London: Rider.

PART II
The Greening of the Land Use Debate

5

UK land use and the global commons

Martin Whitby and Neil Adger

Introduction

Land use has provided a focus for academic activity and has been studied over the last few decades with varying intensity. Land is one of the classical factors of production and hence has been of interest since Ricardo and Malthus first tried to explain its allocation, early in the 19th century. Agricultural economists have included land use on their research agenda: including both the efficiency with which it is allocated to different uses and the institutional structures which regulate it (Coleman, 1990). The post-war productivist phase of agricultural policy directed attention to collection of data for price determination and criticism of agricultural policy became the central concern of agricultural economists; their attention switched to market analysis and the impact of policy on supply.

A group of researchers nevertheless retained land use on the agenda: Best with a series of careful studies of the rate of conversion of land to other uses (Best 1981), and Wibberley viewing the process from a policy perspective (Wibberley 1959; Edwards and Wibberley 1971). The UK literature on economic issues in land use was surveyed by Peters (1970), who emphasized the use of analytical techniques to resolve policy questions, in particular the cost-benefit analysis of land use change. The intensity of interest in land shown by agricultural economists has varied in the 1970s and 1980s and their interest has generally been related to some aspect of policy (see for example the surveys of Hodge (1985), Bowers (1990) and Hanley (1991)).

The last two decades have seen a distinct broadening of the land use debate as policies have been modified to meet new problems, and new skills have been brought to bear upon it, improving the presentation and quality of data for use in economic and other models. An increasing volume of output from sociologists can also be detected during this period, the best known being that of Newby et al. (1978). This broadening process has encouraged the inclusion of environmental issues on the research agendas of those working on land use.

Peaks in the land use/environment debate during the 1980s have centred around a series of key books, many of them provoked by policy issues of various kinds. The debate was also fuelled by the Club of Rome Report of 1972 (arguments summarized in the *Ecologist*, (1972)), by the commodity crisis of 1972/3 and by the first and second OPEC shocks of 1973 and 1979. The rapid rate of agricultural intensification of the 1970s can be attributed to several market events. First, there was a massive injection of income into the industry following the commodity crisis which itself was triggered mainly by the former USSR buying up US grain stocks and causing a sudden doubling of world grain prices (a.k.a. The Great Grain Robbery). At the same time in the UK expectation of entry into the European Community (EC) and adoption of the price levels applying within the Common Agricultural Policy also encouraged investment. The 'countryside debate' emerged from these events during the 1970s. Shoard (1980), Bowers and Cheshire (1983) and Body (1982) all produced books which owe part of their inspiration to concerns over intensification. Most recently, the end of the 1980s has seen the emergence of global warming as a policy issue. Generally the agricultural focus has been on the impact of warming on agricultural production on sea level rise (e.g. Parry, 1990; Jansen et al., 1991) but of immediate importance is the problem of the impact of land use on the emission of greenhouse gases to the global commons (e.g. Adger et al., 1992; Bouwman, 1990; Sedjo, 1989).

Land use and land use policies

The focus of this chapter will be on primary land use, treating urban use as a residual category, despite the fact that it is in value terms the most important sector to which land may be converted from agriculture.

Primary uses such as farming and forestry are typically combined with other important activities including sport, recreation and conservation of wildlife and landscapes. In some cases these secondary uses may be more highly valued than the primary use: for example the annual value of the shooting rights on an area of upland grazing may well exceed that of the sheep produced on the same land. Following a discussion of the ALURE policy package of 1987, we will assess the success of the forestry sector in terms of conversion from agricultural land. We return to the evaluation of multiple uses at the end of this chapter.

Agriculture is the main land using industry in the UK, in terms of space (some 80 per cent); forestry follows close behind (10 per cent); the remaining 10 per cent being mainly urban. These round figures ignore the debate about the rate of conversion of land from agriculture to various other uses which have been summarized elsewhere (Best, 1981).

In the preamble to the 1947 Agriculture Act, the aim of UK agricultural policy was to achieve home production of 'that share of the Nation's food . . . as in the national interest it is desirable to produce at home'. The national interest then was generally interpreted as accepting importations of cheap food from wherever it could be obtained. On joining the European Community in 1973, however, the UK became a participant in the Common Agricultural Policy (CAP) which pursues an explicit policy of importing only food which cannot physically be produced in the EC. Such a policy, combined with technical innovation and downward inflexibility in the policy-determined price level, has led to the production of substantial agricultural surpluses which can only be disposed of through subsidized exports, or stored pending sale. Both of these options have proved extremely costly to both taxpayers in the EC and to the agricultural producers of external countries through the erosion of world commodity prices.

Alternative land use and rural enterprise

The cost of surpluses in the early 1980s moderated political enthusiasm for production at any price. The concern to check surplus agricultural production was also manifest in the so-called ALURE (Alternative Land Use and Rural Enterprise) policy package (MAFF, 1987). This package called, inter alia, for the designation of Environmentally Sensitive Areas (ESAs); the promotion of afforestation farmland through a Farm Woodlands Scheme; and easing the conversion of land from agriculture to urban uses by relaxing the constraints which had hitherto operated through the planning system.

The varying success in achieving these objectives is now becoming clear. The ESAs are widely seen as the most successful recent policy change (e.g. Baldock et al., 1990) although evaluation of policies aimed mainly at conservation must be recognised as premature. Those areas first designated have just completed their first five years of operation and the Minister of Agriculture, Fisheries and Food (Gummer, 1991) has announced an intention to re-introduce new schemes for those areas. The first round of ESAs covered 0.73 million hectares and within them participation in the Scheme involved farming within defined guidelines which were specific to each area. The uptake of the agreements offered was remarkably rapid, reflecting some combination of the farmers' enthusiasm for the objectives of the policy, the level of payments offered to those complying, ease of compliance with scheme prescriptions and the individual farmer's view of future levels of price and income. The balance of these factors may be inferred from the fact that the uptake of agreements has been rapid in almost all ESAs. The total rate of uptake of ESA agreements is plotted in Figure 5.1, which shows that uptake has been very rapid for agreements and the level of participation has levelled off at some 60 per cent of the designated area within three years of the start of the scheme. This rate of uptake has been quite remarkable in comparison with other forms of agreement with farmers where negotiation periods have often been extended, with consequently high administrative costs, often combined with higher levels of payment to farmers as well (Whitby et al., 1990).

The evaluation of the second element of the ALURE package, the Farm Woodlands Scheme, (Gasson and Hill, 1990) reports that the uptake of the Scheme had not reached a quarter of the target area (36 thousand ha) by

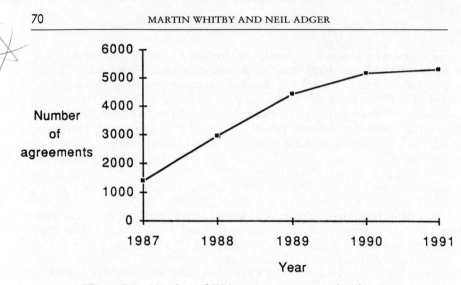

Figure 5.1 Number of ESA agreements operative: by year

Source: Ministry of Agriculture, Fisheries and Food

1990, after two and a half years of operation. The report also emphasizes the importance of non-economic motivation amongst farmers participating in the scheme. From the aggregate Exchequer point of view the cost of the scheme in its first year was £0.83 m., whereas the saving in agricultural support costs estimated was £0.53m. Given that some of this land would have been planted without the scheme, the report concludes that the net annual cost of the scheme was £0.42m. The low uptake of this scheme must be seen as a disappointment. The authors of the evaluation suggest that administrative adjustments to the scheme would improve the results and they advocate a more determined effort to promote it.

The third ALURE element, the attempt to accelerate the transfer of land to urban use, has been much slower in producing results. The pace of land-use conversion has generally been slow, ranging from recession-bound lows in the 1980s, in the region of 10 thousand hectares per year, to the peak of the 1930s when suburban England and Wales was consuming agricultural land at the rate of more than 20 thousand hectares per year. Best (1983) in his last statement on the subject contrasted his perception of the slow rate of conversion of agricultural land to urban use with that purveyed by the media. In a paper which described this 'mismatch of facts . . . in land-use studies' he drew attention to the decline in the rate of conversion of land which was sustained from the 1930s right through to the early 1980s. He estimated that the rate of urban increase in the early 1980s had fallen to 'less than 8 thousand ha, or half the rate of the previous three decades'. He then warned of the likely acceleration in 'land take' as the economy emerged from the recession, because the successive dismantling of planning controls was no longer likely to constrain urban development. The latest data available from the DoE (1989) indicate a net annual rate of increase in the urban area of England of some 7 thousand ha per annum during both 1988 and 1989. The comparable increase for Wales during the period 1985–9 appears to be 3.7 thousand ha. This continued low rate of conversion suggests that the acceleration indicated through the ALURE package and described in DoE Circular (16/87) has not yet materialized. The lesson from this generally slow response to the ALURE initiative must be that land use practices are slow to change. The response of owners to new incentives is slow, partly due to the long-term growth processes involved, but also because of the cautious conservatism of land owners and occupiers.

The speed of urban expansion depends partly on the rate of formation of new homes, which in turn tracks movements in availability of capital (both public and private) affecting new purchasers' ability to buy homes. The planning process serves as an explicit regulator of the transfer of land to urban uses, since the 1947 Town and Country Planning Act 'nationalized' the right to develop land, requiring developers to seek permission for defined changes of use. Policies regarding conversion of agricultural land have been influenced through the whole post-war period by the philosophical position adopted in the Scott Report of 1942. That report, one of the major documents shaping the post-war planning system as it affected rural areas, was committed to the notion that land conversion from agricultural to other uses should be conducted under rules which placed the 'onus of proof', that new uses were in the national interest, on the shoulders of the developer. Operation of that philosophy involved reference of proposals for conversion to the Ministry of Agriculture which generally took the position that better grades of land should not be transferred wherever poorer grades could be used instead. Such a rule, whilst defensible in terms of such homely concepts as 'good housekeeping', also serves to constrain the rate of urban development and add to its costs by directing activity to less appropriate sites. The rule has had a long and influential history and still persists as far as the better grades of agricultural land are concerned. The cost of this, in terms of lost development opportunities and extra development costs, remains to be estimated, although the level of dissatisfaction with congested living in the South East of England appears to be on the increase (Shucksmith, 1990).

In simple areal terms the forestry sector has been a much more significant agent in the conversion of agricultural land, although most of its acquisitions have been at the extensive margin of cultivation, in contrast with urban development which typically takes land at the intensive margin. The annual rate of transfer of land to forestry has varied up to 30 thousand hectares in recent decades and the current official target rate of conversion is somewhat greater than this. The allocative efficiency of this rapid rate of expansion, which has led to a more than doubling of the afforested area during this century, has also been questioned throughout the post-war period.

Although it has now divested itself of some of its established plantings, the Forestry Commission remains Britain's largest single landowner, with the dual responsibility of overseeing the administration of forest grants and licences to private foresters and of managing the state forest enterprise. Its duties and financial obligations have led to regular reviews of its activities (Land Use Study Group, 1966; HM Treasury, 1972; National Audit Office, 1986; Public Accounts Committee, 1987; House of Commons, 1988) through which its own arguments for maintenance and expansion of the forest area in the UK are presented and challenged. Each of these studies is constrained by the availability of adequate economic analysis based on unambiguous data. The latest attempt to remedy these deficiencies has been published under the name of the chairman of the relevant working party (Cunningham, 1991).

The problem for the Commission in justifying afforestation has centred on the fact that temperate forests have a long gestation period (fifty years is not an uncommon notation for even the faster growing species) so that the *present value* of the timber produced by this investment is extremely low. This can be seen from the discount factors to convert a lump sum available in fifty years' time to a present value at various different discount rates.

Table 5.1 Present value of £1, available in fifty years' time, by discount rate

Discount rate per cent	Present value of £1
0	1.0000
3	0.2281
6	0.0543
10	0.0085

With the exception of the zero rate, all of the discount rates shown in Table 5.1 have been applied to official forest investment appraisals at various times and the result has shown forestry to be a dubious investment at rates of discount higher than 3 per cent, if only timber values are brought into the balance.

The search for economic support for the forestry sector has encouraged the Commission to make use of novel techniques (in the UK, that is) for evaluating the benefits arising from its activities. Moreover, it has not always used these techniques rigorously. Thus the Treasury Study of 1972 included, as benefits from forestry, estimates of the value of recreation in the forest, obtained using the travel cost method (Clawson and Knetsch, 1966). Such a use of these estimates is legitimate as a measure of benefits; less legitimate is to ignore the probability that the agricultural land under consideration for planting also provides recreational benefits under agricultural use. The temptation to consider only gross benefits in making cost-benefit appraisals is one of the more obvious methods of 'improving' the result.

The 1972 study referred to applied the 10 per cent Test Discount Rate then in use for all public sector investments, to benefits and costs. This was particularly unfavourable to the forestry case because, applied over a fifty-year rotation, it reduces the present value of the benefits of forestry which do not accrue until the end of the rotation to £0.0085 per £1.00 of terminal value. By adding recreational values the forestry case produced nearly acceptable net present values in some cases at the 10 per cent discount rate. Forestry support has nevertheless continued, despite these poor results, and the Treasury granted the Commission a concession, until recently, to apply a discount rate of 3 per cent in its appraisals. Subsequent official reports have concluded (National Audit Office, 1986), that the Commission's plantings often do not reach even that rate of performance and the required rate of return for forestry has since been raised to 6 per cent.

The most recent study contains estimates of recreation benefits (Benson and Willis, 1991) and of the opportunity cost of land (Harvey, 1991) as well as an aggregation of benefits and costs from all sources (Pearce, 1991). Pearce lists marketed and non-marketed costs and benefits including:

timber values	air pollution value (other than CO_2)
recreational value	water pollution values
landscape value	'greenhouse effect' (trees as carbon stores)
biodiversity value	economic security
watershed protection damage	community integrity
microclimate.	

The study attempts to measure the net benefits of forestry with a summation of those that can be quantified. The list is too long to examine in detail, but it must be noted that there are various points at which conventions are adopted or analytical assumptions made, which enhance the likliehood of positive net present values for particular types of forestry investment. For example, on recreational values Pearce recognizes that some recreational use of farmland will be lost by planting it with trees, but he nevertheless uses the gross recreational benefits of forests estimated by Benson and Willis (1991) without correction for that effect. Examples of the amenity value of agricultural land do exist, though not for the UK, but it would be necessary to have estimates of the amenity value of that land being afforested for direct comparison. This may involve the loss of agricultural land, upland hill farming areas or lowland wetland areas (see Hanley and Craig (1991) for an estimate of the amenity value of the latter).

Similarly, the estimates of the 'greenhouse' contribution of forestry are based on some estimates of carbon sequestration by trees prepared by Forestry Commission scientists (Thompson and Matthews, 1989) which record only the changes above ground during the forest rotation, ignoring important changes below ground, in the root system, as well as the losses of carbon which occur when land is converted from various different uses to forestry (see below).

Several other matters, including community integrity, biodiversity, watershed protection, microclimate and water pollution impacts are not included in the calculations and it may be that the balance of all sources of bias is zero. By producing a long list of impacts Pearce has emphasized the analytical problems of justifying forest planting. Yet his results show, depressingly, that only one form of planting of those tested Sitka Spruce on the uplands, produces a positive net present value when discounted at the current required rate of six per cent.

Aggregate accounts for land use

Whilst Pearce (1991), and the majority of official studies before it, have concentrated on changing land use at the margin, it is also important to be able to assess the output of land in the aggregate. Whereas efficiency is best measured in terms of marginal rates of performance, aggregate measurements show the relative contribution to the national economy of different users. It is even more relevant to do this when undesirable outcomes, such as pollution, are associated with the primary production processes, when it is necessary to measure aggregates in order to assess the scale and rate of accumulation of pollutants in the environment. Such changes are associated with both the existing patterns of land use and with changes to them.

A useful means of assessing the current pattern of land use and the way in which it is changing is now possible because of the greatly expanded capacity to obtain data by remote sensing. Remote sensing is particularly associated with the use of satellite photography, but for longer time series analysis it is necessary to make use of aerial photographs. A set of such photographs for Great Britain (GB) has recently been analysed and presented, for England and Wales by Hunting Surveys (1986) and for Scotland by various regional councils. These have been aggregated into a matrix of change for GB by Adger et al. (1992)[1] which is displayed in Table 5.2. The right hand column in this presentation shows the distribution of all types of land use cover in 1947 and the bottom row the distribution in 1980. The lead diagonal indicates the share of land found in each category at both the beginning and end of the period (which would normally be assumed to have stayed in that category throughout the whole period). The off-diagonal elements in the table indicate the movement of use between categories.

To take an example, the 4.2 per cent of total surface area under coniferous trees in 1980 consists of 0.8 per cent which was in that use at the beginning of the period plus various additions from every other category except urban use. The largest single source of land for coniferous plantation was upland semi-natural vegetation. Another notable source was 0.4 per cent from broadleaved woodland. The matrix also highlights the changes that have taken place in the area of cropped land. The share of area under crops increased from 22.3 per cent in 1947 to 26.9 per cent in 1980, mainly by acquiring 8.8 per cent from improved grassland which was offset by losses to that category of 4.1 per cent.[2]

Table 5.2 Transition land use matrix for Great Britain (1947 to 1980) (percentage of total area)

% Cover in 1947/1980	(a)	(b)	(c)	(d)	(e)	(f)	(g)	(h)	Total (1947)
a) Broadleaved woodland	**2.8**	0.4	0.2	0.2	0.0	0.3	0.5	0.1	4.5
b) Coniferous woodland	0.0	**0.8**	0.1	0.1	0.0	0.0	0.0	0.0	1.1
c) Mixed woodland	0.0	0.1	**0.5**	0.2	0.0	0.0	0.0	0.0	1.0
d) Upland semi-natural vegetation	0.2	2.5	0.4	**29.0**	0.2	0.7	2.4	0.6	36.0
e) Lowland semi-natural vegetation	0.1	0.2	0.1	0.1	**0.2**	0.2	0.2	0.0	1.0
f) Crops	0.1	0.1	0.0	0.5	0.0	**16.6**	4.1	1.0	22.3
g) Improved grass	0.2	0.2	0.1	1.3	0.0	8.8	**17.0**	1.5	29.1
h) Other and urban	0.1	0.0	0.0	0.2	0.0	0.3	0.2	**4.4**	5.1
Total (1980)	3.6	4.2	1.4	31.6	0.4	26.9	24.4	7.6	100.0

Source: Adger *et al.*, 1992.

The insights to be gained from such a matrix are well exemplified by their use in estimating changing carbon balances. In particular it allows separation of the effects of continuing land use from those of changing land use. All changes in land use are fully enumerated and their impacts on the environment can be assessed. As part of a wider study aimed at modifying the accounts for the primary land-using industries, Adger *et al.* (1992) have calculated a series of carbon factors for each important element in the matrix and multiplied them by appropriate areas to yield estimates of the carbon losses and gains from the sector. The study embraces both forestry and agriculture and shows that although substantial volumes of carbon are indeed fixed by trees, amounting to one third of the total amount fixed in retained land use, all changes in land use from one category to another account for a somewhat greater loss of carbon to the atmosphere. To this must be added the effect of agricultural carbon emissions from livestock (as methane), from the burning of fossil fuels, from liming and peat wastage in striking a carbon balance for the sector. The resulting balance is displayed in Table 5.3.

The carbon fluxes reported here are by no means trivial, and may be important if policies to reduce the amount of carbon reaching the atmosphere are to be pursued. However, a better indication of their significance as relevant policy goals can be obtained by setting them in the context of total UK emissions of carbon from all sources which amounted to more than 150 million tonnes in 1988 (Boden *et al.*, 1990). On this basis, the elimination of all carbon losses from the primary land use sector would amount to no more than 3 per cent of total UK emissions. Similarly the 1 million tonnes of carbon fixed by the forestry sector is even less significant.

Table 5.3 Carbon fixation and emissions by GB agriculture and forestry 1988

Fixed	kilotonnes	Emitted	Kilotonnes
Crops for consumption	6,032	From livestock as methane*	2,574
As meat	319	Fossil fuel consumed	707
Livestock products	161	Liming	348
Harvested timber	1,049	Peat wastage	500
Retained land use	2,224	Land use change	903
Total	9,785	Total	5,032

Note: *Methane is measured in carbon equivalent.
Source: Adger *et al*. 1991.

Aggregate estimates of land use 'externalities'

A physical externality is an effect of an activity which imposes or confers a cost or benefit on a person or group. Such effects are external to the market, hence beneficiaries do not pay for them and those bearing costs are not compensated through the market. Pollution is a classic externality which may be of private good or public good nature. By-products can impinge on individuals or on the whole of society, as with global warming. Externalities may be compensated for, regulated, or markets can be created to 'internalize' them. Global warming is a classic public good externality the impact of which is felt, albeit differentially, by the whole of society. The same carbon emission from whatever source equally contributes to the ambient levels of greenhouse gases and though the effects will impinge on regions differently, no individual or group will be exempt from the effects of global warming. The carbon balances above illustrate the role of the land use sector as a source of both positive and negative externalities.

Aggregate estimates of those externalities directly associated with the land using sector can be incorporated in a national accounting framework. As previously discussed by Buttel (Chapter 2), the issue of sustainable income and the depletion of natural resources in aggregate has been brought to the fore with the recognition of the anomalies of traditional measures of economic welfare. It is now widely recognized that economic policy is fundamentally flawed in seeking growth in aggregate income, as conventionally measured.[3] The inclusion of *environmental* costs and benefits is the main feasible alteration that may be incorporated in forthcoming revisions. The underlying premise for these revisions is that the environment is regarded as a stock of natural capital which, like the stock of man-made capital, can be added to or depleted by economic activity. At the aggregate level, those economic activities which deplete the stock of natural capital and flows of services which constitute part of the national welfare can also be estimated, though this moves away from classic definition of sustainable income. An adjustment is also made for defensive expenditures, which are those expenditures of the government and household sectors that are necessarily incurred because of the existence of some negative externality. These expenditures are therefore necessary to maintain the level of aggregate welfare at its previous level.

Adger and Whitby (1991) make such adjustments to the net product of the primary land use sector to allow for defensive expenditure and depletion of natural resources and, by assuming that the land designation process for conservation and recreation is an indicator of the scale of environmental goods valued for existence, option and indirect use, are also able to include estimates of the positive value of environmental benefits from these activities. The study recognizes that the information on the environmental externalities, such as the physical levels of pollution, presented in 'satellite' accounts is the first step to providing policy makers with indicators of the aggregate effects of economic and environmental policies. The identification of marketed defensive expenditures and of non-marketed environmental goods requires boundaries to be set on the sector or type of expenditure estimated. These reflect the essentially arbitrary but evolutionary nature of national and sectoral accounts as presently constituted.

Results from this study are presented in Table 5.4. The two main classes of externality to be included are the positive ones arising from the wildlife and landscape 'goods' produced in the countryside, and the negative externalities arising from pollution. The positive externalities are measured by the contribution of the areas of the countryside designated as important, through the political process, as being of special importance for recreation or conservation. National Parks are primarily concerned with access to a wide public, whereas Sites of Special Scientific Interest provide us with maintained wildlife habitats even if some of us never visit them. Two-thirds of the positive adjustment was due to the Green Belt, but only one-sixth to the much larger area designated for various recreational uses. One-tenth arose from the wildlife designations. The valuations applied to these protected areas are taken from various independent studies of environmental value.

The negative externalities of agriculture and forestry are associated with pollution by them. There are, for example, 841 kilotonnes of nitrates leached into the ground each year from agriculture. The impact of the land use sector on emissions and sequestrations has been explained above and the estimates of aggregate welfare include an adjustment for the net sequestration (modification (1)), valued at an estimated optimal carbon tax rate for the UK (based on Anderson, D. (1991); see Adger and Whitby (1991) for full discussion).

These admittedly incomplete results show net extra flows of benefit from the land use sector of £965m. for 1988, additional to the £4028m. as calculated by MAFF and the Forestry Commission, though omitting many of the adjustments required to give a full indication of the role of the land-using industries in the welfare of Great Britain. Gaps in the estimated benefits and costs remain, such as the incurred costs of nitrate pollution, latent from accumulated agricultural use, and the array of greenhouse gases produced. In arguing for the existence of positive externalities as identified

Table 5.4 Modified agriculture and forestry accounts: Great Britain land use sector

	(£ million current prices) 1988
Net product	4,028
Sustainability modifications	
(1) *degradation of natural capital*	135
(2) *defensive expenditures*	−58
(3) *non-marketed service flows*	888
Modified net product	4,993
of which: Interest	660
Rent and labour	1,664
Farming income	1,816
Forestry income	−112
(1+2) *Sustainability adjustment*	77
(3) *Service flows*	888

Source: Adger and Whitby (1991).

through the protective land designation process, the paper emphasizes that positive external values accrue to society *in spite of* rather than because of modern farming and forestry practices.

A final question remains over our national evaluation of externalities which impact on the global greenhouse. Should these be charged as social costs against UK national income when those sustaining these costs are distributed globally?

Conclusions

This chapter has touched on aspects of the land use debate and the policies emerging from it in Britain. The early economist's definition of land as a factor of production embodying all 'those free gifts of nature' has been replaced by a conception of land as a capital good. However that conception, too, may be being replaced by a broader appreciation of the many and diverse public and private goods produced by land. An attempt to measure these sources of value both in the way projects are appraised in the public sector, using cost-benefit analysis, and in the way in which national income accounts seek to reflect more accurately changes in the national welfare is now needed. Accurate and exhaustive measurement of external and private costs and benefits arising from land use change are required. These must encompass the purely local private impacts as well as the effects of carbon sequestration and release to the global commons, if they are to be relevant to current policy questions.

Notes

1. Although the discussion to date has been applicable to the whole of the UK, the empirical results in the following section are based on data for Great Britain, a subset of the area of the UK which excluded Northern Ireland.
2. It is recognized that the matrix in Table 5.2 is extremely coarse in that it has only eight of the original twenty categories reported by Adger *et al.* That number represented a reduction from the original sources, which were not precisely consistent with each other in all categories. Furthermore the original data were obtained from samples of aerial photographs which are therefore subject to sampling errors in addition to those of interpretation. In the circumstances they provide a reasonable rough guide to events but they cannot be taken as precise: they remain a useful source of data because they reveal so much more than comparison of single-vector frequency distributions about the detail of land use change.
3. The requirement for revision of the System of National Accounts (the international standard) by the UN, has been recognised and has been debated in recent years (Ahmad *et al.* (1989) provide a review of international experience). Other social and environmental issues than those in the study are important and can be measured through aggregate indicators, especially for developing countries (UNDP, 1990; Anderson, V. 1991).

References

Adger N., Brown, K., Shiel, R. and Whitby, M. (1992), 'Carbon dynamics of land use in Great Britain', *Journal of Environmental Management*, 35.

Adger, W. N. and Whitby, M. C. (1991) *National accounting for the externalities of agriculture and forestry*, ESRC Countryside Change Initiative, Working Paper 16, University of Newcastle upon Tyne.

Ahmad, Y. J., El Serafy, S. and Lutz, E. (eds) (1989) *Environmental accounting for sustainable development*, World Bank, Washington DC.

Anderson, D. (1991) *The forestry industry and the greenhouse effect*, Forestry Commission and the Scottish Forestry Trust, Edinburgh.

Anderson, V. (1991) *Alternative economic indicators*, Routledge, London.

Baldock, D., Cox, G., Lowe, P. and Winter, M. (1990) 'Environmentally Sensitive Areas: incrementalism or reform?', *Journal of Rural Studies*, 6(2): 143–162.

Benson, J. and Willis, K. G. (1991) 'The demand for forests for recreation', in Forestry Commission (ed.), *Forestry expansion: a case study of technical, economic and ecological factors*, Forestry Commission, Edinburgh.

Best, R. H. (1981) *Land Use and Living Space*, Methuen, London.

Best, R. H. (1983) *Urban growth and agriculture*, British Association for the Advancement of Science Conference, Brighton.

Boden, T. A., Kanciruk, P. and Farrell, M. P. (1990) *Trends '90: A compendium of data on global change*, Carbon Dioxide Information Analysis Centre, Oak Ridge, Tennessee.

Body, R. (1982) *Agriculture: the Triumph and the Shame*, Temple Smith, London.

Bouwman, A. F. (1990) 'Land use related sources of greenhouse gases: present emissions and possible future trends', *Land Use Policy*, 7(2): 154–164.

Bowers, J. K. and Cheshire, P. C. (1983) *Agriculture, the Countryside and Land Use*, Methuen, London.

Bowers, J. K. (ed.) (1990) *Agriculture and land use into the 1990s*, Economic and Social Research Council, Swindon.

Centre for Agricultural Strategy (1976) *Land for Agriculture*, Report No. 1, Centre for Agricultural Strategy, University of Reading.

Clawson, M. and Knetsch, J. L. (1966) *Economics of Outdoor Recreation*, Johns Hopkins University Press, Baltimore.

Coleman, D. (1990) 'The development, organisation and orientation of agricultural economics in the United Kingdom', in Lowe, P. and Bodiguel, M. (eds), *Rural studies in Britain and France*, Belhaven Press, London.

Cox, G., Lowe, P. and Winter, M. (1985) 'Land Use Conflict after the Wildlife and Countryside Act 1981: the Role of the Farming and Wildlife Advisory Group', *Journal of Rural Studies*, 1(2): 173–183.

Cunningham, I. (1991) Introduction, in Forestry Commission (ed.), *Forestry expansion: a case study of technical, economic and ecological factors*, Forestry Commission, Edinburgh.

Department of the Environment (1989) *Digest of Environmental Protection and Water Statistics*, Government Statistical Service, HMSO, London.

Dillman, B. L. and Bergstrom, J. C. (1991) 'Measuring environmental amenity benefits of agricultural land', in Hanley, N. (ed.) *Farming and the countryside: an economic analysis of external costs and benefits*, CAB International, Wallingford.

The Ecologist (1972) 'Blueprint for Survival', *The Ecologist*, 2(2): 1–44.

Edwards, A. (1986) *An Agricultural Land Use Budget for the United Kingdom*, Department of Environmental Studies and Countryside Planning, Wye College, University of London.

Edwards, A., and Wibberley, G. P. (1971) *An agricultural land budget for Britain*, Studies in Rural Land Use No. 10, Wye College, University of London.

Gasson, R. and Hill, P. (1990) *An economic evaluation of the Farm Woodland Scheme*, Farm Business Unit Occasional Paper No 17, Department of Agricultural Economics, Wye College, University of London.

Gummer, Rt Hon. J. (1991) Opening address, in Miller, F. A. (ed.), *Agricultural policy and the environment*, CAS Paper 24, Centre for Agricultural Strategy, Reading.

Hanley, N. (ed.) (1991) *Farming and the countryside: an economic analysis of external costs and benefits*, CAB International, Wallingford.

Hanley, N. and Craig, S. (1991) 'Wilderness development decisions and the Krutilla-Fisher model: the case of Scotland's 'Flow Country', *Ecological Economies*, 4(2): 145–163.

Harvey, D. R. (1991) 'The agricultural demand for land: its availability and cost for forestry', in Forestry Commission (ed.), *Forestry expansion: a case study of technical, economic and ecological factors*, Forestry Commission, Edinburgh.

Hodge, I. (1985) *Countryside change, a review of research*, Economic and Social Research Council, Swindon.

House of Commons (1988) *Land use and forestry*, House of Commons Agriculture Committee, Minutes of evidence, HMSO, London.

HM Treasury, (1972) *Forestry in Great Britain: an interdepartmental cost/benefit study*, HMSO, London.

Hunting Surveys and Consultants Limited (1986) *Monitoring landscape change*, HMSO, London.

Jansen, H.M.A., Kuik, O.J. and Spiegel, C.K. (1991) 'Impacts of sea level rise: an economic approach', in Organisation for Economic Cooperation and Development (ed.) *Climate change: evaluating the socio-economic impacts*, Organisation for Economic Cooperation and Development, Paris.

Land Use Study Group (1966) *Agriculture, forestry, and the multiple use of rural land*, HMSO, London.

Ministry of Agriculture, Fisheries and Food (1987) *Farming and rural enterprise*, HMSO, London.

National Audit Office (1986) *Review of Forestry Commission Objectives and Achievements*, Reports by the Comptroller and Auditor General, HMSO, London.

Newby, H., Bell, C., Rose, D. and Saunders, P. (1978) *Property, paternalism and power: class and control in rural England*, Hutchinson, London.

Parry, M. (1990) 'The potential impact on agriculture of the greenhouse effect', *Land Use Policy*, 7(2): 109–123.

Pearce, D. (1991) 'Assessing the returns to the economy and society from investment in forestry', in Forestry Commission (eds), *Forestry expansion: a case study of technical, economic and ecological factors*, Forestry Commission, Edinburgh.

Peters, G. H. (1970) 'Land use studies in Britain: a review of literature with special reference to applications of cost-benefit analysis', *Journal of Agricultural Economics*, 21(2): 171–214.

Public Accounts Committee (1987) *Forestry Commission: review of objectives and achievements*, Committee on Public Accounts, HMSO, London.

Sedjo, R. A. (1989) 'Forests to offset the greenhouse effect', *Journal of Forestry*, 87(7): 12–15.

Shoard, M. (1980) *The theft of the countryside*, Temple Smith, London.

Shucksmith, M. (1990) *Housebuilding in Britain's countryside*, Routledge, London.

Thompson, D. A. and Matthews, R. W. (1989) *The storage of carbon in trees and timber*, Forestry Commission Research Information Note 146, Alice Holt.

United Nations Development Programme (1990) *Human Development Report 1990*, United Nations, New York.

Whitby, M. C. (1991) 'Ex post and ex ante views of forest employment: to the future with the wisdom of hindsight', in Bowers, J. K (ed.), *Agriculture and land use into the 1990s*, Economic and Social Research Council, Swindon.

Whitby, M. C. (1991) 'The changing nature of rural land use', in Hanley, N. (ed.), *Farming in the countryside: an economic analysis of external costs and benefits*, CAB International, Wallingford.

Whitby, M.C. and Saunders, C.M. (1990) *Alternative Payment Systems for Management Agreements*, Nature Conservancy Council, Peterborough.

Wibberley, G.P. (1959) *Agriculture and Urban Growth*. Michael Joseph, London.

6

Scandinavian agriculture in a changing environment

Olle Pettersson

Introduction

As in most industrial or post-industrial societies, Scandinavian agriculture has been during past decades, and is today, subjected to major technological, environmental, economic and social changes. The dominating trends in this development are fairly uniform: higher yields and more efficient production by utilization of better plant and animal varieties, together with technical and chemical aids.

A smaller area is utilized for the production required nationally, or for the amount that can be sold on the market with or without government support. In this way, the positive environmental values of agriculture decrease since the open countryside decreases and the flora and fauna of the former agricultural landscape find it more difficult to survive. At the same time, the negative environmental effects of cultivation have increased, principally in the shape of nutrient leaching. This is connected with the Scandinavian climate, with increasingly concentrated production, and with increased intensity. When calculated per kg wheat or per kg milk, the leaching is perhaps not much larger than formerly, but locally it has increased considerably per hectare and per litre of water passing through the agricultural land on its way to lakes, waterways and seas and to the groundwater.

The actual content of agricultural production in terms of area, crops and different habitats is an environmental factor in itself. The influence from the cultivated land on the surrounding nature is another such factor. Between these two factors there is an interaction to the extent that a certain mix of production will lead to a certain type of disturbance. To some extent, they may be regarded as two different aspects of modifications in agriculture and its impact on the environment. Figure 6.1 illustrates the utilization of the Swedish agricultural land and its changes with time.

Million hectares

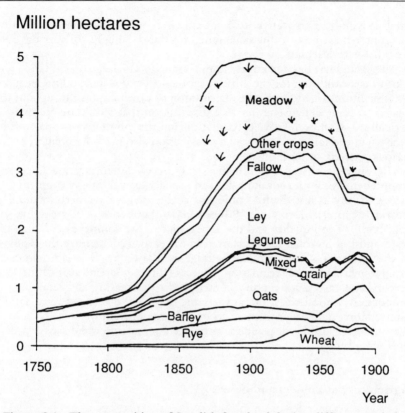

Figure 6.1 The composition of Swedish farmland during different periods

The Scandinavian perspective

Scandinavia is no uniform agricultural area. It includes fertile plainlands in Denmark and southern Sweden with an agricultural structure and yields that are similar to the granaries of Central Europe. It also includes agriculture in sparsely populated areas along the shores of the fjords in Norway and in the deep forests of northern Sweden and Finland.

Many of the examples and discussions in this paper are primarily related to Swedish conditions. However, because of its geography, Sweden covers all the forms of agriculture and environmental problems to be found throughout Scandinavia. They extend from the environmentally fairly harmless ley and cattle-dominated farms in central and northern Sweden, to the intensive grain- or pig-dominated units in the southern provinces. When described in terms of soil types, they vary from heavy clay soils with relatively little leaching of nutrients and an almost negligible soil erosion to the sandy soil areas in parts of south Sweden, similar to parts of Denmark. These areas are exposed to wind erosion, even though the dimensions are small in a global perspective, to some extent depending on the introduction of counter-measures. At the same time, these areas of light soils are the ones most liable to leaching.

All Scandinavia has a relatively humid climate. The large precipitation and run-off is a condition for the diffuse, area-associated water pollution caused by agriculture. In addition, the distribution of precipitation throughout the year is to some extent counter to a distribution that would be optimal for agriculture. Comprehensive precipitation and run-off during the part of the year when the soil is not covered by vegetation also provides conditions for serious leaching of both nitrogen and phosphorus.

The ongoing changes within the structure of agriculture are large and comprehensive, both economically and socially as well as environmentally. However, this is not the first time that such changes have been made. The clearing of forests during the 19th century in Sweden was of great importance both for soil quality and the appearance of the countryside. When the restoration of Swedish forests started in the early 20th century the biomass of the forests was not even half as large as it is today. The large drainage programmes and water regulation projects from the second half of the 19th century and early 20th century contributed to increasing and retaining the production of foodstuffs, but at the same time they destroyed large natural assets. However, the problems and evaluations prevailing in the society of that time put a different perspective on the conflict and the discussion than they would today.

Agriculture as subject and object

At the same time as the changes have taken place in agriculture during past decades, large-scale air pollution in the shape of nitrogen and sulphur deposits, heavy metals and ozone have dominated discussion regarding our environment. Scandinavia has been and is particularly exposed to the industrial discharges of, in particular, sulphur from industrial areas of the United Kingdom and Central Europe. Scandinavia is – again for climatic reasons – a net importer of air pollution. Nitrogen fallout, where traffic is the major source, is by contrast largely a domestic product.

Acidification, sulphur- and nitrogen precipitation, as well as the direct effects of air pollution on vegetation, are among the major environmental problems in Scandinavia. The forest soils, which are already naturally acid and poor in minerals, and of which there are many in Scandinavia, are further depleted. This results in an imbalance in the nutrient supply to trees and indirect damage caused by pollution to the vegetation. Nitrogen precipitation fertilizes the forest as well as fields and meadows. This causes the depletion or disappearance of many natural species as well as of those in the flora of meadows and pastures, species encountering difficulties in situations of good nitrogen supply.

On the other hand, cultivated land is not in general suffering from air pollution. Nonetheless, the acidification is compensated for other reasons by liming and fertilizing. The acid precipitation is small in comparison with what the cultivation measures themselves imply as regards acidification and the need for liming. Nitrogen fallout contributes to an important part of the nitrogen supply of forest trees but is minor in relation to the nitrogen addition by fertilizer and manure to cultivated land. Thus the cultivated land can cope with the pollution of the surrounding world to a better extent than forest and natural areas.

Control and regulation of soil conditions, implied by all cultivation with regard to pH and nutrient level, gives the cultivated land an advantage in comparison with forest and natural land. Air pollution that directly influences the crop is unable to cause any permanent damage to annual plants in agriculture but may perhaps have this effect on forest trees, with their different longevity and life cycle. Although there are examples of damage caused by air pollution on agricultural plants, they do not have the same long-term ecological and economic dimensions as the effects of pollution in other parts of the countryside.

The increasing pollution caused by agriculture has probably had greater effects on society than those caused by society on agriculture. Cultivation measures designed to increase production do not make the soil more vulnerable to external influence but may lead to increased pollution from agriculture to the environment.

To some extent, the environmental influence of agriculture can be decreased by improved technology – for example, by increased precision in the use of fertilizers and pesticides, and by means of special measures such as retaining vegetation cover in order to reduce leaching. Another consideration that must be borne in mind is that environmental influence is an unavoidable secondary effect of cultivation. However, the character and dimensions of the problem vary depending on natural conditions and the structure of the farm and its branch of production.

Origin of environmental problems

The advantages of cultivation to mankind, as well as its disadvantages to nature and mankind, can both be found in the original conflict between nature and cultivation. Since the discussion today is frequently based on a variant of the *paradise myth*, which includes the belief that agriculture has had a 'natural' phase in its development when there was full harmony and no environmental problems, there may be reason to look more closely at the fundamental conditions and problems of cultivation. Cultivation implies the creation of entirely new ecosystems which – in contrast to natural ecosystems – are a result of human endeavour (Figure 6.2).

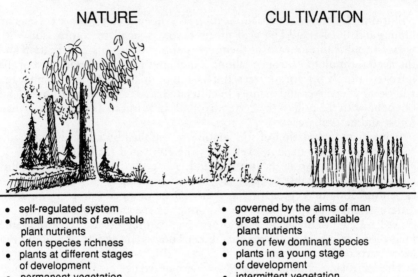

NATURE	CULTIVATION
• self-regulated system	• governed by the aims of man
• small amounts of available plant nutrients	• great amounts of available plant nutrients
• often species richness	• one or few dominant species
• plants at different stages of development	• plants in a young stage of development
• permanent vegetation	• intermittent vegetation
• recirculation, small leakage	• open circulation, great leakage
	• weeds and pests
	• high net production of biomass

Figure 6.2   Differing characteristics of cultivated and natural ecosystems

Ecological Conditions

Whereas the natural ecosystem lacks goals and meaning, and is only the result of evolutionary and ecological forces, the agrarian ecosystem has the task of producing a surplus in order to satisfy the requirements for feed, food or fibre as defined by man. The recirculation and self-regulation of nature is replaced by deliberate measures. The aims and the methods used by the cultivator in order to achieve these targets have consequences for the appearance and properties of the ecosystem in several respects. One of these concerns the selection of species and varieties that are permitted to grow.

In the natural ecosystem, the species composition reflects how individual plants have been able to survive and compete with others. In contrast, with cultivation the criterion is that the plants should produce a sufficiently large surplus. Plants which do not fulfil this requirement are eliminated or kept in check. Natural selection has been replaced by a selection decided upon by the farmer. The equilibrium and harmony that for long periods may occur, or appear to occur, in the natural ecosystem are reflected in the cultivated ecosystem by a more short-term balance which is maintained by continuous measures and inputs.

From this perspective, all forms of cultivation are unnatural. The methods differ, as well as the opinions and descriptions of the character and intention of the cultivation measures, but the objective is largely the same. The farmer's battle against the forces of nature is continuously in progress even though there are defeats and tactical withdrawals among the advances.

An important aspect of the agrarian ecosystem is that of the species and varieties which are allowed to grow. Another aspect is the availability and supply of plant nutrients, which is of major importance in the control of agrarian ecosystems. Plant nutrients circulate in the natural system. The small amounts that are released when the biomass is degraded are taken up by other plants. In nature, the nutrient availability is an important factor, alongside light, air and water, for the self-regulation of the ecosystem.

In cultivated ecosystems there must be large amounts of potassium, phosphorus and nitrogen available in order for the plants to produce a surplus (see Figure 6.3). Through the supply of organic manure and fertilizer, or by release of the nutrients available in the soil, there are relatively high concentrations of several nutrients in the soil, including nitrogen.

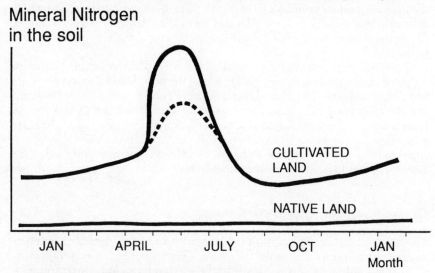

Mineral Nitrogen in the soil

CULTIVATED LAND

NATIVE LAND

JAN   APRIL   JULY   OCT   JAN

Month

Figure 6.3 The level of mineral nitrogen in the soil during the year in cultivated and native land

In fact, this is desirable only during certain times of the year when the plant takes up its nutrition, particularly during the early summer. By means of the measures introduced to achieve the desired nutrient level, the concentration of plant nutrients in the soil will, however, remain high throughout the entire year in comparison with the natural ecosystem. Under the climatic conditions prevailing in Scandinavia, with large precipitation and run-off from the field during spring and autumn, this leads to large amounts of leaching.

The cultivated soil leaches plant nutrients for several different reasons. The high nutrient level compared with natural systems, and the fact that the soil is not vegetated during some parts of the year, are among the most important reasons. To some extent the leaching can be reduced, but in practice it will always be considerably higher than in more natural systems.

Apart from fertilization, soil management and other cultivation measures are of importance for nutrient status. By stimulating the metabolism in the soil and the degradation of organic matter, nutrients are also released. Soil tillage may be regarded somewhat as a 'necessary evil' in order to obtain suitable conditions for the crop both with regard to moisture, temperature and nutrient availability. It also plays a role in achieving uniform and reliable germination and for controlling undesirable vegetation.

In the natural ecosystem, there is a successive transition between the intensive photosynthesis and growth during the summer and the stationary phase during the winter. With cultivation, the vegetation is abruptly terminated by harvesting and removal of large amounts of biomass. In some cases, the harvest residues contain extremely large amounts of nutrients and easily metabolizable organic material. In this way, the release of nitrogen during the autumn may be comprehensive, e.g. in crops such as potatoes and legumes.

The status that is favourable for the cultivated plant is retained through different cultivation measures. As a result of the one-sided selection of plants and other measures introduced, certain other species will be also favoured and the crop plant may be exposed to competition from weeds and attacks from insects and fungus diseases. Countermeasures vary, but all of them are important for the environmental effect of the cultivation. Soil tillage, crop rotation and direct control using technical and chemical methods, for example, all reduce attacks and competition.

Cultivation methods and production structure

The fundamental *ecological conditions* of cultivation are, therefore, important as regards its environmental influence. One way of expressing this is that all cultivation leads to disturbances to the surroundings in comparison with not cultivating at all. There is thus a basic problem or a certain basic level of environmental problems *regardless of the methods used*. The size of the problems on this more basic level depends, in turn, on natural conditions such as climate and soil type. Large-scale precipitation and run-off lead to leaching of plant nutrients, whereas lack of precipitation and large-scale evaporation lead instead to 'internal' problems for the cultivation system in the shape of, for example, salinization.

The size of the environmental influence of agriculture is also determined by factors of a more technological and social character. Thus the *production structure* of the agricultural industry is of importance. This concerns, for instance, such aspects as where and how much organic manure is produced in relation to the needs of crop production. Another of these structural aspects is the one-sidedness of cultivation with regard to grain production and how homogeneous the actual countryside is. The more annual crops in the rotation and the fewer perennial crops, the greater the problems in certain respects.

Protective barriers against uncultivated parts of the countryside which can cope with, absorb or eliminate leaching plant nutrients are of great importance for the negative environmental influence that cultivation may lead to in a more regional perspective. The changes to the countryside that led to eliminated wetlands, to straightened-out watercourses, and which allow water from cultivated areas to flow more rapidly to lakes and to the sea, have also led to greater and faster transportation of nutrients with major consequences in the final receiving body of water.

In Scandinavia as well as in other industrial countries, the changes in the structure of agricultural production have led to intensive livestock-keeping within certain agricultural areas, and an imbalance between livestock-keeping and crop production. To some extent this is a result of the free market and the advantages of large-scale production, but in other respects it has been stimulated by agricultural policy.

The quality of the *technology and the methods* used in cultivation is also of importance for the influence on the surroundings. The degree of precision when spreading fertilizer and pesticides is to some extent decisive for the amount that disappears from the agrarian ecosystem. The suitability of the molecules in the chemicals applied for their task in damaging weeds and pests is also decisive regarding the extent to which they have undesirable secondary effects on plants and animals – in nature and in the cultivation – that are not the target organisms. The quality of buildings and machinery and the availability of technological resources as regards storage and spreading of manure are further factors of importance for how far it is possible to optimize the cultivation in an environmental perspective.

Scandinavian agriculture has been exposed to the same forces and the same structural changes as in other industrial countries. However, inertia has been widespread and the changes that cause problems, e.g. concentrated livestock-keeping and intensive cultivation, have not been as pronounced in Scandinavia as in the Netherlands and in parts of England, Germany and the United States. The variations within Scandinavia are also large.

Forces in agricultural development

The direction and development of cultivation, its methods and production results, as well as its influence on the environment, are governed by many different factors. Some of these originate from nature, whereas others are involved with social, economic or political forces (see Figure 6.4).

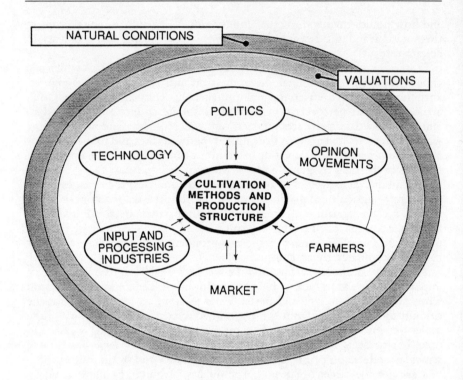

Figure 6.4   Forces and factors important for the development of cultivation
methods and production structure in agriculture

Ecological framework

The natural conditions include factors such as the climate and the soil type.
The amount of available water, the structure of the soils, the composition
and original nutrient availability, together with the amount of light and heat
that can be metabolized in photosynthesis, make up the outer framework
within which agriculture and its methods can be developed. Certain
measures in plant breeding, irrigation and soil preparation can manipulate
the natural conditions but only within certain limits.

Some of the problems and secondary effects of agriculture are connected
with these natural conditions and vary between different parts of the world.
As regards Scandinavian agriculture, this implies that the nutrient leaching is
relatively large whereas erosion problems are usually limited.

Values

The values and attitudes prevalent in society also directly and indirectly influence the direction and methods used in agriculture. What is accepted and permissible varies, because of historical and cultural differences. For example, rules about which animals and plants are considered correct to eat are deeply embedded in tradition and values that vary between individuals and groups. Ethics and values are also extremely important in attitudes to changes in agriculture and in the cultivated landscape. If certain values are more prominent in the Scandinavian countries, then this will characterize the discussion on and assessment of the changes in agriculture.

The specialization of crop production and livestock-keeping on the individual farm depends on several more direct forces in addition to the environment of values and natural conditions. Among these are the market and agricultural policy, which decide what the consumers wish to purchase and the demands placed by inhabitants and society on production.

In Scandinavia there has traditionally been a high degree of confidence in political measures and solutions to different problems in society. This is probably the result of a relatively stable political situation and also with numerous successful examples of the art of 'social engineering'. Consequently, it is natural to expect that both disappointment and worry about the development, as well as demands for changes and the introduction of better times, would lead to political demands and opinions of greater importance in Scandinavia than in other countries.

Technology

Research, education and extension are of great importance for development in most parts of modern and post-modern society. The systematic utilization of both old and new knowledge also has an important role in agriculture. This concerns both developmental work within private companies and government-funded research at institutes and universities.

Many methods and techniques are rapidly disseminated since research and extension have international contacts and since product development and marketing are similar throughout large parts of the world. Large amounts of agricultural technology and changes within agriculture have, consequently, a remarkably similar character in different places, principally in the different industrialized countries.

Changed valuations

An important factor and a condition for the industrial revolution is the view of nature that has dominated for several centuries in western countries. In these countries, physics has been the science that has provided a structure for the dominating philosophy. Consequently, it has also characterized the view of nature and provided a base for the opinion that the surrounding world can be controlled, that nature and individuals are machines and that changes are predictable. This view of nature has also been a condition for the changes in agriculture in an 'industrial' direction. There are tendencies that the position of physics in this respect is being replaced by biology and ecology, at the same time as traditional religion is decreasing in importance and a form of 'eco-religion' arriving in its place.

As regards Scandinavia, we must not forget the exceptional place of agriculture in culture and in the consciousness of the population. A common factor for all the Scandinavian countries is that the more comprehensive industrial revolution came late for many of the inhabitants even though aspects of industrialism – for instance, mining – have long traditions in these countries. Until fairly recently, the Scandinavian countries were peasant countries, and there has never been a pronounced 'big city culture', with accompanying dominating changes in values, such as may be found in the United Kingdom and in Central and Southern Europe.

Most people have relatively close contacts and relationships with the farming culture. This was also characterized to a greater extent than in many other countries by free and independent farmers and to a smaller extent by nobility and large estate owners, even though exceptions from this can also be found in certain parts of Scandinavia. Consequently, it is probable that more people feel affected by the changes in agriculture in Scandinavia than in many other parts of Europe. It is their own cultural inheritance that is being changed, and not just that of other people.

Historically, both the positive and negative environmental effects of cultivation and livestock management have been a secondary effect. The main objects for agriculture, to produce sufficient food for making a living or to supply the demands of the market, have dominated the perspective until recently. The botanically most unique and beautiful parts of the countryside, which form a fundamental part of Scandinavian history and culture, were a result of over-exploitation with regard to plant nutrients. Meadows and wooded pastures were depleted at the expense of the arable field.

With technological development and availability of fertilizer, these areas have lost their economic value and are today disappearing, perhaps just at a time when they are starting to be appreciated by more than the urban upper and middle class when visiting their summer cottages. The 'urbanized' view of nature, which shows less appreciation of production and more appreci- ation of beauty, is extending through society at the same time as these parts of the agricultural landscape are being lost. To some extent, the changes are modified and delayed as a result of the design of the support system in society, but technology, the market and overall economic factors largely maintain the earlier direction of events.

Changes to reality

Major changes to the agricultural industry in Scandinavia have taken place as recently as during past decades. A few data concerning Sweden are given in Table 6.1. They concern both the structure of the industry and the yields from animals and crops and inputs of energy and other external resources, as well as the technology used from seeding to harvest.

Table 6.1 Some data on the changes in Swedish agriculture during the last decades

	1950	1988
Cultivated land, 1,000 hectares	3,600	2,800
Meadow, 1,000 hectares	650	330
Farms, 1,000	280	100
Dairy cows, 1,000	1,700	640
Pigs, 1,000	1,300	2,200
Horses, 1,000	440	60
Tractors, 1,000	70	180
Fertilizer use, kg/hectare		
Nitrogen	15	80
Phosphorus	15	10
Potassium	10	20
Yield		
Winter wheat,100 kg/hectare	24	55
Spring barley,100 kg/hectare	20	35
Milk, kg/cow/year	3,000	6,800

The number of agriculture firms has decreased to one-third of the Second World War level. One-fourth of the area has been withdrawn from production. Inputs of nitrogen fertilizer have increased several times over, and new pesticides are now being used. For the dominating crops, the yields have approximately doubled, as has milk production per cow. In contrast, the number of cows has decreased whereas the production of pork has increased considerably.

Structural changes, increased total production and specialization have led to a considerable increase of certain environmental problems, particularly the leaching of nutrients. At the same time, the aesthetic value of the agricultural landscape has been reduced in some respects both quantitatively and qualitatively (see also Figure 6.1). Mechanization has replaced much of the manual work.

Overall, these changes have resulted in the proportion of the population engaged in direct agricultural production decreasing from about 25 per cent to 3 per cent since 1950. These figures apply to Sweden but the tendencies are similar for all countries, even if the time perspective may be different. Some of the changes have come later in Norway and Finland in comparison with Denmark. In Norway, political measures to preserve the structure of agriculture have had greater impact. In Finland, urbanization and industrialization arrived later than in Sweden. In Denmark, the availability of and success of export markets has been of great importance for retaining the extent of agricultural production in the country.

Character and dimensions of environmental problems

The environmental problems of agriculture have their origin in fundamental ecological factors, in the structure of the industry and in the technique and the methods applied. How the major or minor problems are regarded depends, in turn, on what values are placed on agriculture in relation to what people consider it should be.

When studied more closely, the heading of this section can be divided into four different aspects (Figure 6.5). These concern the *sustainability of production or productive ability*, the *influence on the environment*, thus dealing with environmental effects in a more concrete manner, the *utilization of non-renewable resources*, and *questions concerning product quality and suitability with regard to health*.

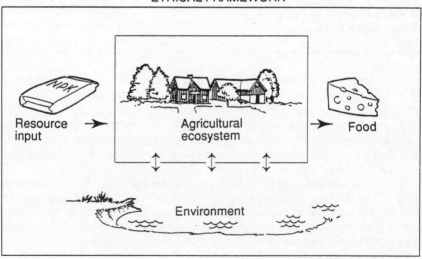

Figure 6.5   Agriculture as industry and ecosystem and its relation to the environment

The problems concerning the sustainability of the production of land and animals include the requirement to preserve the organic and nutrient balance of the soil. In principle, secondary effects of pesticides which may lead to accumulation in soils or may influence the soil life in a negative direction also belong to the same type of effects. Agriculture today uses non-renewable resources in the form of energy for fuels and nitrogenous fertilizers, potassium and phosphorus from limited deposits.

A third type of problem concerns effects on the environment caused by production itself, which are environmental effects of a more concrete nature. The leaching of nutrients from arable land also belongs to this category, together with secondary effects in nature caused by agricultural pesticides. The changes to the appearance of and access to the countryside caused by production methods can also be included in this category of agricultural influence on the environment.

The fourth aspect concerns product quality. Examples include not only nutritional, physiological and technical quality of food, but also the risk of residues of pesticides entering the processed foodstuffs or enhanced concentrations of heavy metals as a result of the applications made to agricultural land.

Conflicts between objectives

As there may be and are conflicts between high yields and efficiency on the one hand and environmental goals on the other, there may also be conflicts between the different 'environmental' objectives that apply to agriculture. Stable, durable agriculture is not necessarily the type that has the least effect on the external environment. Similarly, low-input agriculture is not necessarily the most environmentally orientated. There may also be a contradiction between preserved productive ability and preservation of non-renewable resources.

There are numerous examples of these conflicts. Intensive fertilization contributes to increasing the amount of harvest residues and thereby improves the humus balance in the soil. At the same time, the high intensity may lead to increased pollution through leaching to the surface- and groundwater. Agriculture with low resource requirements and with lower utilization of external supplies of nitrogen may imply that biological nitrogen fixation can be used to a greater extent, something which would probably lead to larger losses to the environment than the use of conventional fertilizer. Utilization of harvest residues for purposes outside agriculture (energy, etc.) may, in turn, lead to a deteriorated humus balance in the field. The use of pesticides may lead to residues in foodstuffs, but at the same time have positive effects on quality in other respects since it contributes to better hygiene and better technical quality of the products.

Certain conflicts between objectives can be reduced or eliminated using sophisticated technology and new knowledge which make it possible to manipulate the ecosystem with smaller secondary effects. Other conflicts are of a more fundamental nature and originate from the original contradiction between nature and cultivation.

Changed environmental impact

What are the changes, then, that have taken place over the years in the influence of agriculture on the environment as a result of the forces and changes within agriculture discussed in earlier sections? Allowing for the generalizations that a survey of this kind must contain, we may state that the productive ability of both the soil and of animals has been retained and improved. This is a result of, for example, the possibility of supplying essential nutrients from external sources but is also a result of general improvements as regards the properties of crop plants and domestic animals.

As a result of the compaction and humus concentrations resulting from our cropping methods, the physical structure of the soil is not optimal, but there are no concrete threats of soil impoverishment and soil destruction. The use of pesticides leads to a powerful ecological influence on the cropping system and a stricter establishment of the objectives of agriculture. On the other hand, the secondary effects are not of a character or dimension to threaten the soil status or the health of the crops.

As regards product quality from agriculture, both technological development and the changes to the varieties available have largely led to improvements. Effects on health from pesticide residues are small and can be coped with. Demands from consumers and the food industry result in a far higher likelihood of poor quality products being rejected than in former times and societies characterized by food deficiencies.

There are many quality problems with regard to the handling of foodstuffs in modern society but few of these involve the quality of the products when they leave the farm gate. An exception may possibly be found in the increasing concentrations of the heavy metal cadmium which comes from both air pollution and from fertilizer, and which in the long term is a potential threat but in the short term implies relatively small modifications to the cadmium concentrations of natural origin.

As regards environmental effects on a more concrete level, on the other hand, the changes in agriculture as a whole, and also in the Scandinavian countries, have led to increased environmental influence. Leaching of nitrogen has increased considerably in pace with the structural changes made hitherto with local surpluses of organic manure and with an increasing proportion of grain production and a reduction in the proportion of grassland and grazing land. The general increase in intensity and the increased total production have also resulted in increased total leaching, although the changes in environmental destruction per produced unit of wheat or milk are not as large.

Similarly, intensification and reduced utilization of 'marginal' cutting- and grazing leys have reduced the positive environmental values of the agricultural landscape. There are fewer grazing cows and they are also further away from the road than previously, and thus are not seen as frequently by people passing through the countryside. The unfertilized meadows and pastures, with their species-rich but low-productive flora and fauna, are now being reduced in extent, which will cause problems in the establishment of nature/culture preservations.

At the same time as agriculture and livestock-keeping require increasingly smaller amounts of land and inputs of work, they require increasing amounts of energy and external non-renewable resources. In both economic and in physical terms, the supply of oil, metals and fertilizers has increased throughout the entire industrial era, even though development during the past decade has passed the maximum and is now turning downwards.

In summary, we may therefore state that food products from agriculture and the basis for production in agriculture are in good shape whereas the environment is in a less good shape, and that agricultural production takes place with the support of resource inputs from outside agriculture. We can also see, as a result of the changes during past decades, that agriculture has become increasingly better in its original role as a foodstuffs producer, but is today producing fewer positive and more negative secondary effects (Figure 6.6). The demand for foodstuffs and the requirements placed on their quality have been dominant, whereas the demands for environmental values have not been concrete criteria for agricultural development, either directly or indirectly via political measures.

Concluding comments

Agricultural development in the various industrialized countries is remarkably similar, not only environmentally but also socially, economically and technologically. This may be interpreted to imply that technology has been a dominating force whereas values and politics have been subordinate. An alternative interpretation is that political efforts in the industrialized countries have also been of a common character and that development has, consequently, been more or less determined by 'fate'.

Although the changes have been fairly similar in different countries, the discussion and evaluations, the enthusiasm and the disappointments with regard to the changes have varied. The specifically Scandinavian approach deals, therefore, probably more with the value of the changes than with the actual content of the changes. All the Scandinavian countries are sparsely inhabited, possibly with the exception of parts of Denmark and southern Sweden. Consequently, the negative environmental effect of agriculture has not reached the same dimensions as in more densely populated regions of Europe.

The history of the Scandinavian countries, with a late industrialization and a short time perspective since the peasant society, has also characterized

Figure 6.6 Agricultural technology is changing and so is the countryside

Scandinavia. It was not the countryside owned by large estate owners or 'other people' that was being changed. It was the peasants' own countryside. It was not 'other people' who suffered, but relatives and friends who had links with agriculture. Consequently, it is probable that the change has been more painful in parts of Scandinavia than in other countries where agriculture has played more of a background role, both politically and culturally, for a longer period. In addition, Scandinavian farmers have long been actively involved in the centre of the political spectrum, which has resulted in continued influence over agricultural policy and agricultural debate.

Slowly but surely, though perhaps painfully, Scandinavian agriculture is finding its place both economically, socially, politically and environmentally in post-industrial society. This may possibly involve a more permanent subordinate status. Perhaps, however, this is a temporary situation while the agricultural sector waits for new tasks in the future bio-industrial society.

7

Agro-environmentalism: the political economy of soil erosion in the USA

Louis Swanson

Introduction

The mid-1980s was a period of qualitative changes in US public policy toward *agro-environmental* issues. For the first time, the 1985 Food Security Act – the Farm Bill – legislated quasi-regulatory and targeted soil conservation policies. Many observers credited the farm financial crisis of this same period with strengthening the capacity of non-farm environmental interest groups to intervene in the making of agricultural policy. The various farm interest groups were politically vulnerable given the need to find new allies in their campaigning for what would be an unprecedented $28 billion bailout of US farms (principally large farms). However, it is more probable that the basis for this qualitative policy shift was already in place and that a restructuring of US agro-ecology policy would have changed eventually.

Historically, US commercial farming practices have produced wastes, or what economists euphemistically call *externalities*, in creating agricultural commodities. But, for a complex array of reasons associated with agrarian myths and misperceptions of US farm structure, public opinion has been opposed to the regulation of what was perceived as a family farm sector (Buttel and Swanson, 1986). By the mid-1980s, considerable scientific information was available for environmental interest groups to persuade much of public opinion, especially middle class urban professionals, that the agricultural environment was once again in danger.

The compelling question, though, is *not* why did such qualitative changes in agroenvironmental policy occur so quickly and decisively, but *why was the farm sector exempt from such State intervention on behalf of the environment for so long*. The explanation developed here relies on a constellation of social, political, and economic forces.

Socially, American agrarian myths assumed both a unity between sustainable agricultural practices and family farming and the dominance of family farming in the US farm structure. The public and farmers alike internalized this myth. This configuration of values and presumptions about the character of US farm structure contributed to a generalized belief that farmers could be trusted to do the right thing by the environment because it was in their best interest to do so.

In terms of national politics, the structure of the US federal government assured the compartmentalization of commercial farm interests, and therefore their impressive hegemony over agricultural policy, within Congressional agricultural committees and the Department of Agriculture (USDA) (Browne, 1988). Culturally protected by the agrarian myth, politically protected by the rules of Congressional law making, and programmatically protected by the bureaucratic self-interest and inertia of the USDA, commercial farm interests had little incentive to impose on themselves public policy which would push them to conserve the agricultural environment, and more incentive to ensure capital accumulation within the sphere of agricultural production (including agribusinesses supplying and purchasing from farmers). As a consequence, conservation policy was more often associated with farm income maintenance than with conserving soil (Reichelderfer, 1992; Browne, 1988).

But the power of the agrarian myth also penetrated the seemingly hard-nosed econometric assumptions of economists, where there has been a belief that prosperous family farms will practise soil conservation. This despite the work of agricultural economists such as Earl Heady and Carl Allen (1951) who inferred from their post-World War II research that conservation behaviour was often economically irrational due to short-term planning horizons and small business management constraints.

Today, most economists and many sociologists believe that the public assumption that farmers, for a variety of market and cultural reasons, will care for the environment does not take into account the economic forces that militated against such desired actions. As Heady and Allen long ago noted, farm management practices tend to have short-term planning horizons coupled with highly competitive markets that reduce the rate of profit per unit produced (Batie, 1986; Mironowski, 1986; Buttel and Swanson, 1986). Add to these formidable barriers to long-term capital investment in low-return conservation techniques inherent natural and market risks and farming becomes an unattractive investment for most large scale firms interested in maximizing capital investments (Buttel and Swanson, 1986). Conservation is often just too expensive for the returns to production it yields. Which is why the State has both an interest and an obligation to intervene to promote soil conservation in some manner to correct such so-called market imperfections.

These social forces (culture, polity, and the economy) have not only contributed to a legitimacy crisis for State intervention to promote soil conservation, but are also associated with other aspects of environmental degradation. In fact, while soil conservation has been the historical focus of US agro-environmental policy, current debates over agro-environmental policies are also equally concerned in ecological crises of water quality (surface and ground water), loss of wildlife habitat, human health (especially farm cancer rates), and food safety.

The public confidence crises for agricultural policies and associated institutions may signal a fundamental shift in public attitudes and perceptions about farming and the environment. If so, the cultural basis for current government entitlements to farmers may encounter fundamental qualitative changes. Reichelderfer (1992) proposes that collectively these agro-environmental issues give greater attention to a serious debate on whether farmers are land *stewards* or *polluters*.

In order to make sense of the dialectical processes with which these complex social forces have been articulated requires a brief historical review. The remainder of this chapter is divided into four sections. First, assuming that most US public policymakers have found some way of attaching their programs to fundamental societal beliefs it seems responsible briefly to examine these, as fractured as they may be. While such beliefs may have legitimized past policies, they may now serve as a basis for agricultural policy change. Second, two descriptive discussions of the historical transformation of US soil conservation policy are analysed. Third, this brief historical backdrop is followed by a closer but still abbreviated examination of two prominent soil conservation policies. These policies, which are the Conservation Reserve Program (CRP) and Conservation Compliance (CC), reflect continuing contradictions within US agriculture and the crisis for State intervention on behalf of the environment.

Agrarian myths and US soil conservation policies

All societies have agrarian myths. They are important cultural legacies of times past, often imparting the hard-earned wisdom of countless previous generations. Myths provide powerful framing assumptions that guide decision making, especially if it involves tough choices. By influencing both individual and societal choices, these particular aspects of culture can shape public policy. They can also be cynically manipulated. Such myths create moral obligations for current members of society to prioritize societal goals and can lead to the dispersement of scarce capital resources.

Myths may have little association with the existing social phenomena they are said to inform. This accounts for the common use of this term to indicate a revered but essentially inaccurate description of current conditions. Agrarian myths certainly represent dominant framing assumptions, but they also may misrepresent current conditions. Both uses of the term myth are applicable to agrarian values.

Variations of the US agrarian myth attribute fundamental values to a specific type of social organization – the *family farm* (Browne et al., 1992; Thompson, 1988). Among current versions of the American agrarian myth, the ideas of Thomas Jefferson and the 19th-century romantic poets Emmerson and Thoreau provide a conceptual and historical glue. Not surprisingly, determining what is a family farm has been a highly contentious debate.

The central tenets of the agrarian myth are a simultaneous emphasis on (1) the unity of ecological sustainability and production of agricultural commodities by household farms; (2) individual responsibility for stewardship of nature's resources; (3) equal emphasis given to the values *equality* and *freedom*; and (4) the sanctity of private property. The importance of these values is such that each stands alone in US culture. However, in combination they are virtually unassailable as guides for a more perfect society. Imagine the legitimacy any particular social institution might have if there were wide agreement that it constituted the embodiment of this cultural powerhouse of values.

In the US the family farm has been seen as both the historic and the modern embodiment of these combined values. The family farmer is assumed to be a *natural steward* of nature, *husbanding* its resources for future generations, and guided by the incentives of a private property owner yet further empowered by personal characteristics of strong individualism based upon the belief that *his* property will be a legacy for generations of his offspring. Moreover, unlike large property owners, such as manufacturing and financial capitalists, their small scale makes any one family farm little threat to the larger society.

Little wonder that Jefferson claimed that yeoman farmers were the backbone of American democracy while attempting to thwart his political enemies' attempt to establish what would become the US Constitution. (It is interesting to note that Jefferson's praise of farmers dims once he becomes president.) The embodiment of this generalized collection of dominant cultural values has given rise to the *myth of the family farm* (see Vogeler, 1981). The trust given to all farm types, on the assumption that family farms dominate US farm structure, accounts for a portion of the phenomena of the late intervention by the federal government into regulating the agro-environment. It also accounts for the emphasis on *voluntary compliance* with societal soil conservation goals.

Are family farms the embodiment of the agrarian myth?

Do family farms warrant these attributions? – probably not. But this is not necessarily their fault; rather the blame, if any, resides in their willingness to be given such high cultural status in America's national myth structure, along with Horatio Alger and George Washington. Farmers have internalized the myth's account of their virtuosity. The evidence suggests, however, that farmers have never practised sustainable agriculture, regardless of their scale of operation; since the New Deal most have not been independent of State entitlement and financial policy, and the majority of farm families since 1920 have not left their farms as an occupational and property legacy to their descendants.

Social historians do not find overwhelming evidence that family farms ever achieved their current status as stewards of the environment (cf. Hahn,

1985; Henretta, 1974). During the 20th century, considerable evidence suggests that as a group family farms have been uneven in their conservation behaviour. The soil erosion crisis of the Dust Bowl was only a single aspect of a much larger scene of environmental degradation. The rapid expansion of US overseas grain markets in the 1970s was accompanied by increases in the rate of soil loss. Furthermore, US farmers have systematically destroyed wildlife habitats and species considered to be pests (ranging from lowly beetles to coyotes). Even Strange (1988), an ardent supporter of family farms, notes that they have not widely practised sustainable farming systems. On the other hand, efforts by farmers coupled with assistance from the Soil Conservation Service (SCS) have greatly reduced the amount of erosion that might have otherwise occurred. In fact, the evidence is that all farmers highly value stewardship. This raises the question of why there is such a great distance between attitudes and behaviour.

There appears to be little difference in the scale of US farms and those practising soil conservation (Swanson, Camboni, and Napier, 1986). Small operations are just as unlikely to practise soil conservation as their larger neighbours. This inconsistency between attitudes and behaviour, though, should not be surprising when the realities of managing a farm in a highly competitive market are taken into consideration. Nonetheless, national myths assume otherwise. Farmer failure to practise conservation is usually attributed either to their willing collaboration with the forces of capitalism against their better interests (cf. Berry, 1977) or to economic forces and public policies beyond their control (Strange, 1988). When the myth is challenged by the evidence, it is the farmer who is found wanting, not the myth (Berry, 1977).

Farmers' actual independence and their ability to ensure the farm as a family legacy also fail to meet the expectations of national mythology. Most farmers are very dependent upon federal government programmes, whether they be direct entitlements such as some commodity programmes, licences to produce through marketing orders, federal export policies, or financial assistance through federal financial institutions. This dependence has made reform of the programmes quite difficult. Moreover, since the benefits are not targeted to particular types of farms, such as small but commercial family farms, a disproportionate amount of capital resources have gone to the largest farms (Browne et al., 1992). It is ironic that farmers are often portrayed as staunch individualists yet rely on government subsidies for a high proportion of their profits (Browne et al., 1992).

The issue of legacy also falls short of mythical expectations. While the US has experienced on average the loss of about 2,000 farms a week since 1945, for mid-sized commercial farms this loss has been due to the children not choosing to stay in farming but inheriting the farmland. For sharecropping families in the South, who have virtually disappeared, families were forced off land they did not own by the restructuring of old plantations for industrial agriculture. For the former group of children, those of the mid-sized farms, the legacy has been to keep the land but not to farm. A consequence of this tradition is that today almost half of all land cultivated is owned by someone other than the people producing on it. Most of these landowners are former farm kids. The latter group of sharecropper kids, often African Americans, received no land (no golden parachute) but did inherit the legacy of poverty and ignorance.

Cynical use of the agrarian myth

Bonnen and Browne (1989) propose that both the agrarian myth and the myth of the family farm have been cynically manipulated by populist and corporate interests alike to achieve their policy objectives. This, too, is unsurprising given the power of these connected myths. Ideological confrontations aimed at capturing these myths are a continuing feature of US farm politics.

As societal framing assumptions, dominant myths provide an important generalized basis for creating and evaluating performances of agro-environmental policies. No farm policy is likely to emerge or persist without some linkage to these myths and the public legitimacy they render. Capturing them becomes an intricate and often unconscious endeavour of agricultural interest groups. But myths are not set in concrete. They too change. For example, the sanctity of private property and assumptions of family legacy as dimensions of the agrarian myth have weakened in importance as some of the recent agro-environmental policies make claims for public rights to supersede private property rights.

Agro-environmental policies cannot be understood outside their cultural context. But this cultural context should not be assumed to be monolithic and unchangeable. As agro-environmental policies have shifted, so too has the cultural basis for these policies.

Historical paths of US soil conservation policy

The *greening* of US agro-environmental policy has been described by Thigpen (1988) in terms of four historical periods. Reichelderfer (1992) identifies three periods. While Thigpen's stages relate to shifting emphasis in policy assumptions and participants in policy-making in soil conservation policy, Reichelderfer divides her periods into differing assessments of who, if anyone, is given care of agro-environmental policy. Together, these descriptions of historical change provide a very useful foundation for analysing this dialectical process.

Thigpen proposes that US soil conservation policy can be roughly divided into four periods: (1) the Colonial period to 1920; (2) 1920–1960; (3)1960–1985; and (4) 1985 to the present. For each of these periods Thigpen examines the interaction among spheres of influence on farmer conservation behaviour. Four general spheres are identified: (1) requirements of production agriculture; (2) the context of US society concern for the natural environment; (3) public soil conservation policy; and (4) individual characteristics of farmers.

Colonial period–1920: continual exploitation of the land

The colonial–1920 period was characterized by no State soil conservation policy. Common agricultural practices during this period had the greatest influence on farmer behaviour. These farming systems were sustainable only in stories of the agrarian myth. The noted agricultural historian Wayne Rasmussen (1982) argues that soil erosion was relatively high throughout this period. Henretta (1974) goes as far as to say that soil exhaustion due to yeoman farming was an important factor encouraging migration into the frontier of the rural South. Margolis (1975) notes that the frontier farming systems of the US were similar to frontier patterns of soil exploitation around the world. In short, farming systems of this period, large and small scale alike, tended to consume soil resources at a relatively high rate.

Concern for soil exhaustion formed the basis for numerous private soil conservation societies among more wealthy farm interests. Genovese (1967), in his study of the Southern *antebellum* political economy, notes the occurrence of numerous agricultural societies that were primarily concerned about the loss of soil productivity and exhaustion. Even Thomas Jefferson was aware of soil exhaustion on his hilly plantation in western Virginia (Rasmussen, 1982). Rasmussen (1982) also states that one of the most significant periods of severe soil erosion in the Midwest and the South occurred during the restructuring of agriculture after the American Civil War (which occurred 1861–1865).

Throughout the late 19th century and well into the first two decades of the 20th century soil conservation practices were subordinated to the perceived requirements of production agriculture. Soil conservation was important only to the extent that it threatened production. This viewpoint held little concern for the environment. Nonetheless, declining soil productivity was threatening the wealth creation process and gradually encouraged widespread interest in soil conservation.

Other types of environmental concerns were gaining national prominence prior to 1920. President Theodore Roosevelt introduced environmental concerns by establishing the political basis for the US Department of Interior and the national parks system. But this concern was for the preservation of what was left of the nation's pristine beauty, and not for the wastes associated with industrial or agricultural production.

1920–1960: conservation crisis and state intervention

The 1920s was a decade of farm depression and increasing exploitation of the nation's soil resources. The ecological consequences of this heightened resource exploitation became most visible during the drought of the early and mid-1930s which exposed the soil to wind erosion (Svobida, 1986). The Dust Bowl era forced Americans west of the Rocky Mountains to admit the existence of an agro-environmental crisis of immense proportions as they washed the dust off their cars and homes. This was also the darkest period of the Great Depression for US farmers. The combination of an agro-environmental and farm income crisis triggered qualitative changes in the State's role in the agricultural economy.

From the outset President Franklin Roosevelt's New Deal agricultural programmes were considered to be temporary relief. That these programmes have survived into the last decade of the 20th century is a testament to the political power of key farm interests and the capacity of those interests to perpetuate these programmes despite their high costs to the public treasury and low benefits to medium and small farm operations (Browne, 1988; Reichelderfer, 1992; Zinn, 1992).

Cornerstone conservation assumptions of the New Deal

The USDA was given authority for managing this dual crisis as overseer of farm commodity programs and of the newly founded Soil Conservation Service (SCS). Three policy assumptions guided SCS programme development and implementation. First, the primary problem was believed to be one of farm income. It was assumed that once the farm income crisis was abated farmers would *return* to environmentally sound farming practices. Second, the cost of soil erosion was believed to be principally borne by the farmer through lost productivity. Therefore, it was in the interest of farmers to implement soil conservation measures. SCS programmes were focused upon *on-site* conservation problems. Third, programme implementation relied on a combination of voluntary farmer compliance and the establishment of local conservation districts composed of farmers and community leaders to help SCS diffuse conservation practices.

Each of these assumptions are firmly rooted in the cultural and political economy of that period. Publicly the conservation programmes were seen as common sense assistance to financially hard-pressed family farmers. Farmers accounted for almost a third of the US population in the mid-1930s, which made farm income programmes a type of welfare or rural development programme. Given the economic and agro-environmental emergencies these programmes represented good politics, even though ten years earlier such programmes would have been decried as Bolshevik.

Despite the publicity accompanying their creation and implementation, the aim of the New Deal conservation programmes was not primarily conservation. Rather, their focus was on productivity, though not necessarily increased production. This seemingly contradictory policy goal was at the time quite apparent. Farm markets, especially world markets, had severely contracted during the Great Depression but farm production had not. This caused farm prices to decline even further. Overproduction, not increased production, was seen as the determining economic cause of low farm income during the Great Depression. Farm income adjustment programmes were composed of a combination of supply management and price support. Farm income was to be supported by direct State intervention in farm markets. Conservation provided a means for reducing supply by reducing some of the acreage in production through practices such as terracing, developing grass waterways, and intercropping.

Conservation traditionally a second consideration to income support programmes

The agrarian and family farm myths proved useful in justifying the programmes, since farmers were culturally entitled to special benefits, such as direct subsidies for their crops. But these programs were only secondarily conservation programmes.

[B]ecause these early conservation programs were designed with agricultural interests in mind, they were easily integrated with concurrent efforts to adjust agricultural production and stabilize prices. As its title suggests, the Soil Conservation and Domestic Allotment Act of 1936 closely correlated soil conservation objectives with the production adjustment goals. One could say, in fact, that it exploited soil conservation goals to achieve production adjustment goals. . . . Nevertheless, the programs established in 1936 introduced what became a longstanding practice of using resource conservation programs to complement agricultural market interventions (Reichelderfer, 1992:5).

Conservation programmes, then, were subservient to income maintenance programmes. They provided a mechanism for either increasing productivity by easing their restriction or for reducing surplus production by taking land out of production. Conservation policies continue to be multi-objective, with one objective often countering another. Again, Reichelderfer (1992:5) provides insight into this policy tap dance.

As agricultural demand began to outstrip supplies during World War II, the Agricultural Conservation Program was an important source of subsidies for production-enhancing capital investment. This close linkage between conservation programs and productivity goals was retained despite a recurrence of problems with surplus production and low farm prices in the late forties.

1960–1985: eclipse of New Deal conservation assumptions

The substantial veneer of rhetoric protecting farm policy and agro-
environmental issues from public scrutiny wore down as the environmental
degradation of US farming systems became more apparent. Throughout
the 1970s and early 1980s non-farm environmental interest groups became politically more powerful at both local and national levels. But their
attention to agro-environmental issues lagged behind their industrial and
wildlife habitat concerns. While Earth Day 1971 is considered to mark the
advent of environmental politics in the US, the agro-environment was
ignored until the high soil erosion of the late 1970s and early 1980s became
more apparent.

The three cornerstone assumptions of New Deal soil conservation policy
remained unassailed into the 1980s, despite creditable research opposing
them. As noted above, the most reputable was the work of Heady and Allen
(1951) which effectively dismissed the first assumption that soil erosion was
a function of low farm income. Their on-farm research identified the
combination of short-term planning horizons from farm managers and the
very low profit returns on conservation practices as inherent barriers to
effective use of such practices by farmers. They pointed out that the economic incentive for farmers was *to not practise soil conservation, even when
farm prices were relatively high*. They went so far as to state that farmers
would be acting irrationally if they independently transferred scarce capital
resources to conservation. Therefore, while these research results did not
influence agricultural conservation policy, they did provide evidence that
combining income support programmes with conservation programmes in
no way assured a reduction in soil erosion. But their work did underscore
the political forces at work such that good research did not lead to good
policy. Later research confirmed their findings (see Swanson, Camboni, and
Napier, 1986).

The assumption that farm productivity was strongly associated with soil
erosion was not questioned until Crosson's work in 1982. Lost productivity
due to soil erosion could be, at least for several decades, cheaply made up
by increased applications of so-called land saving technologies such as nitrogen fixing fertilizers, pesticides, and new high-yield seed varieties.
Consequently, productivity actually increased during periods of high soil
erosion. Moreover, not all land was subject to high soil erosion and, as a
result, profits lost to soil erosion were often negligible. In short, lost profits
due to soil erosion in the post World War II period were offset by technological advances that increased productivity even on highly erodible land.
Therefore, despite the previous assumption that profits lost to soil erosion
would lead to widespread use of soil conservation techniques by farmers,
this did not occur nationally.

The final New Deal cornerstone assumption to be eclipsed was the notion
that the primary costs of soil erosion were within the farm gate. Again, it
was Crosson's work that demonstrated that *off-farm costs* due to soil erosion

were as much as three to four times as high as *on-farm costs*. Pollution of roadside ditches and waterways, as well as the chemical run-off into rivers and lakes, were associated with wildlife kills and costly dredging.

1985–present: passage of the conservation provisions of the 1985 Farm Bill

Since the early 1980s other types of agricultural pollution have also become visible to the public, including the chemical pollution of surface and ground water, the primary sources of drinking water for rural and urban populations. The early 1980s marked a watershed period in which agro-environmental degradation was no longer seen as a farm issue but as a public environmental issue. By the passage of the 1985 Farm Bill, and its conservation provisions, each of the three New Deal cornerstone conservation assumptions had been eclipsed. With the advent of the Conservation Compliance, Sodbuster and Swampbuster provisions, agro-environmental policy became quasi-regulatory. Even the official title of the 1985 Farm Bill, the *1985 Food Security Act*, reflected fundamental shifts in who wrote public agricultural policy.

Both Swampbuster and Sodbuster provisions are essentially regulatory but ambiguous pieces of legislation. While the ambiguity was by design – aimed at assisting passage through Congress and at avoiding a Presidential veto – the lack of clarity in both bills has become a focus of intense conflict between environmental interest groups and farm organizations – between environmentalists and producers.

Perhaps the most visible debate is over the definition of what constitutes a *wetland* in the Swampbuster legislation. Such a definition is critical to any discussion of enforcement, yet the principal agencies overseeing wetlands, the Environmental Protection Agency and SCS, still cannot agree that they know a wetland when they see one. While this is an interesting political issue, both Conservation Compliance (CC) and the Conservation Reserve Program (CRP) represent better examples of the shifting political economy of agro-environmental debates in the US. The remainder of this chapter will briefly compare these as examples of fundamental shifts in the US agro-environmental conservation policy.

Conservation Compliance and the Conservation Reserve Program as examples of qualitative shifts in conservation policy

Conservation Compliance and the Conservation Reserve Program represent the schizophrenic character of US agro-environmental policy options. Each represents qualitative shifts in assumptions of US agro-environmental policy, yet quite different political solutions to seemingly problematic conservation dilemmas. The emphasis of CC is on negative incentives to force farmland owners to practise conservation, while CRP is more within the tradition of multi-objective voluntary policy where the State is ready to pay for curbing pollution. They are important for these differences, since they represent fundamentally different policy options for the future. CC represents a regulatory path, while CRP represents a quasi-voluntary path requiring greater pollution policing by farmers and greater costs to the State.

Conservation Compliance

Conservation Compliance introduces the policy option of *cross-compliance*, or more simply a carrot and stick approach to conservation. For farmers, the carrot of State agricultural programmes has been quite lucrative since the New Deal. The stick, the withholding of programme benefits, has been seen by some farmers as an attack on previously unencumbered entitlements. They are correct in this perception.

In order for farmers to receive any government benefit, they must demonstrate that their operations do not seriously contribute to soil erosion. They must have filed a plan with SCS by 1 January 1990 and must implement the plan by 1 January 1995. It was reasoned that if farmers were to be the beneficiaries of public entitlements and financial assistance they should in turn practise greater stewardship. Implicitly, this policy assumes that farmers are not to be completely trusted to perform conservation in their own or the public interest. But this policy did not attempt to recognize market and farm management disincentives to practise conservation. That is, the policy assumes that farmers will internalize costs of pollution without corresponding changes in the prices they receive for their agricultural commodities. Moreover, little *cost-sharing money* was made available to farmers to implement their new conservation plans. While this approach is consistent with industrial environmental policies of letting the polluter pay, offending farmers do not have the option of passing on conservation costs to the consumer as would an electric utility or large manufacturing firm. Hence this legislation is a partial departure from traditional perceptions of farmers as economically hard pressed families struggling for subsistence while conserving the environment.

This legislation also assumes that federal farm policies will persist, since without these programmes there would be no carrot or stick. Such an assumption may be based on a weak foundation, since the very public legitimacy issues that weakened traditional notions that farmers practise good stewardship can easily be turned against the programmes themselves. Nonetheless, the importance of this new policy is the introduction of a *quid pro quo* relationship between private property owners who receive expensive public entitlements and programmes and the public sector.

Consequently, CC altered many of the relationships between SCS field staff and farmland owners and producers from voluntary to quasi-regulatory. SCS did not become the regulatory agency *per se*, since its responsibility only was to assess soil erosion on a farm and then develop a plan in cooperation with the farmer. Rather, the regulatory agency is the Agriculture Stabilization and Conservation Service (ASCS) that oversees the payment of farm programme benefits. But ASCS relies on SCS to make the judgement on compliance, thus giving SCS its quasi-regulatory status.

This sounds complicated, but it is even more so, since SCS is also associated with local Conservation Districts (CDs) that up until the 1985 Farm Bill provided SCS with a great deal of its local legitimacy. The CDs, though, are usually made up of elected officials with close ties to production agriculture. As SCS began to develop the conservation plans with farmers, farmers and other private property owners began to see SCS as environmental police and accordingly began to distance themselves from SCS. This tended to reduce SCS's local and national legitimacy among landowning farm producers. But non-environmental groups began to see SCS as an agency worthy of support since it was required to determine conservation compliance and therefore these groups provide a different, and possibly from SCS's perspective an unwanted source of legitimacy. Which is where the political issues over CC stand in 1992.

The policy shift from voluntary to quasi-regulatory relationships undermined the third New Deal conservation assumption – that conservation policy should rest on voluntary private and public relationships. And it is the eclipse of this assumption that most represents a qualitative shift in the State's strategy to improve conservation in the agro-ecology. Embedded in this shift is the eclipse of the social value which holds property owners as the primary arbiter of what happens to their land. While property owners of other industries had lost the right to pollute in the 1970s, it took until 1985 for the State to institute new public versus private domains over the use of agricultural private property. While the State provided ten years (1985 to 1995) to accomplish this shift, and therefore transferred enforcement to a future generation of lawmakers and bureaucrats, it nonetheless sent conservation policy into a new arena of actors and gave agriculture policy what Paarlberg (1980) called the *New Agenda*.

Conservation Reserve Program

Unlike CC, CRP represents a modification of New Deal conservation policies. This legislation pays farmland owners to take highly erodible land out of production for a period of ten years. But it deviates from earlier conservation policy in two significant ways. First, this legislation is *targeted* toward highly erodible land that had been put in production during the 1970s and early 1980s. Second, it represented an omnibus collection of farm and environmental policy goals.

Targeting is one of the least appealing policy mechanisms the Congress of the United States employs – at least from Congress's perspective. In Congress each legislator strives to divert as much money as possible to their state (in the case of Senators) or their Congressional District. The US political slang for this process is *pork barrel* politics. It is simply the practice of syphoning federal government money into special interest projects. Because targeted programmes greatly restrict the characteristics of beneficiaries, Congressmen are not assured of getting their *fair share* of targeted programme monies. Therefore, the passage of CRP represented a significant departure by the Congress in dealing with an agricultural conservation problem.

CRP is also multi-oriented in its goals, which in several instances are in contradiction with one another. True to traditional farm legislation, the primary goal of CRP is to restrict total farm production in order to support higher farm prices. CRP was drafted at a time when the US had excess grain production and there were economic forecasts of even more overproduction during the next decade. By pulling highly erodible land out of production Congress was able to reduce total production and pay about $40 million to farmland owners while seeming to address serious problems of soil erosion. Compared to the total farm programme costs, about $28 billion in 1988 and $13 billion in 1991, this made CRP a relatively small proportion of farm programme costs.

What makes CRP particularly interesting from a policy perspective is the politically diverse coalition that produced it. Six general goals can be identified: (1) supply control of several major agricultural commodities through acreage reduction; (2) reduction of soil erosion on previously cropped highly erodible land; (3) improvement of ground and surface water quality; (4) reduction of the federal budget deficit; (5) increased farm family income during a period of farm recession; and (6) enhanced wildlife habitat.

This impressive list makes for good politics but not particularly good policy since emphasis on any one dimension may dilute the effectiveness of other dimensions. Swanson *et al.* (1991:253) maintain:

> As might be expected CRP has been criticized for trying to do too much and thereby not doing anything well. For instance, the goals of reducing erosion on highly erodible land and improving water quality would seem to be highly compatible. However, . . . [it has been noted] that by not sharply distinguishing between wind erosion in a state like Colorado and sheet and rill erosion in Tennessee, the program is less targeted upon the latter type of erosion which most directly affects groundwater. Moreover, a multi-goal conservation policy also might conflict with other goals of the 1985 [Farm Bill], such as improving international trade.

There is a general concern (see Napier, 1991) that CRP's omnibus character may hinder the goal of reducing soil erosion by attempting to make CRP politically palatable to a divergent number of interests. Furthermore, this legislation does not diverge from the traditional path of subordinating conservation to the political goal of income maintenance, in this case by reducing the number of acreage under tillage. Swanson *et al.* (1991:262) conclude that 'the muddling-through process of compromise in putting together this multi-goal program also may have doomed it to only muddling successes'.

Why this qualitative shift in policy?

Again, two questions seem to arise from this discussion. As stated earlier, why did regulation of production pollution take so long to encompass the agro-environment? and who were the primary actors formulating this change?

The partial answer to the first question, as argued earlier, are the contradictory views of US agriculture. As long as farming was considered to be a household enterprise practised by hard-working, self-exploiting men, women and children for long-term benefit of society and the environment, then a great deal of latitude in pollution was given. The US agrarian myths shaped such a vision, and therefore provided a powerful cultural imperative for the public to look the other way. However, as agro-environmental degradation became increasingly evident in unacceptably high rates of soil erosion and more recently evidence of surface and ground water pollution by agricultural chemicals *and* as the public became more aware of US agriculture's *dual farm structure*, the inequalities of the farm commodity policies and the lack of effectiveness of the conservation policies (given increased rates of soil erosion) forced a reassessment of the myth. The rapid loss of medium-sized commercial family farms begged the question of whether or not farm policies were successful, and eventually provoked the question of whether trust had been misplaced in the family farm.

But such an immanent critique is extraordinarily difficult at a societal level, especially when much of the population is not directly concerned with the agro-environment. This suggests a partial answer to the second question of key actors. Here Browne's (1988) description of US farm policy and more specifically the *farm bloc* is instructive. Browne portrays the farm bloc as a highly regionalized political coalition that traditionally has eschewed party affiliation, thus making both ideological positions and party discipline almost irrelevant. Rather, politicians of all ilks have found it in their interest to support expensive farm programmes given the low public resistance to them but high pay-offs to often wealthy and influential people. As long as environmental interests did not question the cultural assumptions that family farms were both ubiquitous and good stewards, there was little incentive for non-farm groups to take the time necessary to comprehend the dense world of commodity-specific rules and regulations.

An often humorous effect of farm politics is the degree to which politicians support farm legislation that runs counter to their otherwise stongly held political ideologies. For instance, an arch-conservative and free market advocate like Senator Jesse Helms of North Carolina makes continuous pleas for retaining a tobacco programme that is totally regulated by the State and industry and protected from foreign competition. Similarly, a liberal populist farm sector Senator like Tom Harkin of Iowa will argue for price and production controls and then support the dumping of excess US grain in the third world – a policy that not only encourages soil erosion in the US by paying for excess production, but also undermines the development of household farming systems in the developing world.

Browne proposes that the farm bloc historically has achieved both cultural and policy hegemony by nurturing and even cynically manipulating the various forms of the agrarian myth. Moreover, the bloc has benefited in making farm programmes so intricate and commodity-specific that anyone without a direct interest in these programmes would not take the time to understand them. This form of cultural and institutional protection has ensured almost sixty years of relatively stable farm policies, best characterized by a political process of muddling through. However, by the 1980s the cultural norms legitimizing these policies were beginning to erode as the public was informed of the decline in family farms, the increasing scale of commercial farms, and a deteriorating farm ecology. Revelations of the emergence of a *dual farm structure* and the decline of small family farms have begun to expose the degree to which farm programmes transfer wealth from the middle class to rich landowners. The continued deterioration of the natural environment attracted the interest of non-farm environmental groups. However, a key catalyst influencing political and institutional change has been the deepening fiscal crisis of the federal government – the federal debt.

Given the farm financial crisis in the early 1980s, there was concern on the part of farm groups that they could muster enough strength in Congress to support what would be one of the most expensive farm bills ever. The farm depression of the early 1980s was triggered by a constellation of related economic events ranging from the over-capitalization of farm production in the 1970s as farmers speculated on expanding world markets to Federal Reserve (the US's equivalent to a central bank) financial policy shifts that sought to reduce the high rate of inflation and thereby increase what were then very low real rates of interest. The consequence of the latter policy was to make the US economy an attractive place for foreign capital to invest, thus driving up the value of the dollar and simultaneously driving down US export trade due to its greater expense on world markets (since the dollar was being valued higher). Since US agricultural trade is sensitive to the value of the dollar, the sharp increase in the value of the dollar drove down US farm exports as the country became the supplier of last resort.

In addition to these socioeconomic forces, the US government was embarking on a fiscal policy of lowering taxes on the wealthy and greatly expanding military spending. Since the lower tax rates did not significantly increase total revenues by generating additional economic growth the federal government's budget deficit ballooned throughout the 1980s. As the deficit expanded, greater attention was given to federal entitlement programmes as politically the least painful areas for cuts. Social service programmes were severely cut.

Faced with the real possibility of limited support, farm bloc legislators and interest groups looked for new political allies. Such allies emerged in the form of powerful environmental groups who would support efforts to *save the American family farm*, if, in turn, the farm bloc would agree to new agro-environmental legislation. This political compromise produced Swampbuster, Sodbuster, Conservation Compliance, and the Conservation Reserve Program.

It is probably a mistake to assume that had the farm financial crisis not occurred the environmental groups would have delayed their entry into the farm policy arena. The environmental groups had already begun to study farm policies and their consequences for the environment, but the farm crisis provided an opportunity for a more cooperative initial association. Since 1985, and particularly during the 1991 Farm Bill legislative process, the relationship between farm commodity groups and environmental groups has become more strained.

An uncertain future

The future of the 1985 Farm Bill conservation provisions is uncertain. While 1995 will continue to be a deadline for the implementation of CC conservation plans, the long-term continuation of this programme depends upon the persistence of the other farm programmes – the carrots. At this time continuation of these programmes is more in doubt than at any time since their creation during the New Deal. Should farm commodity programmes be modified, or decoupled, such that entitlements of the past sixty years are abolished, cross-compliance as a policy option will be greatly weakened if not eliminated. Such a scenario would leave Congress and the Executive Branch with a rather polarized set of options. These would include direct regulation of the agro-environment, as is increasingly the case for Swampbuster and Sodbuster, and the Conservation Reserve Program with its emphasis on targeting highly erodible land and the temporary purchase of production rights.

A third but untried option is for micro-targeting highly erodible land. If the general targeting of CRP is seen as unpleasant by Congress, micro-targeting is even more so. However, it may provide the most efficient use of scarce State resources. Micro-targeting programs can be developed to include both voluntary and coercive relationships between private landowners and the State. Simply stated, micro-targeting would be limited to specific types of highly erodible land. The State would have the option to negotiate a permanent production easement with property owners. If owners were to resist, then the land could be condemned via imminent domain laws and a permanent easement settlement imposed. What is certain about the future is that soil erosion will continue to be a major agro-environmental issue. A hopeful sign is the increased popularity of sustainable agriculture farming systems, even among Land Grant Universities. However, soil erosion has played less a role in this unfolding agro-environmental issue, than has chemical pollution of surface and groundwater supplies. But any effort to move toward sustainable farming systems necessarily must include conservation of the soil.

For the next decade, Paarlberg's *New Agenda* will become the norm of agriculture policy making and enforcement. Farm Bills are no longer the exclusive domain of well-financed farm and agribusiness interest groups. Non-farm environmental groups with their urban-based local and national political support will demand and be given a powerful negotiating position in future policy formulation. But it will be the farm interests that will continue to be the most powerful actors in agriculture policy. For it is they who continue to influence the institutional law making structures of Congress and who have the greatest economic interest in wealth creation in agriculture. Should these interests continue to resist agro-environmental pollution and food safety issues, more political fights over farm pollution will occur.

In conclusion, given the great potential for a major shift in public attitudes and understanding of farming it is equally possible that the 1990s will witness qualitative changes in all aspects of US agricultural policy. These might include a restructuring, and even elimination, of commodity programmes and revision of the missions of public Land Grant Universities. If so, agro-environmental policies are likely to change once again, but with the potential for highly polarized choices, and therefore the potential of becoming a highly politicized national issue. The certainty of future agro-enviromental policy is that it will be different than current policies that rely on a combination of cross-compliance and voluntary compliance.

References

Batie, Sandra (1986) 'Why soil erosion: A social science perspective', Chapter 1 in Stephen Lovejoy and Ted Napier (eds) *Conserving Soil: Insights from Socioeconomic Research*, Ankeny, Iowa: Soil Conservation Society of America.

Berry, Wendel (1977) *The Unsettling of America*, San Francisco: Sierra Club Books.

Bonnen, James T. and William Browne (1989) 'Why is agricultural policy so difficult to reform?' Chapter 2 in Carol Kramer (ed.) *The Political Economy of U.S. Agriculture*, Washington, D.C.: Resources for the Future.

Browne, William P. (1988) *Private Interests, Public Policy, and American Agriculture*, Lawrence, Kansas: University of Kansas Press.

Browne, William P., Jerry R. Skees, Louis E. Swanson, Paul B. Thompson, and Laurian J. Unnevehr (1992) *Sacred Cows and Hot Potatoes: Agrarian Myths in Agricultural Policy*, Boulder, Colorado: Westview Press.

Buttel, Frederick and Louis Swanson (1986) 'Soil and water conservation: A farm structural and public policy context', Chapter 3 in Stephen Lovejoy and Ted Napier (eds) *Conserving Soil: Insights from Socioeconomic Research*, Ankeny, Iowa: Soil Conservation Society of America.

Crosson, Pierre (1982) 'The long-term adequacy of agricultural land in the United States', Chapter 1 in P.R. Crosson (ed.) *The Cropland Crisis: Myth or Reality*, Baltimore, Maryland: Johns Hopkins University Press.

Genovese, Eugene D. (1967) *The Political Economy of Slavery: Studies in the Economy and Society of the Slave South*, New York: Vintage Books.

Hahn, Steven (1985) *The Roots of Southern Populism: Yeoman Farmers and the Transformation of the Georgia Upcountry, 1850–1890*, New York: Oxford University Press.

Heady, Earl and Carl Allen (1951) *Returns from Capital Required for Soil Conservation Farming Systems*, Research Bulletin No. 381. Experiment Station, College of Agriculture, Iowa State University, Ames.

Henretta, James A. (1974) 'Families and Farms: Mentality in Preindustrial America', *William and Mary Quarterly* 35(1):3–32.

Margolis, Maxine (1975) 'Historical perspectives on frontier agriculture as an adaptive strategy', *American Ethnologist* 4(1):42–64.

Miranowski, John (1986) 'Macro-economics of Soil Conservation', Chapter 2 in Stephen Lovejoy and Ted Napier (eds) *Conserving Soil: Insights from Socioeconomic Research*, Ankeny, Iowa: Soil Conservation Society of America.

Napier, Ted L. (1991) *Implementing the Conservation Title of the Food Security Acts of 1985*, Ankeny, Iowa: Soil and Water Conservation Society of America.

Paarlberg, Don (1980) *Farm and Food Policy: Issues for the 1980s*, Lincoln, Nebraska University of Nebraska Press.

Rasmussen, Wayne (1982) 'History of soil conservation, institutions, and incentives', Chapter 1 in Harold Halcrow, Earl Heady, and Melvin Cotner (eds) *Soil Conservation Policies, Institutions and Incentives*, Ankeny, Iowa: Soil Conservation Society of America.

Reichelderfer, Kathern (1992) 'Land stewards or polluters?: The treatment of farmers in the evolution of environmental and agricultural policy', Chapter 1 in Louis E. Swanson and Frank Clearfield (eds) *Farming and the Environment*, Ankeny, Iowa: Soil and Water Conservation Society of America.

Strange, Marty (1988) *Family Farming: A New Economic Vision*, Lincoln, Nebraska: University of Nebraska Press.

Svobida, Lawrence (1986) *Farming in the Dust Bowl*, Lawrence, Kansas: University of Kansas Press.

Swanson, Louis and Frank Clearfield (eds) (1992) *Farming and the Environment*, Ankeny, Iowa: Soil and Water Conservation Society.

Swanson, Louis, Silvana Camboni and Ted Napier (1986) 'Barriers to adoption of soil conservation practices on farms', Chapter 9 in Stephen Lovejoy and Ted Napier (eds) *Conserving Soil: Insights from Socioeconomic Research*, Ankeny, Iowa: Soil Conservation Society of America.

Swanson, Louis, Kurt Stephenson and Jerry Skees (1991) 'Participation in the Conservation Reserve Program in Kentucky: Implications for Public Policy', Chapter 17 in Ted L. Napier (ed.) *Implementing the Conservation Title of the Food Security Act of 1985*, Ankeny, Iowa: Soil and Water Conservation Society of America.

Thigpen, John F. (1988) *The Sociology of Soil Conservation*. Unpublished dissertation. Department of Sociology, University of Kentucky, Lexington.

Thompson, Paul B. (1988) 'The philosophical rationale for U.S. agricultural policy', Chapter 3 in M. Ann Tutwiler (ed.) *U.S. Agriculture in a Global Setting*, Washington, D.C.: Resources for The Future.

Vogeler, Ingolf, (1981) *The Myth of the Family Farm*, Westview Press, Boulder, Colorado.

Zinn, Jeffery (1992) 'Agricultural Policy and the Congress: A view to the future', Chapter 2 in Louis E. Swanson and Frank Clearfield (eds) *Farming and the Environment*, Ankeny, Iowa: Soil and Water Conservation Society of America.

8

Bio-technology: Rural policy implications of bovine growth hormone adoption in the USA

Charles Geisler and Tom Lyson

Introduction

Agricultural biotechnology made a turbulent debut in the 1980s. Nowhere was this more obvious than in the controversies surrounding bovine growth hormone (bGH), the insulin-like substance given to cows to increase their efficiency in milk production. Since 1985, the sale of milk from dairy herds experimentally treated with bGH has been legal in the United States and commercialization of bGH was widely taken for granted. Late in 1990, however, the respected Consumers Union (publisher of *Consumer Reports* magazine) joined other consumer, environmental and small farm advocates in calling upon the US Food and Drug Administration to investigate further the social and environmental impacts of bGH use (Ingersol, 1990). Because bGH is the first major trial of genetic engineering in the food domain, the future of biotechnology in agriculture hangs on the scope and thoroughness of such research.[1]

The intent of this chapter is to investigate a range of social and environmental effects likely to take effect if bGH is commercialized. To date, most research on bGH has been limited to public health concerns or dairy price reductions resulting from further milk glut, despite early warnings of other social dislocations (Kalter, 1985). Of overriding interest to us are the impacts related to the further erosion of family-based dairying, to which bGH adoption will contribute (OTA, 1986; Knoblauch, 1987). Though some have argued that bGH will benefit large and small dairy farmers equally, its effective use requires technologies and practices that are not size neutral and which, when combined with bGH, will accelerate the exit of small and medium size operators from the industry (Fallert *et al.* 1987). Each of the impacts we consider follow from the restructuring of the dairy industry – that is, the replacement of smaller operators by large, regionally concentrated and industrially organized dairies.

In their 1984 book, *The Second Industrial Divide*, Michael Piore and Charles Sabel present a framework for examining changes in industrial

production in the late 20th century. Their work, with useful extensions for
rural as well as urban policy, contrasts two modes of industrial organization:
large-scale, standardized, mass production and smaller scale, flexibly specialized, craft production. Mass production gained prominence across many
industrial sectors during the late 19th and early 20th centuries. Relatively
small-scale, technologically diverse and regionally dispersed production
units persist in areas such as construction, machine tools, apparel manufacturing and some areas of production agriculture.

Historically, virtually all segments of agriculture in the United States were
typified by an entrepreneurial, innovative, relatively small-scale form of
economic organization closely resembling Piore and Sable's 'craft production'. However, in recent years the mass production, industrialized
mode of organization has made major inroads in the areas of poultry, hog,
fruits and vegetables. Most of the fruits and vegetables grown in California
and Florida come from larger-than-family farms, and are vertically integrated with processors and distributors (Wallace, 1987). According to the
1987 Census of Agriculture, less than 3,000 very large farms account for over
70 per cent of all fresh vegetable sales in this country. Poultry production,
which was once geographically and organizationally dispersed, is now controlled by just four large processors; beef cattle production has undergone
drastic concentration in the last three decades (Knutson, Penn and Boehm,
1983).

Dairying as a craft industry

Dairying, too, has experienced widespread consolidation and reorganization
along mass production lines, especially in the sunbelt states. There, dairy
farms with 500 or more cows are the fastest growing segment of the dairy
industry (Table 8.1). In Arizona, over 80 per cent of the dairy cattle are
found on large, industrial type farms, while over 60 per cent of California
dairy cows are found on these types of farms. Yet in other regions the large-
scale, mass production model has yet to displace the heterogeneous, craft-
based approach by smaller family farms (Albrecht and Ladewig, 1982).
Among US farms dedicated mainly to dairying (i.e., milk accounts for at
least half of commodity sales), 75 per cent had herd sizes under 72 cows and
produced 36 per cent of aggregate milk sales in 1987 (Stanton and Bertelsen,
1989).

Thus, dairying in the United States maintains a dual character in both an
organizational and a regional sense. Compared to most sunbelt dairying,
average herd sizes in traditional dairybelt states are an order of magnitude
smaller and the number of dairy farms dramatically larger.[2] It is these latter
states which still hold most closely to a small-scale, extensive system of dairy
farming representative of Piore and Sabel's 'craft' industry. Although farm
numbers have decreased considerably over the past forty years, the total
number of dairy cattle has also decreased. Thus, average herd size has grown

Table 8.1 Characteristics of dairy farms in the sunbelt and the dairybelt

	Average herd size		Number of farms with 500 or more cows		Number of cows (000)		Percentage of cows in state on farms with 500 or more cows		Number of dairy farms	
	1978	1987	1978	1987	1978	1987	1978	1987	1978	1987
Sunbelt States:										
California	344	424	482	725	940.0	1067.3	42.1	62.9	2,730	2,519
Arizona	475	638	46	67	80.3	85.5	52.9	80.2	169	134
Texas	104	150	32	84	304.0	346.2	8.6	19.2	2,931	2,510
New Mexico	267	476	17	37	34.7	57.2	55.0	73.7	130	120
Florida	479	508	131	108	189.9	174.8	70.0	74.7	396	344
Dairybelt States:										
Wisconsin	47	51	2	9	1754.0	1693.3	.07	.3	37,181	32,870
Minnestoa	43	46	1	0	758.9	680.4	.07	0	17,792	14,629
Michigan	58	68	4	9	372.4	332.5	.8	1.8	6,436	4,905
New York	57	68	8	29	851.9	802.9	.6	2.5	14,792	11,722
Pennsylvania	51	55	6	7	661.5	651.6	.5	.7	12,946	11,872

Source: Census of Agriculture 1978 and 1987. Data are for dairy farms with 20 or more cows.

only slightly. Among the dairybelt states, only New York is beginning to experience an increase of very large dairy operations. If bGH is not approved for commercial distribution and use, restructuring of the industry within the dairy belt would be less dramatic and less rapid, as would the impacts associated with this restructuring.

Restructuring and vulnerability

The shift in milk production away from the heterogeneous, regionally dispersed system of family-based dairying closely conforming to Piore and Sabel's craft industry is likely to have numerous social and environmental impacts. Our view is that bGH commercialization will contribute substantially to these impacts by accelerating such a shift and making it irrevocable. The nation will gain a more efficient dairy industry at the expense of biological diversity, technological heterogeneity, and organizational flexibility. In what follows, we focus on various system-level risks and vulnerabilities accompanying a radically restructured dairy industry at the expense of craft producers. We illustrate each impact using recent surveys of dairy operators in New York State and relevant secondary sources from other sunbelt and dairybelt states.

Vulnerability 1: accident proneness

In 1984 Charles Perrow published *Normal Accidents*, a landmark book in which he argues that error-inducing properties are embedded in the very nature of large-scale, highly technical and complex production systems. Interactive complexity, wherein system failures induce other system failures, and tight coupling – i.e., reduced error margins by which systems recover from failure – are two such system properties. Ironically, operator skill and management ability make no difference in preventing accident proneness of this type. The catastrophes at Three Mile Island, Chernobyl and Bhopal illustrate Perrow's point.

The food system in general and production agriculture in particular are especially vulnerable to normal accidents. Especially instructive is the PBB contamination of the milk supply in Michigan in 1973. Fire retardant was inadvertently mixed with cattle feed supplies delivered to an unknown number of dairy farms throughout the state. By the time the accident was discovered, nearly nine million people in the state had eaten contaminated meat and dairy products. Michigan farmers were forced to destroy 30,000 head of contaminated cattle in the wake of the accident (Eggington, 1980).

The economic, environmental and health consequences of the Michigan tragedy would have been more serious had it not been for a highly dispersed system of milk production that diluted levels of contamination over many small herds throughout the state. Low-level contamination of virtually the

entire dairy food chain resulted only when PBB milk was mixed by processors with non-contaminated milk – that is, the point at which the scale of
operation in Michigan's production system greatly increased. If the same
accident occurred in, say, Arizona or California, the potential for a normal
accident affecting far larger consumer populations with less warning would
have multiplied.

The likelihood of normal accidents in the dairy industry will increase, if
Perrow is correct, with the scale of dairy operations. California offers
something of a test case in this regard, with its average of 400 cows per dairy
farm. That state's high-density, mass-bred dairy herds are particularly sus-
ceptible to epizootics of trichomoniasis, an animal disease for which there is
no effective treatment (Goodger and Skirrow, 1986) and other illnesses such
as vesicular stomatitis (Thurmond et al., 1987), udder infections and mastitis
(Gonzales et al., 1988). Trichomoniasis may pose a risk for the state's dairy
system as a whole to the extent that California comes to rely exclusively on
large, high density, mass-bred operations. A higher frequency of organizationally differentiated, intermediate size dairies offers preventive treatment
for the accident proneness described by Perrow.

Another conceivable normal accident related to large-scale dairying and
therefore to bGH is widespread human resistance to antibiotics adminis-
tered to animals and consumed, in one form or another, by humans. Over
half the antibiotics produced in America go to farms, not hospitals. They
enhance animal growth rates and animal feed conversion and control diseases (Cohen and Tauxe, 1986). As cows are hyperstimulated in conjunction
with bGH treatments, animal stress levels rise and susceptibility to illness
increases. In four surveys by independent researchers since 1987, anywhere
from 63 to 86 per cent of the milk sampled in the United States was shown to
be tainted with a mix of sulfa drugs and antibiotics. Commenting on the
latter, Princeton biochemist Karim Ahmed warned of a serious public health
problem in which humans will be less likely to benefit from antibiotic
therapies. The reason is that veterinary antibiotics can build up human
resistance to antibiotics made for humans and render them ineffective
(Ingersol, 1989). The problem will only worsen if dairymen intensify their
antibiotic dependency as a health maintenance strategy associated with
bGH.

Vulnerability 2: loss of technological diversity

The advent of technologies conducive to industrialized dairy production will
greatly narrow the diversity among the nation's dairy farmers. Dairy technologies are noticeably different on large and small herd-size farms. Milking
parlours are only economically efficient on large farms, for example.
Working with fewer animals, most small and medium sized operators are
better able to monitor the performance of their animals and hence maximize
milk production with their own size-specific technologies and management

strategies. The fact that there are highly efficient small producers and inefficient large ones is evident in Table 8.2 and suggests that the technologies of the former are not inferior to those found on larger farms (see also Fallert *et al.*, 1987).

If only the operators of large herds remain profitable after bGH is introduced, then the heterogeneous and diverse dairying strategies that characterize small-scale, family-run dairy farms will give way to technological monocultures. In a critique of 'one-size-fits-all-farming', a recent study by the International Institute for Applied Systems Analysis noted that there may be inherent value in the maintenance of technological diversity that is analogous to the value of genetic diversity in ecosystems (Brooks, 1986). The pending loss of diversity in dairy production mirrors concern typically directed at the narrowing genetic base of the world's staple foods (e.g., Kloppenburg, 1988).

Alternatively, a system of diversified, family-based dairying takes continuous advantage of spontaneous technological innovation in multiple places and of diverse, *in situ* field trials. These relatively low-input systems keep value added on farms and in rural communities rather than in the laboratories and factories of input suppliers (Hassebrook and Hegyes, 1989). Farmer experimentation, for example, led to free-stall dairy barns. Where the craft mode dominates, innovations which fail are localized and contained by the very lack of standardization. Innovator rents from inventions (the profits realized by early adopters) are modest and seldom lead to dramatic restructuring of the industry.

Vulnerability 3: dependence on wage labour

Organizationally, very large dairy farms look radically different from smaller, family-run units. Gilbert and Akor (1988) recently compared dairy farm structure in Wisconsin and California, with an interest in what the future held for states like Wisconsin and other dairybelt states should bGH be commercialized. They found that the labour processes on the dairy farms of each state differ dramatically. On a typical large, dry-lot California dairy farm (800–1,000 cows) labour is divided between the owner/manager, a herdsman, three to five milkers, a calf manager, a feeder, a breeder and relief workers. Milking takes place virtually around the clock. In Wisconsin, dairy operators and their families perform all the functions noted above, plus growing crops, but with smaller herds. These dairy families typically milk twice a day. The study concludes that specialization reinforces expansion whereas its absence contributes to the reproduction of family dairy farms.

The average dairy herd in America hovers around seventy cows. This is largely determined by what a single family (two members or one member plus a hired person) can manage (Stanton and Bertelsen, 1989). Iowa corn farmers, Montana wheat producers and Georgia soybean farmers can expand their operations by buying new labour-extending technologies.

Table 8.2 Herd size and herd average for State of New York (1987)

Production per cow per year	Herd size				
	<40	40–59	60–79	80–119	⩾120
	(Per cent)				
a. <12,000 lbs.	53	32	21	24	7
b. 12,000–13,999 lbs	23	22	22	17	32
(a + b combined)	**76**	**54**	**43**	**41**	**39**
c. 14,000–15,999 lbs	9	21	27	24	21
d. 16,000–17,999 lbs	10	17	20	21	25
(c + d combined)	**19**	**38**	**47**	**45**	**46**
e. 18,000–19,999 lbs	4	6	9	10	11
f. ⩾20,000 lbs	1	2	2	3	3
(e + f combined)	**5**	**8**	**11**	**13**	**14**

Source: Data tabulated from the New York Farm Management and Energy Survey, 1987, courtesy of the Department of Agricultural Economics, Cornell University.

Larger tors or more powerful combines allow a family to work larger amounts of land. Family-organized dairy farms, as opposed to industrial dairies, are constrained more by labour than by land, however. Even with sophisticated technology and management skills, the above family unit can realistically handle up to eighty cows without an otherwise imperative shift to wage labour dependency.

Based on recent projections that the smallest, economically viable, post-bGH dairy in the traditional dairy belt will be two to three times what a traditional operator can handle (Kalter *et al.*, 1985), we must infer that labour management will compete with animal management among the dairy operators who survive the restructuring of the industry. Such managers will be forced to hire part-time, full-time or seasonal labour to milk cows and grow forage and concentrates. Table 8.3 shows the results of two recent studies in New York State reviewing labour requirements of different size dairy operations.[3] The three largest categories show high dependency levels on both part-time and year-round employees. For the nation as a whole, wages and benefits tend to be a minor cash expense for dairy farms of less than seventy-two cows, but the second largest expense for farms of over ninety cows. For smaller herds, wages and benefits are 6–7 per cent of cash expenses, whereas they range from 13–15 per cent when herds surpass 90 animals.

Central to wage labour vulnerability is the inadequate supply of skilled dairy labour in most rural areas. Such labour is in short supply, requires fringe benefits, and often fails to take the personal interest in cow health and well-being that owners formerly took with smaller herds. Nor is it certain that dairy farm operators who are considered 'good managers' of animals will be good managers of labour. If they are not, and hired labour in the

Table 8.3 Employment patterns of dairy farms by herd size for New York State (1987) and western New York (1989)

Labour Characteristic	Herd size				
	<40	40–59	60–79	80–99	>100
	(Per cent)				
Part-time employees					
a. New York State	26	27	49	43	62
b: Western New York	17	21	20	64	67
Temporary employees					
a. New York State	24	32	28	26	20
b. Western New York	30	48	27	7	25
Year-round employees					
a. New York State	23	33	55	69	87
b. Western New York	4	24	20	71	83

Source: Data tabulated from a) same as Table 8.2, and b) from the Dairy Competitiveness Project, Department of Rural Sociology, Cornell University.

dairy industry becomes unionized, strikes and work stoppages known to other wage-based commodities may impede the supply of dairy products to consumers at home or abroad. Recalcitrant wage labour will quickly grasp the fact that dairy products, among the most perishable of household foods, make dairy owners highly vulnerable to cash-flow interruptions and weak collective bargaining positions.

In sum, as dairy farms become larger in the wake of bGH commercialization and the intra-family division of labour gives way to arrangements in which dairy producers depend on wage labour and professional managers, specialized skills will replace the generalized talent on which the industry has traditionally relied. Entry into dairy farming by those who acquired generalized skills in family units will become ever more restricted as the pool of dairy operators shrinks and as management qualifications escalate.

Vulnerability 4: overcentralized decision making

A significant increase in average dairy farm size will lead to the dissolution of local community ties. As the system of family-based dairying passes, the likelihood increases that social and economic vitality in rural communities and counties will be lost (Goldschmidt, 1978; MacCannell, 1983; Swanson, 1980; Carlin and Green, 1989). Large-scale agriculture is believed to result in greater inequality of income distribution and the loss of social cohesion (Flora *et al.*, 1977). Moreover, local credit, services, and markets will be replaced by externally controlled counterparts. Commenting on the problems associated with vertical integration, the Office of Technology Assessment states that contract integration with corporations, and sometimes cooperatives, radically changes the role of the independent farmer. More often than not, the farmer loses control of, if not legal title to, the commodities grown under a production-integrated arrangement (OTA, 1986).

As a dairy system composed of relatively small-scale units is replaced by a large-scale, industrialized one, surviving operators will depend on ever larger processors and distributors. Many local fluid and manufacturing plants will go out of business, consolidate, or become part of larger national or regional agribusiness firms. Only niche markets will be left for the smaller-scale producers and processors. Like poultry and other commodities, dairy products will relinquish quality control and other decision making to large non-farm corporations like Carnation or Kraft. A production system adapted to myriad forces and benefitting a wide array of local owner-producers will be supplanted by a system designed almost exclusively for 'economic efficiency' (Sagoff, 1988).

Two other consequences of weakened local control and decision-making related to a radically restructured dairy industry are noteworthy. Land concentration leaves a few very large landowners or tenants where multiple operators once farmed and changes the legal nature of local land use, ownership and control. In place of decentralized land use planning wherein a broad range of rural residents decide the location of roads and facilities, industrial parks or waste disposal locations, key land use decisions will become more centralized and redefined as the domain of a few large (and often absentee) landowners (Popper, 1978).

Secondly, the heavy debt associated with large-scale, industrial dairy production has the potential to attenuate local control over significant farm assets. Among dedicated dairy farms in the nation, the average debt-to-asset ratio was 21 per cent in 1987 (Stanton and Bertelsen, 1989). Table 8.4 suggests that smaller dairy operators in New York tend to be debt free or enjoy low debt-to-asset ratios. This contrasts to large herd dairymen, among whom 46 per cent had a quarter million dollars of debt or more. At the expected rate of $.50 per day per cow, bGH will cost an operator with 500 cows an additional $66,500 a year. Thus, as size increases, non-local interests can dictate many critical decisions in dairy production and will have even more external power in such matters if, as anticipated, bGH contributes significantly to upward size shifts in the industry.

Vulnerability 5: environment and amenity decline

Advanced dairy technologies like bGH are likely to lead to interstate as well as intrastate shifts in dairy production (OTA, 1986; Reilly, 1989). This new geography of dairying is apparent in sunbelt states such as California, where large-scale dairying has concentrated near metropolitan centres. The Chino

Table 8.4   Total farm debt by herd size, New York State (1987)

Total debt	Herd size				
(000)	<40	40–59	60–79	80–119	≥120
	(Per cent)				
0	43	23	24	11	20
<$50	33	22	20	22	7
$50–99.9	18	28	14	15	5
$100–249.9	5	26	37	34	24
$250–499.9	0	1	5	18	22
≥$500	0	0	0	0	22

Source: New York Management and Energy Survey, 1987

Valley outside Los Angeles now has the largest concentration of dairy cows in the world; the 375 dairy farms in the area milk over 200,000 cows (Gilbert and Akor, 1988). In New York, the dispersed pattern of dairying is on the verge of abrupt change as farmers expand their herds in anticipation of the economies of scale associated with bGH. Ten years ago there were eight New York herds over 500 cows. Today, there are twenty-nine herds this large and twenty-three of them are regionally concentrated in a small number of counties between Rochester and Syracuse (Table 8.1). Craft-type dairying in the North Country, the West and the Southern Tier of New York – all traditional dairy strongholds – will be severely disadvantaged as bGH commercialization takes hold.

Perhaps the foremost current concern over large-scale, industrialized dairy farming is disposal of the waste streams such strategies necessitate (Molnar and Wu, 1989). On the one hand, cows treated with bGH are more efficient. Because bGH cows partition their energy so as to yield more milk from a fixed amount of feed (Bauman *et al.*, 1985), less manure overall is being generated as a byproduct of the new technology. However, this somewhat reduced waste stream will be geographically concentrated rather than dispersed. Though more efficient, bGH cows consume more food and consequently generate more manure than non-bGH cows. That is, because they are valuable producers, bGH cows will be kept lactating as much as possible – a source of greater feed intake and faeces output (Colucci *et al.*, 1982). Thus the spatial redistribution of dairying between and within states is likely to be accompanied by substantial net increases in manure in zones such as New York State's Northern Tier counties or California's Chino Valley and by related threats to ground and surface water quality.

Vulnerability 6: anti-biotechnology backlash

As noted earlier in this chapter, consumer groups, environmentalists, animal rights activists and small farm advocates have registered deep concerns over bGH adoption and use. Retailers and cooperatives have taken a cautious approach to bGH products and state legislatures in some dairybelt states have passed laws requiring bGH products to be labeled (Marion *et al.*, 1988). Other countries, intent on protecting their own dairy industries, may seize the bGH controversy as a convenient excuse to follow the EEC example of banning American beef treated with selected hormones. The possibility is far from remote that public scepticism over the 'blockbuster' benefits of bGH will spill over to other biotechnologies now being developed.

Such a backlash may have political impacts. When confronted with the prospects of regional decline, concentrated land ownership, threats to environment and amenities, normal accidents and less viable rural communities associated with bGH commercialization, the interest groups named above may seek political remedies at the ballot box. In an era of single-issue politics, a plausible target might be political incumbents championing bGH.

In New York, for example, the composition of the state legislature could change significantly if voters went on an anti-bGH offensive. Following research recently performed by Green and Carlin (1985), which projected potential party change related to farm crisis conditions in 700 farm counties nationwide, we identified eighteen out of fifty New York counties in which majority and minority parties in the country legislature are separated by three or fewer legislative seats. In twelve of these eighteen, dairying was an important part of the local economy. Thus, if only three members of the party in power in these counties were replaced by their opponents, political realignment could occur in roughly one-fourth of New York's counties, increasing the pressure at the state level for such things as milk testing, product labeling, or more generic anti-biotechnology regulations.

Concluding thoughts

In this chapter, two contrasting systems of dairy production in the US are identified. One is characterized by relatively small-scale, heterogeneous producers and is found in the traditional dairybelt states. The other is organized around large-scale, highly specialized, industrialized dairy factories. Although this model of dairy farming is found primarily in the southern and western United States, it will make rapid inroads in the dairybelt states if bGH is commercialized.[4] If this occurs, there will be a strong tendency for dairy farming throughout the United States to restructure itself at the expense of craft-based dairying. If such is the case, the emerging model of dairy production will be subject to social, economic, political and environmental impacts far beyond health and price effects and having extensive rural policy ramifications.

BGH is of course not the only 'super cow' technology contributing to the restructuring of the dairy industry, nor is the list of impacts resulting wholly or in part from bGH reviewed here exhaustive. The land grant college system, organized to provide assistance and advice to a cross-section of farmers, could lose a vast constituency of dairymen. The cultural image of dairy farming, and of milk as 'nature's perfect food' will also change. The pastoral aesthetic cows grazing on family farms, jealously guarded by tourist-conscious states, will give way to a rural factory system in which the technology and the cows will rarely be seen by the public (Johnson, 1988). Milk substitutes may gain favour just as margarine has successfully competed with butter due to consumer reactions to cholesterol.

There is considerable irony in the technology-induced restructuring of the dairy industry treated in this analysis. At a time when countries and corporations alike are turning away from large-scale, rigid, mass production modes of industrial organization and seeking innovative, flexible, diversified alternatives, dairy farming seems headed in another direction. The eroding position of the US in the world industrial order may be due to slavish adherence to hi-tech Fordism and Taylorism. On the other hand, the highly experimental and innovative system of American agriculture based on heterogeneous technology and management style is the model the world has emulated. In an industry plagued by overcapacity and increasingly oriented toward niche markets for its survival, the latter organizational path warrants serious reconsideration among rural policy makers at all levels.

Notes

1. The bGH controversy extends to Europe as well. Monsanto applied unsuccessfully for approval of its version of recombinant bGH in Britain in July of 1990 and the European Committee for Veterinary and Medical Products is under instruction by the European Parliament not to license bGH until more is known about its effects on health, the environment and the farm community (Cherfas, 1990).
2. Dairybelt states include Vermont, New York, Pennsylvania, Ohio, Wisconsin, Michigan, Illinois, Minnesota, Iowa, Washington, and Oregon.
3. New York data were jointly produced by the Department of Agricultural Economics of Cornell University and the New York Agricultural Statistics Service's '1987 Farm Management and Energy Survey' which sampled 10,050 dairy farmers in the State. County data came from New York's 'Dairy Competitiveness Project' in which one of the authors (Lyson) was involved in 1989.
4. Kalter et al. (1985) surveyed New York dairy farmers who were shown a simulated advertisement of the production gain from using bGH and concluded that between 63 and 85 per cent would be likely to adopt bGH within three years of commercialization.

References

Albrecht, D. and H. Ladewig (1982) 'Corporate agriculture and the family farm', *The rural sociologist*, 2: 376–383.
Bauman, D., P.J. Eppard, J.J. DeGeeter and G.M. Lanza (1985) 'Responses of high

producing dairy cows to long term treatment with pituitary- and recombinant-somatotropin', *Journal of Dairy Science*, **68**: 1352.

Brooks, H. (1986) *Sustainable development of the biosphere*, Clark, and Munn, R. (eds), IIASA, Luxemburg, Austria.

Carlin, T. and B. Green (1989) 'Farm structure and nearby communities', *Rural development perspectives*, **5** (16): 16–20.

Cherfas, J. (1990) 'Europe: Bovine growth hormone in a political maze', *Science*, **249**: 852.

Cohen, M. and R. Tauxe (1986) 'Drug-resistant salmonella in the United States: an epidemiological perspective', *Science* **234**: 964–69.

Colucci, P., L. Chase, P. Van Soest (1982) 'Feed intake, apparent diet digestibility, and rate of particulate passage in dairy cattle', *Dairy science*, **65**: 1445–1456.

Eggington, J. (1980) *The Poisoning of Michigan*, W.W. Norton, NY.

Fallert, R., T. McGuchkin, C. Betts and G. Bruner (1987) *bST and the dairy industry*, Agricultural Information Bulletin 535, Economic Research Service-USDA, Washington, DC.

Flora, J., I. Brown and J. Conboy (1977) *Impact of type of agriculture on class structure, social well being and inequalities*, Department of Sociology Report, Kansas State University, Manhattan, KS.

Gilbert, J. and R. Akor (1988) 'Increasing structural divergence in US dairying: California and Wisconsin since 1950', *Rural sociology*, **53**: 56–72.

Goldschmidt, W. (1978) *As you sow*, Allanheld, Osmun, Montclair, NJ.

Gonzalez, R.N., D.E. Jasper, T.B. Farver, R.B. Bushnell and C.E. Franti (1988) 'Prevalence of udder infections and mastitis in 50 California dairy herds' *JAVMA*, **193**: 32–327.

Goodger, W.J. and S.Z. Skirrow (1986) 'Epidemiologic and economic analyses of an unusually long epizootic of trochomoniasis in a large California dairy herd', *JAVMA*, **189**: 772–776.

Green, B.L. and T.A. Carlin (1985) *Agricultural policy, rural communities and politics*, Staff Report AGES850429, Economic Research Service, U.S. Dept. of Agriculture, Washington, DC.

Hassebrook, C. and G. Hegyes (1989) *Choices for the heartland: alternative directions in biotechnology and family farming, rural communities and the environment*, Center for Rural Affairs, Walthill, NE and Iowa State University Research Foundation.

Ingersol, B. (1989) 'Milk is found tainted with a range of drugs farmers give their cattle', *Wall Street Journal*, **126**: A1–2 (December 29).

Ingersol, B. (1990) 'Growth drug for milk cows draws more fire', *Wall Street Journal*, **183**: B1 and 4 (December 4).

Johnson, S. (1988) *New York Times*, **137**: (February 14).

Kalter, R., R. Milligan, W. Lesser, W. McGrath and D. Bauman (1985) *Biotechnology and the dairy industry: production costs and commercial potential of the bovine growth hormone*, A.E. Research 85–20, Cornell University, Ithaca.

Kalter, R. (1985) 'The new biotech agriculture: unforeseen economic consequences', *Issues in science and technology*, **2**(1): 125–133.

Kloppenburg, Jr.J. (1988) *First the seed*, Cambridge, Cambridge University Press.

Knoblauch, W. (1987) *The impact of bST on dairy farm income and survival*, Office of Information and Publications, University of Maryland, College Park, MD.

Knutson, R., J. Penn and W. Boehm (1983) *Agriculture and food policy*, Prentice-Hall, Englewood Cliffs, NJ, 1989, National Academy Press, Washington, DC.

MacCannell, D. (1983) 'Agribusiness and the small community', background paper to *Technology, public policy and the changing structure of American agriculture*, Office of Technology Assessment, Washington, DC.

Marion, B.W., R.L. Wills and L.J. Butler (1988) with contributions by Kloppenburg, Jr., J., Novak, P., Robertson, M., Bailey, W.K., Barns, R., Kleinman, D.L., *The social and economic impact of biotechnology on Wisconsin agriculture*, College of Agriculture and Life Sciences, University of Wisconsin, Madison, WI.

Molnar, J. and L. Wu (1989) *Environmental consequences of animal waste disposal: farm operator perspectives and practices*, Alabama Agricultural Experiment Station Circular 297, Auburn University, Alabama.

OTA (1986) *Technology, public policy, and the changing structure of American agriculture*, Office of Technology Assessment, Washington, DC.

Perrow, C. (1984) *Normal accidents*, Basic Books, NY.

Piore, M.J. and C.F. Sabel (1984) *The second industrial divide: possibilities for prosperity*, Basic Books, NY.

Popper, F. (1978) 'What's the hidden factor in land use regulation?', *Urban land*, 4 (December): 8–11.

Reilly, J. (1989) *Consumer effects of biotechnology*, Agriculture Information Bulletin. USDA, Washington, D.C.

Sagoff, M. (1988) 'Biotechnology and the environment: what is at risk?', *Agriculture and human values*, 5, 3 (Summer): 26–35.

Stanton, B.F. and D. Bertelsen (1989) *Operating results for dairy farms classified by size*, A.E. Research 89–23, Cornell University, Ithaca, NY.

Swanson, L. (1980) *A study in socioeconomic development: changing farm structure and rural community decline in the context of technological transformation of American agriculture*, unpublished Ph.D. Dissertation, Department of Economics, University of Nebraska, Lincoln, NB.

Thurmond, M.C., A.A. Adrans, P.P. Picanso, T. McDowell, B. Reynolds and J. Saito (1987) 'Vesicular stomatitis virus (New Jersey.strain) infection in two California dairy herds: an epidemiologic study', *JAVMA* 191: 965–970.

Wallace, L.T. (1987) *Agriculture's futures*, Springer-Verlag, New York, NY.

PART III

The Greening of Settlement and Society

9

The changing nature of settlement policy in the USA: a theoretical and case study review

Harvey Jacobs

Introduction

In the United States rural settlement policy is in a state of great flux. The 1990 census of population has confirmed that the century-long decline of rural population has continued; the much-heralded reverse migration of the 1970s now appears to have been nothing more than a blip in a long-term trend. Continuing changes in the mode of agricultural production, the widespread failure of rural banks, and the decline of rural manufacturing have all contributed to producing an official rural population which is less than one-quarter of the total US population.

But this does not mean that there are no significant rural settlement planning and policy issues. Quite the contrary. If rural America in general has declined, urban-fringe America has boomed. Also continuing a century-long pattern, American families, and now American business centres, push towards the far edges of cities (see, for example, Pivo, 1990). As urban land uses sprawl over the countryside, issues of rural-urban land use conflict emerge with force. The most enduring of these issues is the conflict over the protection of America's agricultural land base. Added to it are more recent concerns over groundwater quality, soil erosion, river and stream pollution, and the social transformation of distinctive rural places into a homogenous suburban culture (Lapping *et al.*, 1989).

The locus of rural settlement policy in the United States has been land use planning. Land use planning is the mechanism by which the public sector establishes the rules for individual location and use decisions. Traditionally, this authority has been extremely decentralized, resting with the most local of governmental bodies, and subject to little oversight or required integration from more central authorities. Traditionally, this authority has also been a consensual, non-conflictual, and semi-technical process. All of this is now changing.

This chapter explores the changing nature of settlement policy in the US by focusing on two aspects: the changing theoretical construct of land use planning itself, and an illustration of this change via a case study of Lancaster County, Pennsylvania, a locale known worldwide for its community of Amish farmers.

The changing theoretical nature of land use planning

Land use planning has been practised in the US throughout the twentieth century, in both urban and rural areas. Irrespective of the place, the paradigm which underlies this practice is essentially the same. This paradigm is now shifting and in some cases is under active attack. Thus the land use planning which is practised in the future will, of necessity, be fundamentally different from that of the past.

In order to understand how and why land use planning in the US is changing, it is useful to explore its establishment. First, it is important to acknowledge that land use planning was *invented* at the turn of the century. The specific model for land use planning grew out of the German forest management and city planning movements of the late 1800s. These movements promulgated the idea of an analytical, scientific, and systematic approach to determining how land should be used. These movements also put forward the idea that the general public interest could not be served by each individual pursuing their own self-interest, and that there was a need for a social structure which identified and integrated the goals and activities of individuals. Overall, this idea was reinforced by a general interest in Taylor's scientific operations-management movement in the early 1900s. In the cities, these movements gave birth to modern city planning (Scott, 1969; Hall, 1988); in rural America modern land-use settlement policy can be traced to efforts in Wisconsin in the 1920s to resettle farmers from marginal northern forest lands (Rowlands, 1933; Wilson, 1957–1958).

The land use planning model invented at the turn of the century contained certain presumptions. These presumptions are now under attack and at the base of the coming change. They can be summarized in seven points: 1) it is possible to perform a complete physical and social analysis of the capacities of, and demands on, land; 2) this analysis will yield information that will lead to better individual and social decision making; 3) this process of analysis and information generation will be heavily reliant on professionals and experts; 4) the result of this analysis will be a single best pattern of land use and settlement (this is best expressed in the policy tool of zoning with its single use districts); 5) while there is a strong cultural inclination toward local control, there is a professional orientation toward centralization in administrative authority for land; 6) urban society is at the height of the social hierarchy, and other land use concerns need to be subsumed to it; and finally, 7) land is, at base, a private commodity and resource; the presumption is that land use-rights begin with the private owner and social intrusion is only allowed to the extent it is clearly necessary to protect public health and safety (Jacobs, 1992).

This land use planning model is now challenged by three different but interrelated and sometimes contradictory phenomena: the rise of a diverse, populist citizen movement, a decades-long redefinition of private property rights, and the adoption and accessibility of geographic information systems.

The citizen movement of the last several decades is the most obvious push on the changing nature of land use planning. Citizens find themselves challenging many of the underlying presumptions of the long-standing model. Among the most contentious of these is the presumption of experts' pre-eminent knowledge. Citizens are no longer willing to cede to an expert's analysis and opinions just because that person, as a land use or environmental planner, is presented as an expert. Citizens have ample evidence of the failure of experts and feel empowered to conduct their own analysis. This is especially true with regard to land issues, which are so immediate and accessible. As part of this empowerment citizens are willing to assert that their feelings about the transformation implied in land use and settlement planning decisions are as relevant and important as the use of economic rationality and scientific method, the traditional bases for decision making.

As part of their scepticism about experts and their advice, citizens are also often dubious about the long-standing call to centralize management to achieve sound resource objectives. Americans have a profound love-hate relationship with governmental authority. While the cultural value of local control is often touted, it is also common to bemoan its shortcomings. Yet governmental reorganizations over settlement policy seem, more often than not, to yield less citizen access to the decision process (Popper, 1974).

More than anything else, this diverse, populist citizen movement is making clear that land-use and settlement planning and policy is as much a social and political issue as it is a physical and economic one. Land use decisions are not just about economic efficiency, land values, traffic flows, and municipal tax bases. They are as much about community stability, neighbourhood character, individual and family well-being, and the ability of an individual and a family to find their place in the American dream (Logan and Molotch, 1987).

This citizen challenge is reinforced by the long-standing redefinition of private property rights. Starting most ostensibly with the US Supreme Court decision of *Euclid v. Ambler Realty Co.* in 1926, which affirmed the public's right to institute zoning power to protect the public health, safety, welfare, and morals, the public sector in the US has redefined the sticks in the private property bundle so that there is a larger and larger public share to it (McClaughry, 1975; Hunter, 1988).

The US, perhaps more than any other nation, is culturally and legally oriented to respect for private property. The very establishment of the United States was premised on the need for a strong set of private property rights which the public (the government) could intrude upon only when the public interest clearly called for it. And even this intrusion could occur only under strictly set conditions and with established guarantees (contained within the final clause of the Fifth Amendment of the Constitution) (McClaughry, 1976).

What has occurred in the last twenty-five years, parallel to the rise of the modern environmental movement, is an expansion of what is deemed to be the public share of the property rights bundle. The modern environmental movement is itself a movement premised on a redefinition of these rights. The movement stresses how the public interest is not served by private property ownership and how it could be better served by a shrinking private bundle and an expanding public one (Hunter, 1988). Examples of this change abound, from 1950s-style urban renewal activities, to citizen movements for historic building, site, and landscape preservation, agricultural land protection, and wetland preservation. In each case, citizens point to the failure of private property ownership to serve the public interest, and thus the need to redefine the social bounds of acceptable private property use.

The third challenge to traditional land use and settlement planning is the advent of 'user-friendly' geographic information systems. In the early 1990s it can be hard to remember that the first IBM personal computer was introduced in 1981, and the Apple Macintosh in 1984. Computers in general, and personal computers, modems, electronic networks, and bulletin boards in particular, have become ubiquitous (as of 1992 there are an estimated 80 million personal computers in use in the US). In the last decade there has been widespread and increasing adoption of geographic information systems (GIS) among local governments and planning offices (Dangermond, 1989; Jacobs, 1989a).

Before the advent of GIS technology land use and settlement analysis was conducted through a cumbersome and inefficient method of map overlays, in which the differences in base scales and boundary lines among resource maps were often fudged. Not only has GIS allowed a higher degree of accuracy in analysis, but it has opened up the opportunity of 'alternatives-analysis' in the same way that spreadsheet programs have for economic, fiscal, and demographic data (Ventura *et al.*, 1988).

But GIS has done something else; it has opened the process of land use analysis from the office to the street. Under the old way of conducting land use analysis, in essence, it was impossible for anyone other than professionals to perform alternative analyses. This is no longer true. Just as citizens now show up at municipal budget hearings with alternative budgets reflecting alternative priorities, because they have taken the base figures and manipulated them in their own computers, GIS provides the same possibility in settlement planning. Exclusive access to information, and the ability to rely upon it as a base for professional expertise in proffering land use and settlement advice, is fast eroding (e.g. Gurwitt, 1991).

Two brief examples may clarify the first two of these forces; the third force is so emergent that its impact has yet to be documented. Statistics on the rate of conversion of agricultural land to non-agricultural uses in the post World War II period, and debates about these statistics and their import, have been actively bandied about for nearly twenty years (National

Agricultural Lands Study, 1981; Gustafson *et al.*, 1984). Regardless of the 'correct' figures, agricultural land protection continues to be the most prominent urban-fringe land use planning issue in the US (Lapping and Moser, 1992).

It came to prominence when citizens challenged the conventional wisdom of traditional agricultural economics and agricultural economists regarding the loss of prime agricultural land to shopping malls and housing developments. These professionals suggested that there was no problem with the conversion of this land because land as a resource was being substituted by technological and managerial innovations.

Historically, this analysis is, in fact, correct. The decline in the US farm population and the shifting pattern of agricultural land use has not resulted in a decline in farm output – just the opposite. Fewer farmers are producing more food products more 'efficiently.' But for many citizens, particularly those on the urban fringe, the protection of agricultural land is not an issue to be assessed solely on the basis of economic theory, through the lens of a concept such as efficiency.

Rather, for these citizens, agricultural land protection is an issue to be assessed on its landscape, aesthetic, and quality-of-life attributes. They contend that agricultural land is not just a private resource, about which farmland owners can make personal decisions, but that it is in fact a public resource, with implications for regional open space, national and international food security, and intergenerational environmental equity. The enduring and wide-ranging existence of agricultural land protection as an urban-fringe land use planning issue represents a poignant example of the conflict between the judgments of professionals and those of citizens. The fact that every state in the US now has at least one programme directed at agricultural land protection illustrates citizen power in the redefinition of property rights.

The second example has to do with the so-called quiet revolution in land use control. The quiet revolution is a movement begun in the 1960s, much supported by land use professionals, to remove land use planning authority from local governments and transfer it to more central regional or state agencies (Bosselman and Callies, 1971; Popper, 1988). To some extent this can be seen as the next step in what first occurred in the early part of the century when modern land use planning was invented and, through policy instruments such as zoning, land use authority was removed from the individual to the local government.

The classical examples of the quiet revolution include the creation of the Adirondack Park Agency in New York State, similar kinds of agencies for the California coast and the Lake Tahoe area in California and Nevada, and statewide planning acts in Florida, Vermont and Oregon. There has been a recent resurgence of activity in Florida and Vermont, with revisions of their previous legislation. Substantive explorations of similar activities and agencies have also occurred in Maine, Georgia, Rhode Island, Maryland, New Jersey and Washington (Fulton, 1989; Meeks, 1990).

In all of these instances, the argument is the same – local people and local governments (where authority initially rested) will always be elitist, discriminatory, parochial, and anti-ecological in their approach to planning and policy. The presumption of these acts and agencies is that the new central authority will be none of these things – it will act in the greater public interest. So, drawing on the new property rights theories, action is promoted which suggests traditional private property rights should not be recognized, and instead new, regional 'public interest' perspectives on property rights need to be instituted.

Affected citizens – members of the public – aren't so sure. Why? Because they are often troubled with the removal of local control over their land and their neighbourhoods to the authority of distant, hard-to-access professional bureaucrats. So, concurrent with the rise of a new regionalism in land use planning is a new localism, again largely citizen driven (Jacobs, 1989b; Heiman, 1990).

What does all this mean for the future of land use and settlement planning in the US? It means that it will be fundamentally different. Land use and settlement planning will no longer be viewed as a technical exercise, but will be recognized for its strong social character (see, as illustrations, Jacobs, 1989c and Beatley, 1991). This fact, the democratization and socializing of land use and settlement planning, may change it more in the next ten years than it has changed in the last seventy.

A case study of settlement policy in transition[1]

Lancaster County is located in the southeastern corner of the state of Pennsylvania, within 100 miles of major urban centers in Pennsylvania, Maryland, Delaware, and New Jersey. It is a county of nearly 423,000 people and over 600,000 acres (approximately 950 square miles). Historically it has been relatively removed from the pressures of growth along the eastern megalopolis. In the last several decades, and especially in the 1980s, this changed dramatically. In the 1980s Lancaster County citizens found growth and settlement issues thrust upon them.

Lancaster County is a place that strikes the first-time visitor as rich in contrast. It is best known for the community of Plain Sect people, the Old Order Amish and Mennonites, that inhabit the townships in the eastern portion of the county. The Old Order Amish, with their horse and buggy transportation, plain and uniform clothing, shunning of electricity and telephone use, apparent nineteenth century farming practices, and withdrawn lifestyles, harken to a simpler and purer way of living from America's past (Kraybill, 1989).

In contrast is the Three Mile Island Nuclear Power Plant. Located just over the northwestern border of the county, here is a pinnacle of modern technology, both in its best dreams and worst nightmares. The Amish and their 'cousins', the Old Order Mennonites in the northeastern portion of the county, represent stability and resoluteness in community and land steward-ship. Three Mile Island, the only nuclear power plant in the US ever to reach the brink of meltdown, represents the ability of humanity to invent the means of its own destruction.

Lancaster County offers other contrasts as well. It is one of the most productive agricultural counties in the US. In fact, it is the top-ranked non-irrigated county in the US. As such, it out-performs thirteen states in value of agricultural production. And it is a county with an extremely healthy family farm structure. There are approximately 5,000 family farms in the county, 20 per cent of which are owned by the Old Order, Plain Sect families, with an average farm size of eighty-five acres.

But the economy of Lancaster County is not built on farming alone, even though approximately two-thirds of the land is devoted to agriculture. The county has over eight hundred industrial establishments, including the headquarters of some multinationals. It also has over six hundred tourist facilities, which serve five million tourists per year. Many of these visitors are drawn by the unique Pennsylvania Dutch flavour of the county, a function of its Amish population. Its heritage is that of a beautiful land and gentle people who share an ethic about land use and management; but Lancaster County also suffers from serious traffic congestion, groundwater pollution, and housing affordability problems.

Since 1950 the county has grown at an average rate of 16 per cent per decade, with slightly larger growth spurts in the 1950s and the 1980s. Yet something about the amount and rate of growth in the 1980s seemed to trigger a reaction among the county's citizens different from that of earlier decades. By the decade's end this reaction ranged from caution to alarm over continued intensive growth and its threat to the social fabric of the community.

Citizen concern

Citizen concern about growth began around 1980 with a focus on the loss of agricultural land to non-agricultural uses. Since 1950 the number of farms in the county has shrunk, from around 9,000 to about 5,000. Over the last forty years land has been converted from agricultural use at an average rate of about 2,800 acres per year. In response to citizen concerns about this trend, the county government established an Agricultural Preserve Board in 1980. Beginning in 1984, the board became active in acquiring agricultural conser-vation easements (Daniels, 1991).

The county's programme has become the model for a current statewide effort in Pennsylvania. When a citizen-initiated referendum on statewide funding for agricultural land protection was proposed, it was the activities in Lancaster County that provided the example of the need, the approach, and the possibilities for success. The county's programme in agricultural land protection is now one of the most active in the US and has spawned a parallel private-sector land trust that also works for farmland protection.[2] These two efforts provide a focus for citizen concern about land conversion, protection and preservation.

But citizen and governmental efforts in agricultural land protection have proved insufficient, by themselves, to abate the pressures and negative impacts of growth. Between 1980 and 1992 nearly 50,000 acres of farmland have been converted to non-agricultural, primarily residential, uses; in this same period only about 12,500 acres have been permanently preserved.

One of the reasons for this is the strong private property ethic in the county. Lancaster County is politically very conservative. Its long-time representative in the US Congress is one of the most conservative members of that body, and the religious doctrine of the Plain Sect people favours conservative over liberal government. One manifestation of this is a strong respect for private property, which supports an individual's right to receive market value for property and resists government interference with individual property use decisions. Thus, when confronted with a social need to address agricultural land loss, Lancaster County elected an approach that is voluntary and fully compensates agricultural land owners for the market value of their non-agricultural development rights. This approach is balanced with a regulatory programme restricting non-farm use on over 270,000 acres of agricultural land. Together, these efforts reflect both the traditional strength of the farming community in county politics and the changing structure of these politics.

The 1980s were a boom period throughout much of the US and especially in Lancaster County. Whereas housing construction rates in the county over a twenty-year period are, on average, 1,100 units per year, in 1985–1987 houses were built at the rate of 3,500 per year. Rural residential growth occurred at a pace and in a style unlike anything of the past. During the 1980s the same number of people moved into the county as live in the city of Lancaster. Yet, the city of Lancaster occupies only 7.5 square miles, whereas between sixty and seventy square miles of county land were converted out of agricultural and open land uses during the 1980s to absorb in-migrants. Also, before the 1980s, much of the population growth occurred in natural extensions of existing urban centers. During the 1980s the county found itself subject to 'leap-frog' development in which new residential projects peppered the landscape with no relation to existing villages. Land prices escalated rapidly, and land changed hands quickly.

Traditionally, Lancaster County has the lowest unemployment rate in Pennsylvania; in the 1980s the county accounted for 58 per cent of all of Pennsylvania's economic growth. During this decade, Lancaster County's place as an 'Economic Superman', a phrase used by economists in Pennsylvania, was reinforced. But there was a cost to this. In a six-year period in the middle 1980s the number of retail outlet stores built to serve tourists rose from seventeen to 175. The feel of the county, the sense of citizens about their place, their home, was changing.

If a healthy local economy was the 'up' side of growth, social tension was the 'down' side. Lancaster County is a locale with a strong sense of place. Lancaster County citizens are very aware of the special nature of their region. To some extent they cannot help being so. The existence of the Old Order communities is a constant reminder of the county's unique quality. And, of course, everyone is very aware of the role that the Old Orders, especially the Amish, play in the county's tourist industry. The millions of visitors per year and the bumper-to-bumper traffic in the Amish townships east of the city during the summer are clear evidence of this. Add to these external reminders the fact that many families have roots in the county that go back generations and the sense of place becomes almost palpable.

The growth of the 1980s challenged this sense of place in many ways. One of the most significant challenges came from the source of the growth. While historically the county was removed from the major urban centres to the east, southwest and southeast, commuting patterns, improvements to the interstate and state highway systems, changes within the cities themselves, and the quality of life offered by the county combined to bring a demand for county land from people willing to relocate or to commute long distances.

These in-migrants brought a source of change that was more than physical, in the way land was used; it was also sociological. New migrants to the county were often at the root of citizen organizations for land protection, preservation, and growth management. Some of this might be interpreted as a "gang-plank syndrome" (now that I've got mine let's lock others out), but it also suggests that newcomers realize how quickly a special quality of life can be destroyed (Healy and Short, 1979). Thus, citizen activism by new residents represents a desire to manage change so that the very qualities which drew the migrants to the community do not disappear. In the 1980s new migrants began to speak out more and demand more from local government (King and Harris, 1989).

Many of the migrants of the 1980s moved in for the specific qualities offered by life in this particular place. Often, migrants of this sort are unaware of the contradiction embodied in the fact that their migration is one of the reasons the county may be unable to continue being the place that drew them. At the same time, these migrants are very willing to organize and agitate for public policy action supportive of agricultural land protection and managed growth. They frequently come from more urban places and are more astute at using the mechanisms of government to achieve their agendas (Healy and Short, 1979; Garkovich, 1982). In a county with a history and tradition of conservative, rural-style politics, this kind of social change represents a significant transition. While some of this change will likely be positive for land and environmental resource protection, it is also likely to generate significant social tension as the expectations and styles of 'old-timers' and 'newcomers' clash (Graber, 1974).

Transformation within the Old Order communities

Perhaps the most dramatic manifestations of these changes are the transformations within the Old Order communities. The Amish and Mennonites
have lived in Lancaster County for more than two-and-a-half centuries.
They have helped to define the county's distinctive character and are a
significant part of both its agricultural strength and its tourist industry.
Traditionally, both the Amish and Mennonites have been farmers; farming
reinforced their religious, familial, educational, work and community values.
Old Order families remained on the land for generations and considered it
an obligation and a bond to help provide farms to their newly married
children. In fact, the community was so strongly agricultural that as recently
as twenty years ago any Amishman who chose not to be a farmer was looked
down upon. Now this has changed, and dramatically so.

In the 1990s it is estimated that fewer than half of the Amish men in
Lancaster County are employed in agriculture. The rest are business people,
established in a variety of cottage industries, day labourers who work for
them, or clerks and service people in the general community. This rapid
change in the employment structure of the Amish came about for a variety
of reasons. Those directly related to growth include the shrinking amount of
farmland, due to the leap-frog suburbanization, the increased price of the
farmland that remained, and the increased supervision of farming by the
state and localities as a function of new environmental and public health
regulations.

The responses of the two Old Order communities are different. The
Mennonites are largely choosing to leave Lancaster County, feeling pushed
out by social and economic factors they cannot control. They are moving to
other parts of the US where land is cheaper and they can continue their
traditional lifestyle. The Amish have chosen to resist and negotiate with the
forces of change. For them, continuity of place with community and family
outweighs the need to reform occupational structure. Tourism and growth,
once a bane of the Old Order Amish, may now provide the seeds for their
continuation in Lancaster County. The question on everyone's minds,
though, is whether the Amish are themselves changing. As Hostetler (1989)
has asked can they can continue to represent the conscience of the county
and an alternative to the modern world?

The fact that farming is becoming increasingly difficult, expensive and less
attractive to younger members of the Old Order communities means that
those communities will transform. The fact that a generation ago 90 per cent
of newly married couples started farming and now the figure is only 10 per
cent says that the Old Order communities of the future will not and cannot
be analogous to those which endured nearly three centuries of pressure and
change. In the past, the farm was, quite literally, a shelter from the outside
world; this shelter is now crumbling As it crumbles Amish social structure is
transforming from an egalitarian, community base to one with distinct and
identifiable economic classes.

Very practically, the transformations within the Old Order communities need to be of concern to the county because of the central role of these communities in the county's agricultural and tourist industries. Future rural land and tourist developments similar to that of the recent past bode ill for these unique cultural communities.

Citizen movement for growth management

The culmination of these events came together in a citizen movement for growth management in Lancaster County. Growth management is a movement to use public-sector authority creatively to formulate and implement a set of public interest objectives toward land and environmental resources (Meeks, 1990). Most often growth management programmes emerge in communities like Lancaster County that are experiencing rapid rates of growth. A rapid growth rate often includes rapid increases in the rate of population growth and land prices, the perception of rapid changes in the composition of land owners, and an impression that the traditional way of life, or the specialness of the community, including its environmental quality, is threatened. Growth management programmes usually focus on utilizing regulatory and other powers of local and state government to decrease the rate of change and direct the change that does occur.

Lancaster County citizens did not take on their interest in growth management without struggle. The current process, which is marked by a strong and wide degree of consensus, began mired in controversy. Prominent community members adopted forceful positions on the issues of growth and growth management. An ex-director of the Lancaster Chamber of Commerce and Industry (a private, business advocacy organization) became a symbol of the growth-at-any-cost mentality. Conversely, activist citizens at the borough, township and county levels staked out positions for growth management ranging from no-growth to managed growth.

The very existence of consensus is unusual. Growth and its management, and the attendant issues it raises – such as land use planning, the imposition of social rules on individual private property rights, and the conflict between what one author has called the forces of expansion and exclusion (the forces promoting growth and those seeking to protect existing locales) – are often at the very centre of local government controversy (Plotkin, 1987; Molotch, 1976; Logan and Molotch, 1987).

Evidence of consensus on growth management and agricultural land protection emerged through a number of events. The most obvious were changes in key personnel with power to affect county policy. In the late 1980s the county hired a new professional director for its planning agency and a new director for the Agricultural Preserve Board. These individuals were given the mandate to revamp and upgrade their agencies, and they in turn hired new professional personnel. Supporting this, a new, pro-growth management candidate to the three-person county board was elected, as were new members to local township boards. In addition, the pro-growth director of the business advocacy organization was forced out, and a new compromise-oriented director was hired.

Working together, these individuals began preparing a new comprehensive plan for the county. The plan is itself an interesting example of the power of citizen organizations in land and settlement planning and policy and the stresses brought on by the attempt to redefine private property rights.

The planning process underlying the new plan was designed to further develop and reinforce consensus on goals. Quite consciously, the County Planning Commission broke down the process of preparing the new plan into four major components and steps. The first component consists of a set of vision statements about the future of Lancaster County. It was formally adopted after two-and-a-half years of extensive public meetings, public discussions and local media coverage.

The second component is a growth management plan. It builds on the first by making specific settlement planning recommendations. The key part of this plan is the establishment of urban growth boundaries for all urban areas within the county. The boundaries are set to accommodate development for the next twenty years. The conceptual scheme is to try to maintain the county's traditional development pattern of small villages surrounded and separated by productive farmland.

Bowing to the high degree of citizen interest in these issues, the planning commission has exercised a patient, dialogue-based approach to the plan's formation. In essence, the planning commission wrote the plan from the bottom up rather than from the top down. All the major interest groups in the county were able to participate and 'sign off' on its development. Interest in growth management is so high that, quite literally, neither the governing body of the county nor the professional agency charged with the actual drafting of the plan can do anything without it appearing prominently in the local newspapers.

Yet the issue of whose public interest is being served by the draft plan is unclear. Since the planners do not believe they can precisely predict development patterns, and since they wish to put forth a plan that will be acceptable to as many individuals and groups in the county as possible, the area encompassed by each urban growth boundary line includes at least a 25 per cent, and in some cases as much as a 100 per cent 'surplus' of land predicted to be needed for development. In addition, the boundary lines are not being put forward as rigid or concrete, but rather as 'shifting lines in the sand'. The actual location of individual urban growth boundary lines will be subject to yearly revision based on review by the County Planning Commission. This approach is quite conscious. It is designed to present the plan as both reasonable and flexible. At its best it represents a compromise between conflicting concepts of private property rights; at its worst it may mean that the plan is nothing more than a charade whose implementation has little real impact on the rate, pace or place of new residential development.

A final and significant challenge to growth management in Lancaster County is the existing institutional structure for governance and planning in the county. Lancaster County is made up of sixty municipalities, including townships, boroughs and a city. As in many states in the eastern part of the US, substantive authority for land use planning and regulation has been, in essence, relegated by the state legislature to these sub-county governments. In practice, the actual power for implementing a growth management programme is fragmented among these sixty localities. Local governments can, if they choose, ignore the needs of their immediate neighbours and the county as a whole. At this point, to be successful, the proposed growth management plan will require a high degree of voluntary cooperation and coordination among these local governments.

In 1992 the citizens of Lancaster County are in the midst of this process. The growth management plan has yet to be adopted, and the implementation plan, step three, has not even been drafted. They appear to be on a track which will allow them to balance a unique heritage with strong economic pressures for change. However, it would be unusual if Lancaster County were to succeed. Countless locales in the US, when caught between the opportunity to increase individual and collective wealth and the desire to hold onto their heritage, have found it difficult, if not impossible, to resist the social forces of economic expansion and growth (Plotkin, 1987; Logan and Molotch, 1987). But Lancaster County is an atypical place. The real test will be time. As one person observed: 'the county is at the starting gate with growth management; come back in ten years and see how it is really doing'.

Conclusion

Three interrelated trends underlie the future of land use and settlement planning in the US. First, such planning is becoming more pluralistic. More types of individuals and groups are asserting more types of interests in settlement issues. And all of them will argue, with increasing sophistication, that their perspectives on the public interest are the appropriate ones. Second, because of this, settlement planning is becoming more conflictual, among these individuals and groups, and among the groups and land professionals. Third, land use planning is becoming more political. The era of settlement planning dominated by professionals, with exclusive access to information, is over.

The cutting edge of settlement policy will be characterized by two approaches. First, it is necessary to recognize the limited perspective that most participants bring to the settlement debate; work will need to be done to broaden participants' perspectives to assure that all legitimate concerns and interests are taken into account, and to mediate among these varied interests. Second, it is important to approach land use planning as a process of generating alternatives, where the costs and benefits, the winners and losers, the economic, environmental and social impacts of alternative plans are made clear as the basis for informed and vigorous public discourse.

Twenty-first century settlement planning in the US will have to acknowledge and confront the complexities and contradictions within it, and attempt to unveil this to all those who do, and who should, share a concern about them. Such planning will not only respond to interest groups, it will also need to mobilize interest groups. And then, such planning will seek to present to participants options for addressing issues, and assist in assessing options that are brought forward by participants.

This means that the analysis performed in land use and settlement planning needs to change. Such planning will need to be more proactive and strategic in identifying participants to the planning process. And such planning will need to conduct analyses that reflect not just the economic and ecological characteristics of land, but also its social characteristics. Analysts will need to ask not just 'what is the economically efficient use of the land?' and 'what is the ecological carrying capacity of the land?', but 'what is a socially equitable way to plan for the land's use?'.

In general, the future of land use and settlement planning will be in acknowledging that planning is not and cannot be a technocratic, scientific exercise. Land is a unique economic and ecological resource, but it is also a unique social resource. Land use and settlement planning often act as the stage for fundamental and complex social debate about individual and social rights and the articulation of ideals about democracy and social justice.

Land use planning is an exercise in social planning masked as technical planning. To be truly successful, to create an enduring, efficient, and equitable pattern of settlement relationships, it will be necessary to recognize it as such, and act accordingly.

Notes

1. The case study in this chapter was condensed from a manuscript prepared for the Minnesota Extension Service, University of Minnesota and the Lincoln Institute of Land Policy, as part of a project funded by the Economic Development Administration of the US Department of Commerce. Most of the source materials for this case were interviews and internal documents from agencies and organizations in Lancaster County, Pennsylvania, and are not cited here. The complete case study can be obtained from the author.
2. Land trusts are a booming non-profit, private sector, public-interest component of land and settlement planning in the US. Abbott (1989) and Foti and Jacobs (1989) discuss their history, growth and role in two regions of the country.

References

Abbott, G., Jr. (1989) 'Land trusts: innovations on an old New England idea', *New England Landscape* 1: 13–24.

Beatley, T. (1991) 'A set of ethical principles to guide land use policy', *Land Use Policy* **8** (1): 3–8.

Bosselman, F. and D. Callies (1971) *The quiet revolution in land use control*, United States Government Printing Office, Washington, D.C.

Dangermond, J. (1989) 'Trends in geographic information systems', *Ekistics* **56** (338/339): 318–31.

Daniels, T.L. (1991) 'The purchase of development rights: preserving agricultural land and open space', *Journal of the American Planning Association* **57** (4): 421–31.

Foti, P.E. and H.M. Jacobs (1989) 'Private public-interest land use planning: land trusts in the upper mid-west', *Journal of Soil and Water Conservation* **44** (4): 317–19.

Fulton, W. (1989) 'In land-use planning, a second revolution shifts control to the states', *Governing* **2** (6): 40–45.

Garkovich, L. (1982) 'Land use planning as a response to rapid population growth and community change', *Rural Sociology* **47** (1): 47–67.

Graber, E.E. (1974) 'Newcomers and oldtimers: growth and change in a mountain town', *Rural Sociology*, **34** (4): 504–13.

Gurwitt, R. (1991) 'The decision machine', *Governing*, **4** (8): 51–4.

Gustafson, G.C. and N.L. Bills (1984) *U.S. cropland, urbanization and landowner-ship patterns*, Agricultural Economic Report No. 520, U.S. Department of Agriculture, Washington, D.C.

Hall, P. (1988) *Cities of tomorrow: an intellectual history of city planning in the twentieth century*, Blackwell, New York.

Healy, R.G. and J.L. Short (1979) 'Rural lands: market trends and planning impli-cations', *Journal of the American Planning Association*, **45** (3): 305–17.

Heiman, M. (1990) 'From 'not in my backyard!' to 'not in anybody's backyard!': grassroots challenge to hazardous waste facility siting', *Journal of the American Planning Association*, **56** (3): 359–62.

Hostetler, J.A. (1989) 'Toward responsible growth and stewardship of Lancaster County's landscape', *Pennsylvania Mennonite Heritage*, **12** (3): 2–10.

Hunter, D.B. (1988) 'An ecological perspective on property: a call for judicial protection of the public's interest in environmentally critical resources', *Harvard Environmental Law Review*, **12** (2): 311–83.

Jacobs, H.M. (1989a) 'Implementing multipurpose land information systems: political-economic research issues', *Computers, Environment and Urban Systems*, **13** (1): 3–13.

Jacobs, H M. (1989b) 'Localism and land use planning', *Journal of Architectural and Planning Research*, **6** (1): 1–17.

Jacobs, H.M. (1992) 'Planning the use of land for the 21st century', *Journal of Soil and Water Conservation*, **47** (1): 32–4.

Jacobs, H.M. (1989c) 'Social equity in agricultural land protection', *Landscape and Urban Planning*, **17** (1): 21–33.

King, L. and G. Harris (1989) 'Local responses to rapid growth: New York and Vermont cases', *Journal of the American Planning Association*, **55** (2): 181–91.

Kraybill, D.B. (1989) *The riddle of Amish Culture*, Johns Hopkins University Press, Baltimore.

Lapping, M.B., T.L. Daniels and J.W. Keller (1989) *Rural planning and development in the United States*, Guilford Press, New York.

Lapping, M.B. and J. Moser (1992) '1990 in Review', in *Progress in rural policy and planning*, (2) A. Gilg (ed.) Belhaven, London (forthcoming).

Logan, J.R. and H.L. Molotch (1987) *Urban fortunes: the political economy of place*, University of California Press, Berkeley, CA.

McClaughry, J. (1975) 'The new feudalism', *Environmental Law*, 5 (3): 675–702.

McClaughry, J. (1976) 'Farmers, freedom and feudalism', *South Dakota Law Review*, 21 (3): 486–541.

Meeks, G., Jr. (1990) 'Growth management: a renewed agenda for the states', *Journal of Soil and Water Conservation*, 45 (6): 600–4.

Molotch, H. (1976) 'The city as a growth machine: toward a political economy of place', *American Journal of Sociology*, 82 (2): 309–22.

National Agricultural Lands Study (1981) *Final Report*, U.S. Department of Agriculture, Washington, D.C.

Pivo, G.E. (1990) 'The net of mixed beads: suburban office development in six metropolitan regions', *Journal of the American Planning Association*, 56 (4): 457–69.

Plotkin, S. (1987) *Keep out: the struggle for land use control*, University of California Press, Berkeley.

Popper, F.J. (1974) 'Land use reform: illusion or reality?' *Planning*, 41 (9):14–19.

Popper, F.J. (1988) 'Understanding American land use planning since 1970: a revisionist interpretation', *Journal of the American Planning Association*, 54 (3): 291–301.

Rowlands, W.A. (1933) 'County zoning for agriculture, forestry and recreation in Wisconsin', *Journal of Land and Public Utility Economics*, 9 (3): 272–82.

Scott, M. (1969) *American city planning since 1890*, University of California Press, Berkeley.

Ventura, S.J., B.J. Niemann Jr., and D.D. Moyer (1988) 'A multipurpose land information system for rural resource planning', *Journal of Soil and Water Conservation*, 43 (3): 226–29.

Wilson, F.G. (1957–1958) 'Zoning for forestry and recreation: Wisconsin's pioneer role', *Wisconsin Magazine of History*, 41 (2):102–6.

10

Social impacts of energy development in the western USA: the case of the boom town

Richard Krannich and Lori Cramer

Introduction

During the 1970s and 1980s large-scale energy resource developments became widespread throughout the northern Great Plains and Rocky Mountain regions of the United States.

In most instances these developments occurred in geographically isolated and sparsely populated rural areas, reflecting both the location of unexploited reserves of energy resources and the social, economic and political vulnerabilities of traditionally resource-dependent rural areas (see Krannich and Luloff, 1991; Lovejoy and Krannich, 1982). In addition to concentrating the environmental consequences of such development in rural areas, these activities caused many rural communities to experience extremely rapid population growth. In many instances the population of small communities doubled or tripled over the course of just two or three years, setting the stage for a broad range of social impacts associated with rapid population growth.

Nearly two decades of research on the social changes associated with boom town conditions have resulted in a substantial body of literature and research on this topic. However, there is little to indicate that a reasonable degree of closure has emerged out of that research. This chapter attempts to assess the potential for attaining such closure out of the accumulated knowledge base. It provides a summarization and synthesis of the literature addressing social consequences of energy developments and associated rapid growth. Major themes and trends in the conceptual orientations and research results that have characterized the boom town literature are explicated. Results reported in the literature are used as a basis for evaluating the validity of the oft-cited and widely debated 'social disruption' hypothesis. Finally, drawing on two case studies, shifts in the conditions and context of boom towns, especially those linked to impact mitigation programmes and policies, are examined as a possible explanation for some qualitative changes in the nature and severity of impacts reported in more recent boom town literature.

Major themes and trends in boom town research

Early research: 1974–80

The first real evidence of social science interest in what would come to be described as 'boom town' research began to appear around 1974, following a surge in domestic energy resource development spurred in part by the 1973 Arab oil embargo. One of the first and most widely cited reports of social problems associated with rapid growth was Kohrs' (1974) paper focusing on boom growth associated with coal mining and power plant developments in Gillette, Wyoming. Kohrs characterized the changes observed as the 'Gillette Syndrome', which he described as being manifested by dramatic increases in the incidence of divorce, depression, school dropout rates, suicide attempts, juvenile delinquency, criminal activity, anomie, mental disorders and other social problems.

During this same period, Gold (1974) reported on early results of research conducted in and around the boom towns of Colstrip, Montana and Gillette, Wyoming. Gold focused his attention largely on effects involving lifestyles and informal social linkages among established residents, and argued that those most seriously affected by resource development and related growth effects were ranchers, whose lifestyles were most significantly threatened by such changes. He also observed that rapid growth, or 'people pollution,' was associated with 'the weakening of neighborly ties, rural community social structure and the like' (1974: 9). Finally, Gold observed a sense of helplessness or powerlessness among local residents confronted by changes induced by large, powerful, externally-controlled corporate interests.

In another early study, Gilmore and Duff (1975) reported widespread social disarray and a deteriorating quality of life associated with boom growth accompanying resource development activities in the area surrounding Rock Springs, Wyoming. A doubling of population during 1970–74 was reportedly accompanied by an increase of 857 per cent in the caseload of the mental health center, along with increases in alienation, social isolation, and school dropout rates (see Gilmore, 1976).

The types and magnitude of effects reported by these early authors differed greatly from earlier findings regarding the relatively benign socioeconomic consequences of large-scale rural industrialization projects in other regions of the US (see Summers *et al.*, 1976). Such accounts of dramatic growth and the apparent emergence of serious social problems stimulated a rapid expansion of social science interest in the boom town phenomenon. Between 1975 and the early 1980s, research describing the adverse social consequences of boom growth was reported for literally dozens of rural study communities throughout the northern Great Plains and Rocky Mountain West.

Several authors reported that boom growth contributed to adverse mental health effects among both new inmigrants and long-term residents (Dixon, 1978: Freudenburg *et al.*, 1982; Lantz and McKeown, 1977; Weisz, 1979).

Others reported dramatic increases in the level of community crime, violence and other forms of deviance (Dixon, 1978; Lantz and McKeown, 1977; Little, 1977; Freudenburg, 1978). Widespread community conflict and tensions between growth advocates and opponents were reported in some settings (Gold, 1974, 1976). Shifts in indicators of community social integration were also reported (Boulding, 1981; Jirovec, 1979; Little, 1977), as were declines in the levels of satisfaction expressed by boom town residents (Murdock and Schriner, 1979). Many of these changes were attributed to the collapse of established informal social structures that are often observed in rural communities, and a failure of new formal institutions and structures to adequately provide for social integration, social control and well-being of local residents (Cortese, 1982; Cortese and Jones, 1977; Little, 1977; Moen et al., 1981).

Critiques and re-evaluation: 1980–84

By the early 1980s, the accumulated literature on social consequences of boom growth appeared to many observers to establish clearly that boom towns were characterized by the emergence of numerous, and often quite serious, social problems. Boom town problems were a focus of journalistic and media accounts (see Feldman, 1980; Kittredge, 1981), as well as scholarly research. Most research reports appeared to both accept and provide empirical support for 'the assumption that local social effects of western energy development are severe and negative' (Wilkinson et al., 1982). Indeed, one author observed that the 'social disruption hypothesis has become the conventional wisdom' (Finsterbusch, 1982).

Despite this widespread acceptance of assertions that social malaise and disruption were all but inevitable consequences of boom growth, expressions of cautious scepticism if not outright disagreement began to emerge around 1980 (see Wilkinson et al., 1980; Thompson, 1979). The most comprehensive critique of the 'social disruption' hypothesis, set forth by Wilkinson and his associates (Wilkinson et al., 1982), focused on several shortcomings that characterized much of the early boom town research. First, they noted that many of the early studies, especially those by Kohrs and by Gilmore and Duff, relied heavily on weak empirical evidence, poorly documented data and undocumented assertions about boom-induced social problems. They also pointed out that many subsequent analyses were too quick to accept and to rely uncritically upon the limited or flawed findings of these and other early studies. The literature was characterized as reflecting a widespread tendency to accept the 'disruption' hypothesis, even in the absence of sufficiently rigorous data collection and analyses. Also noted was a tendency among some analysts to conclude that disruption was present, even when the data they reported appeared either inconclusive or even inconsistent with such contentions.

During this same period, limitations of research designs also came under scrutiny as a possible source of bias in analyses of boom town consequences (Gale, 1982). The heavy reliance on single-community case studies rather than comparative studies of multiple communities was noted as one important limitation (Krannich and Greider, 1984). Another limitation, only recently addressed in the literature, was a tendency to rely on cross-sectional data collected at a single point in time, rather than developing longitudinal data to track social responses to community change over an extended period of boom growth (see Brown et al., 1989).

These and other critiques of the conceptual and empirical foundations of the social disruption hypotheses stimulated equally critical rebuttals and countercriticisms (Albrecht, 1982; Finsterbusch, 1982; Freudenburg, 1982; Gale, 1982; Gold, 1982). As frequently occurs when an established paradigm is challenged (see Kuhn, 1970), critics of the social disruption perspective (Wilkinson et al., 1982) were accused of 'sociological mischievousness' (Gold, 1982: 356), 'careless scholarship' (Murdock and Leistritz, 1982: 357), and scholarship that was 'misleading or simply incorrect' (Freudenburg, 1982: 323).

Such intense reaction and counter-reaction is a reflection of the degree to which many social scientists were committed to or 'invested' in the established social disruption perspective. However, the intensity of the controversy generated a very considerable shift in the path of most boom town research, and scholarly debate quickly gave way to a new wave of empirical analyses directed to resolution of the 'boom town question'.

New approaches, multiple indicators and contrasting results: 1984–present

Since about 1984, the research on contemporary boom towns has been characterized by several shifts away from the assumptions, methods, and conclusions that characterized the early phase of boom town studies. Paralleling the gradual conceptual and methodological maturation of the broader field of social impact assessment (see Freudenburg, 1986a), boom town research has shifted away from the sense of urgency and 'alarmed discovery' that characterized early scholarly interest and research. What appeared instead has been a more cautious and systematic exploration of the social consequences of rapid growth.

One of the most obvious shifts that differentiates recent research from that pursued during the 1970s is an almost self-conscious effort to avoid uncritical acceptance of the social disruption assumptions. This shift in conceptual orientation is indicative of the substantial impact of the criticisms and debates that emerged during the early 1980s. Most analyses published since 1984 have made explicit reference to the controversy and uncertainties linked to the disruption framework, and have set forth empirical analyses specifically designed to provide at least a partial test of the disruption hypothesis (see, for example, Brown et al., 1989; England and Albrecht,

1984; Freudenburg, 1986b; Greider and Krannich, 1985a; Krannich and Greider, 1984; Krannich et al., 1985, 1989).

A second important shift in focus relates to research design and methodology. With relatively few exceptions (e.g., Brookshire and D'Arge, 1980; Freudenburg, 1981), very few of the early boom town studies involved research in more than one study community. As a result, interpretations of findings were constrained by an inability to determine whether or not similar transitions and conditions might also characterize other non-boom communities, possibly as a result of broader social change processes affecting both boom and stable communities. However, nearly all of the research reported since 1984 has relied on data that permit comparisons across several study communities, usually examined simultaneously (e.g., Berry et al., 1990; Brown et al., 1989; England and Albrecht, 1984; Freudenburg, 1984, 1986a; Greider and Krannich, 1985a, 1985b; Krannich and Greider, 1984; Krannich et al., 1985, 1989; Wilkinson et al., 1984).

Another key factor distinguishing some of the recent boom town research from that conducted earlier is the movement toward analyses of community change patterns based on longitudinal data. The cross-sectional study designs that have characterized most boom town research (even the more recent studies based on multiple study communities) inevitably limit the degree of confidence that can be placed in conclusions about the relationship between community growth patterns and various indicators of social well-being or ill-being. The early and mid-1980s saw a handful of studies based on longitudinal examination of data such as crime statistics and divorce records (Wilkinson et al., 1983; 1984). More recently, several studies based on longitudinal data addressing the attitudes and perceptions of boom town residents have also been reported (see Brown et al., 1989; Krannich et al., 1989; Berry et al., 1990).

The conclusions derived from these more recent studies of boom town social change differ markedly from those that characterized the early boom town research. For the most part, findings have suggested that rapid growth is not consistently or uniformly associated with extreme levels of disruption, disorganization, or social malaise. For example, studies based on available data suggest that in western counties characterized by energy development and rapid population growth, crime rates (Brookshire and D'Arge, 1980; Wilkinson et al., 1984) and divorce rates (Wilkinson et al., 1983) have generally not increased markedly during boom periods. There is, however, some evidence that rates of delinquency have increased in conjunction with such boom growth (Wilkinson and Camasso, 1984). Studies of self-reported criminal victimization experience have also provided mixed evidence. Freudenburg's (1986b) research in Craig, Colorado suggested increased victimization, while research by Krannich et al. (1985, 1989) proposed that victimization experiences did not increase during periods of rapid growth in several Wyoming and Utah communities.[1]

Evidence based on more recent examination of social integration, satisfaction, and various dimensions of subjective well-being, provides somewhat more mixed support for the disruption hypothesis. Several studies have suggested a virtual absence of some oft-cited disruptive consequences. England and Albrecht (1984), for example, studied several variables linked to the concept of disruption. They concluded that, contrary to assertions in earlier boom town literature (e.g., Cortese and Jones, 1977; Cortese, 1982), boom growth did not result in a replacement of informal social ties with formal associations. Similarly, these same authors observed that the 'life-world' of boom town residents did not shift dramatically in response to rapid growth and community change (England and Albrecht, 1985). Seyfrit and Sadler-Hammer (1988) reported only limited association between rapid growth and shifts in youths' attitudes toward community, family and home relations, perceived integration, or community participation. In a recent longitudinal study, Berry et al. (1990) indicated that neighbouring inter-actions remained relatively stable over time, even in the face of substantial shifts in community growth patterns. Similarly, a longitudinal study by Greider et al. (1990) indicated that levels of generalized distrust exhibited little variation in the face of rapid community change.

Other studies have suggested that disruptive outcomes occur differentially across social groups. For example, Freudenburg (1984) reported that while there were virtually no attitudinal differences between adult residents of a boom town and surrounding stable communities, boom town adolescents exhibited lower levels of satisfaction and higher levels of alienation. Krannich and Greider (1984) noted a deterioration in the levels of perceived social integration among the relatively transient segment of boom town newcomers residing in mobile home parks. Similarly, neighbours were looked to less frequently as a source of social support among boom town residents, than among those living in stable communities (Greider and Krannich 1985a).

Other recent research has also provided support for the disruption hypothesis. Several studies have indicated a negative relationship between community growth and community satisfaction (Brown et al., 1989), particularly satisfaction with local facilities and services (England and Albrecht, 1984; Greider and Krannich, 1985b; Murdock and Schriner, 1979). Also, several analyses have documented a tendency for boom town residents to express significantly higher fear of crime than is generally evident in more stable rural communities (Freudenburg, 1986b; Krannich et al., 1985, 1989). Boom growth has also been shown to be associated with reduced local friendship ties and increased residential transiency (Brown et al., 1989) and heightened perceptions of social isolation (Greider et al., 1990).

At the same time, it is important to note that evidence derived from longitudinal studies suggests that disruptive effects of boom growth on various indicators of social well-being are often fairly short-lived. Gold (1986) has suggested that communal association and affiliation have rebounded fairly quickly in communities affected by large-scale resource developments, without long-term or permanent destruction of community social structures. Indeed, he has observed that while rapid growth may generate tensions and conflict between some segments of affected communities, it can also contribute to increased solidarity and integration within specific groups sharing common interests and perspectives regarding community change. Krannich *et al.* (1989) have noted that while fear of crime tends to 'spike' during periods of very rapid population growth, it also is quickly attenuated when boom towns enter a period of either stability or population decline. Similarly, recent research on neighbouring relations in boom towns indicates a tendency for levels of familarity and provision of social support among neighbours to decline during rapid growth, but to rebound quickly when boom gives way to population decline and the outmigration of temporary residents (Berry *et al.*, 1990). Longitudinal research on the relationship between rapid growth and levels of social isolation has also indicated a tendency for isolation to increase during a period of very rapid growth, followed by a trend toward decreased isolation when the community became more stable (Greider *et al.*, 1990).

Synthesis of disparate findings

Cumulative evidence regarding disruptive social change

In 1980, Brookshire and D'Arge posed the rhetorical question, 'Are boom-towns bad?'. On the basis of the preceding discussion, it appears that our answer must be a rather heavily qualified 'maybe – but only sometimes, in some places, during some periods, for some dimensions of community life and personal well-being, and for some segments of the local population'. The accumulated evidence is not sufficient to reject the social disruption hypothesis, but neither is it sufficient to accept it fully. As noted by Murdock *et al.* (1986), some disruption evidently does occur, but it appears to be less widespread and less extreme than was suggested in the early boom town research.

In general, analyses of so-called 'objective' social indicators, whether they involve agency records and statistics (e.g., Wilkinson *et al.*, 1983, 1984) or self-report data on criminal victimization (Krannich *et al.*, 1985; 1989) and social interaction (England and Albrecht, 1984; Greider and Krannich, 1985a; Berry *et al.*, 1990) have provided relatively little support for the disruption hypothesis. This may possibly be a consequence of the limitations inherent in such 'objective' measures. Social scientists have repeatedly observed that there is often a substantial disparity between 'objective' conditions and 'subjective' dimensions of social reality (see Berger and Luckman, 1966; Green, 1975; Greider and Krannich, 1985b; Greider and Little, 1988). Regarding boom town research, Gold has argued that analyses based on such allegedly objective data are inherently flawed, both because such data are often unreliable and because they fail to address social problems 'from the point of view of . . . the residents' (1982: 350; also see Albrecht and Thompson, 1988).

Analyses based on various subjective indicators have also failed to provide clear-cut support for the disruption hypothesis. However, the evidence derived from such studies does suggest a greater tendency for disruptive outcomes. In general, such studies have provided fairly consistent evidence of a deterioration in community satisfaction levels, reduced levels of perceived integration and community attachment, and heightened fear of crime. Boom towns may not automatically result in a collapse of social linkages, and may even facilitate the development of some new types of social relations (England and Albrecht, 1984; Krannich and Greider, 1990). Nevertheless, the cumulative weight of available evidence suggests that residents of boom towns generally come to evaluate their communities less positively, at least during the course of the boom growth period.

Factors accounting for disparate findings

There are several factors involved in the transformation from the earlier context, in which the disruption perspective was so widely accepted as to be considered 'conventional wisdom', to the current context of mixed results and more cautious interpretation.

There has recently been a shift away from uncritical reliance on assumptions of disruption and poorly documented assertions, towards more careful interpretation of, and reliance on, empirical evidence. Another major factor is the emergence of methodologically more rigorous research designs in recent boom town research. Whether due to methodological shortcomings or ideological biases, such an interpretation suggests that early boom town literature may have simply been wrong in its assertions of widespread social malaise and a collapse of community social structures. Of major importance have been a shift in conceptual and methodological approach, and a change in the boom town conditions themselves.

However, there are equally plausible alternative explanations for the transition that has characterized the boom town literature. One such explanation involves changes in the nature of boom towns themselves. In a sense, social scientists have been aiming at a moving target. During the roughly two decades during which research on contemporary boom towns has been conducted, there has been considerable evolution in the degree to which rural communities have been prepared for 'coping with rapid growth' (see Weber and Howell, 1982). As a result, there is reason to suspect that, even if boom towns *are* 'bad', in many cases they have become less so as a result of lessons learned from efforts to respond to and resolve the more or less catastrophic conditions described in earlier boom town research.

Early boom town research focused on a handful of communities that were, according to virtually all accounts, overwhelmed by very rapid and poorly anticipated growth – places like Gillette and Rock Springs, Wyoming and Craig, Colorado. In each instance, the magnitude of population growth was extremely large, there was little advance warning or accurate forecasting of the size or timing of the growth, and there were few efforts to implement advance planning and up-front mitigation programs to absorb the increased demands which rapid growth placed on housing, public facilities and services, and other aspects of local infrastructure (see Murdock and Leistritz, 1979; Weber and Howell, 1982).

In these 'first generation' boom towns, efforts to implement impact mitigation programmes were often of limited scope, and most mitigation efforts came well after the boom had commenced. Inevitably, the inadequacy of housing, schools, medical facilities and services, public safety and law enforcement services, social service programmes, local fiscal resources, and other elements of local infrastructure resulted in less than optimal operation of formal and informal community structures, activities and processes. It is hardly surprising that such conditions would lead in turn to reduced levels of satisfaction and personal well-being (see Little and Krannich, 1989).

'Second generation' boom towns: Evanston, Wyoming

If the boom towns of the mid-1970s represent the first generation of communities impacted by rapid growth related to resource development, a 'second generation' of contemporary boom towns began to emerge during the late 1970s and early 1980s. By that time, many important lessons had been learned from after-the-fact efforts to confront problems in earlier boom towns. Experiences gained in places like Rock Springs, Gillette and Craig provided a basis for improved planning and mitigation efforts in newly-evolving boom towns.

One such place was Evanston, Wyoming, which grew rapidly from about 1979 to 1984 as a result of widespread development associated with oil and gas exploration, drilling, development, and processing activities. Like many earlier boom towns, Evanston's growth occurred in a haphazard and unpredictable fashion because it was generated by the activities of literally dozens of operating firms. However, unlike most earlier boom situations, a coordinated industry organization called the Overthrust Industrial Association was formed during the early phase of the boom to provide impact assistance to affected communities and counties. Although this organization did not begin to actively pursue mitigation planning and programme implementation until the boom was well underway, the infusion of new funding and programme development efforts appeared to turn what was initially an uncontrolled and unmanageable boom into a relatively well-managed growth process. Several analyses suggest that social disruption was clearly evident during the initial years of Evanston's boom, as reflected in heightened fear of crime (Krannich *et al.*, 1985), reduced community satisfaction (Greider and Krannich, 1985b), shifts in neighboring patterns (Greider and

Krannich, 1985a), and reduced levels of perceived social integration (Krannich *et al.*, 1984). However, some of these indicators of social disruption, including fear of crime and perceived social isolation, actually exhibited signs of improvement during 1982–84, when the boom was still in progress (Krannich *et al.*, 1989; Greider *et al.*, 1990). Such shifts are suggestive of an ameliorative effect of mitigation and growth management efforts on residents' perceptions of, and responses to, community conditions.

'Third generation' boom towns: Delta, Utah

By the early to mid-1980s, a slowed pace of energy resource development throughout the western states resulted in the cancellation of many planned development projects. As a result, after about 1982–84 there were relatively few newly-emerging boom towns. However, places that did experience large-scale resource developments and associated rapid growth during this period tended to represent a 'third generation' of contemporary boom towns. In virtually all instances, rapid growth that occurred during this period was accompanied by substantial advance planning and the implementation of a broad range of impact mitigation programmes. In most cases these included pre-development mitigation to provide expanded local infrastructure capacity in anticipation of growth, as well as additional levels of mitigation during the course of project activities, triggered by continuous monitoring of project development and growth-related impacts.

Delta, Utah represents one of the more thoroughly-researched examples of these 'third generation' boom towns. Delta was affected by the nearby construction of a large coal-fired electric power plant, which caused the population to more than triple from 1980 to 1984 (see Brown *et al.*, 1989). In sharp contrast to observations in earlier boom towns, available evidence suggests that such extreme growth was accompanied by only minor problems with infrastructure overload, and only limited social impacts. Interviews with local key informants suggested that both the organization responsible for power plant development and local officials and community leaders went into the pre-development planning process with considerable awareness of the problems reported in previous boom towns. Community leaders in particular exhibited a surprising familiarity with the social science literature on the topic. That knowledge base provided a major impetus to local demands, and responsive actions by the organization responsible for power plant development, to initiate a detailed monitoring and mitigation programme in advance of construction activities.

Development of new school facilities, expansion of public safety, health and social services, and provision of both in-town and on-site housing for workers and their dependents, met virtually all growth demands even during the height of the boom. In many earlier boom towns physical evidence of unmanageable growth has been widely apparent in the form of ramshackle temporary RV parks and mobile home parks, hastily-erected temporary housing, overcrowded public facilities, and so forth. In contrast, during the peak of boom growth, Delta appeared only slightly different from the predominantly Mormon agricultural village that had persisted for most of the twentieth century (see Nelson, 1952).

Paralleling the relative lack of infrastructure overload and related inadequacy of facilities, services and fiscal resources, Delta exhibited only moderate shifts in various indicators of social well-being during the course of the boom period. This may be attributable in part to the success of mitigation programmes in reducing most socioeconomic consequences to fairly moderate levels. Also, public knowledge and awareness of problems in other boom towns, gleaned largely from media accounts and some social science analyses, created a situation in which many residents feared for the worst, and were then more or less pleasantly surprised to find that changes were far less catastrophic than anticipated. For example, although fear of crime did increase significantly over pre-boom levels, the levels of fear measured in Delta at the point of peak impact were considerably lower than had been observed at similar stages in other, earlier boom towns (Krannich et al., 1989). A substantial decline in community satisfaction occurred, but the bulk of that decline occurred in the period *before* the commencement of rapid population growth, reflecting the effects of community conflict over water transfers (Greider and Little, 1988) and anticipation of community change (Brown et al., 1989). Similarly, there were declines in perceived social integration, the number of local friendship ties, and familiarity with neighbours during the course of the boom, but for the most part the magnitude of change in these indicators was not extreme even at the point of peak growth, and a rebound toward more normal levels was evident by 1986 when the boom was winding down (see Berry et al., 1990; Brown et al., 1989 ; Greider et al., 1990).

Perhaps more importantly, recent survey data collected in Delta[2] indicate that, four years after Delta's boom had run its course, there are very few long-lasting adverse effects on the attitudes, perceptions or general subjective well-being of local residents. Levels of community satisfaction are quite high, as reflected by a mean response value of 6.8 on a scale ranging from 0 (completely dissatisfied) to 10 (completely satisfied). Over 70 per cent of respondents indicated that, on balance, the development of the power plant had beneficial effects on the community; improved employment opportunities and general economic development effects were the most frequently cited reasons for such beliefs. Respondents were also asked whether or not, given the information available to them now, they would choose to build the power plant if they could return to a pre-development time period. Nearly 85 per cent said they 'definitely' or 'probably' would choose to build the project, with almost two-thirds (62 per cent) saying they 'definitely' would build it. About 5 per cent indicated uncertainty, while only 6.6 per cent said they probably would not build the project, and just 3.6 per cent said they definitely would not build it.

Conclusions

The issue of whether social disruption is an inevitable consequence of rapid growth in rural villages and small towns has occupied the attention of social scientists, planners and policy makers, the media, and affected publics for nearly twenty years. Initially, research findings suggested that boom growth led almost inevitably to a collapse of community social structures and widespread social disarray. However, more recent research has called such conclusions into question, or at least suggested that rapid growth has somewhat less sweeping effects than suggested initially. While many questions remain unanswered, the cumulative evidence suggests that, while disruption may not be as serious or as widespread as initially reported, at least some dimensions of well-being do deteriorate for many if not most boom town residents.

That observation must, however, be carefully qualified. First, it is important to keep in mind that social disruption is a multidimensional concept (Krannich and Greider, 1984). It is therefore unreasonable to assume that all possible indices of disruption will exhibit deterioration in response to rapid growth. Similarly, it is unreasonable to assume that all segments of a local population will experience disruptive consequences of the same type and magnitude. Some residents may experience severe social and economic dislocations, while others may be relatively unaffected or may experience positive shifts in social and economic well-being (see Krannich and Greider, 1990).

It thus appears important to consider the social consequences of boom growth as an evolving and changing phenomenon. The knowledge accumulated from previous research as well as successful and unsuccessful efforts at boom town growth management have provided a basis for changes in the nature of boom consequences, and residents' reactions to those consequences. Increasingly effective approaches to mitigation of growth effects have provided a means of minimizing many of the problems linked to inadequate community carrying capacity. Moreover, improved public understanding of and preparation for the changes associated with rapid growth may help to attenuate some of the anticipatory fears, concerns and misunderstandings which appear in many instances to have fuelled local conflict and dissatisfaction over boom growth.

From the perspectives of many established residents of rural towns and villages affected by boom growth, the rapid growth associated with large-scale resource developments undoubtedly represents a serious threat. Residents of rural places tend generally to place a high value on the small-town informality characteristic of rural lifestyles, and are likely to express concern and ambivalence if not outright opposition to projects that threaten to cause what Gold refers to as 'people pollution' (1974). Thus, in advance of a boom, it is reasonable to anticipate that many, if not most, residents would agree that boom towns are 'bad', and to be fearful of changes that might alter locally-valued ways of life.

The economic opportunities provided by resource development projects, however, can provide residents of affected communities with attractive trade-offs; help to reduce ambivalence; and generate positive changes which, at least indirectly, compensate for the changes in social structure and in lifestyles that result from increased population size. This is particularly the case if mitigation programs are designed to assist local communities through provision of local employment benefits and improved public facilities and services. When such programmes are implemented, it is likely that, retrospectively, most boom town residents will conclude that the boom was not so 'bad', after all. That such responses have occurred in more recent boom towns of the 1980s suggests that our answer to the question, 'are boom towns bad?,' is in need of modification. In addition, the fact that we can propose a more optimistic response to that question reflects positively on the ability of social science research to help guide and shape planning efforts that have improved the well-being of rural towns and villages affected by large-scale developments.

Notes

1. Freudenburg's research relied on a measure of personal criminal victimization, while the research by Krannich and his associates used a measure of both direct victimization and indirect victimization experience involving crimes against family members and close friends.
2. This survey, conducted in May, 1990, involved a self-completion questionnaire that was personally delivered to and collected from a randomly-selected sample of 150 adult residents of Delta. A total of 141 usable questionnaires were returned, representing a response rate of 90.5 per cent.

References

Albrecht, Stan L. (1982) 'Commentary', *Pacific Sociological Review* 25 (July): 297–306.
Albrecht, Stan L. and James G. Thompson (1988) 'The place of attitudes and perceptions in social impact assessment', *Society and Natural Resources* 1(1): 69–80.
Berger, Peter L. and Thomas Luckmann (1966) *The Social Construction of Reality*, Garden City, NJ: Doubleday.
Berry, E. Helen, Richard S. Krannich and Thomas Greider (1990) 'A longitudinal analysis of neighboring in rapidly changing rural places', *Journal of Rural Studies* 6(2): 175–186.
Boulding, E. (1981) 'Women as integrators and stabilizers', pp. 119–149 in E. Moen *et al.*, (eds), *Women and the Social Costs of Economic Development: Two Colorado Case Studies*. Boulder, CO: Westview Press.
Brookshire, D.S. and R.C. D'Arge (1980) 'Adjustment issues of impacted communities, or are boomtowns bad?', *Natural Resources Journal* 20 (July): 523–546.
Brown, Ralph B., H. Reed Geertsen and Richard S. Krannich (1989) 'Community

satisfaction and social integration in a boom town: A longitudinal analysis', *Rural Sociology* **54**(4): 568–586.

Cortese, Charles F. (1982) 'The impacts of rapid growth on local organizations and community services', pp. 115–136 in B. Weber and R. Howell (eds), *Coping with Rapid Growth in Rural Communities*, Boulder: Westview Press.

Cortese, Charles F. and Bernie Jones (1977) 'The sociological analysis of boom towns', *Western Sociological Review* **8**(1): 76–90.

Dixon, Mim (1978) *What Happened to Fairbanks? The Effects of the Trans-Alaska Oil Pipeline in the Community of Fairbanks, Alaska*, Boulder, CO: Westview Press.

England, J. Lynn and Stan L. Albrecht (1984) 'Boomtowns and social disruption', *Rural Sociology* **49** (Summer): 230–246.

——— (1985) 'Boomtowns and lifeworld disruption', presented at the annual meetings of the Rural Sociological Society, Blacksburg, Virginia, August.

Feldman, D. (1980) 'Boomtown women', *Environmental Action* (May): 16–20.

Finsterbusch, Kurt (1982) 'Commentary', *Pacific Sociological Review* **25** (July): 307–322.

Freudenburg, W.R. (1978) 'Toward ending the inattention: A report on social impacts and policy implications of energy boom town development', presented at the annual meeting of the American Association for the Advancement of Science, February.

——— (1981) 'Women and men in an energy boom town: Adjustment, alienation and adaptation', *Rural Sociology* **46**(2): 220–244.

——— (1982) 'Commentary.' *Pacific Sociological Review* **25**(3): 323–338.

——— (1984) 'Differential impacts of rapid community growth', *American Sociological Review* **49**(5): 697–705.

——— (1986a) 'Social impact assessment', *Annual Review of Sociology* **12**: 451–478.

——— (1986b) 'The density of acquaintanceship: An overlooked variable in community research?', *American Journal of Sociology* **92** (July): 27–63.

Freudenburg, W.R., L. Bacigalupi and C. Young (1982) 'Mental health consequences of rapid growth: A report from the longitudinal study of boom town mental health impacts', *Journal of Health and Human Resources Administration*, **4**(3): 334–352.

Gale, Richard P. (1982) 'Commentary', *Pacific Sociological Review* **25** (July): 339–348.

Gilmore, John S. (1976) 'Boom towns may hinder energy resource development', *Science* **191** (Feb.): 535–540.

Gilmore, John S. and Mary K. Duff (1975) *Boomtown Growth Management*, Boulder, CO: Westview Press.

Gold, Raymond L. (1974) 'Social impacts of coal-related development in southeastern Montana', Missoula: Institute for Social Science Research, University of Montana.

——— (1976) 'Trespass and other social impacts of northern Plains coal development', presented at the annual meeting of the American Association for the Advancement of Science, February.

——— (1982) 'Commentary', *Pacific Sociological Review* **25**(3): 349–356.

——— (1986) *Ranching, Mining, and the Human Impact of Natural Resource Development*, New Brunswick, NJ: Transaction Books.

Green, Arnold (1975) *Social Problems: Arena of Conflict*, New York: McGraw-Hill.

Greider, Thomas and Richard S. Krannich (1985a) 'Perceptions of problems in rapid growth and stable communities: A comparative analysis', *Journal of the*

Community Development Society **16**(2): 80–96.

―――― (1985b) 'Neighboring patterns, social support and rapid growth: A comparison analysis from three western communities', *Sociological Perspectives* **28** (January): 51–70.

Greider, Thomas, Richard S. Krannich and E. Helen Berry (1990) 'Perceptions of distrust and social isolation in changing rural communities: A comparative longitudinal analysis', unpublished manuscript, Institute for Social Science Research on Natural Resources, Utah State University.

Greider, Thomas and Ronald L. Little (1988) 'Social action and social impacts: Subjective interpretation of environmental change', *Society and Natural Resources* **1**(1): 45–55.

Jirovec, R. (1979) 'Preparing a boom town for the impact of rapid growth', pp. 79–90 in J.A. Davenport and J. Davenport (eds), *Boom Towns and Human Services*, Laramie: University of Wyoming Press.

Kittredge, W. (1981) 'Overthrust dreams', *Outside* (June/July): 68–79.

Kohrs, Eldean V. (1974) 'Social consequences of boom town growth in Wyoming', presented at the regional meetings of the American Association for the Advancement of Science, Laramie, Wyoming.

Krannich, Richard S., E. Helen Berry and Thomas Greider (1989) 'Fear of crime in rapidly changing rural communities: A longitudinal analysis', *Rural Sociology* **54** (Summer): 195–212.

Krannich, Richard S. and Thomas Greider (1984) 'Personal well-being in rapid growth and stable communities: Multiple indicators and contrasting results', *Rural Sociology* **49** (Winter): 541–552.

―――― (1990) 'Rapid growth effects on rural community relations', pp. 61–73 in A.E. Luloff and L.E. Swanson (eds), *American Rural Communities*. Boulder, CO: Westview Press.

Krannich, Richard S., Thomas Greider and Ronald L. Little (1985) 'Rapid growth and fear of crime: A four community comparison', *Rural Sociology* **50** (Summer): 193–209.

Krannich, Richard S. and A.E. Luloff (1991) 'Problems of resource dependency in U.S. rural communities', forthcoming, *Progress in Rural Planning*, Vol. 1, No. 1.

Kuhn, Thomas (1970) *The Structure of Scientific Revolutions* (second edition), Chicago: University of Chicago Press.

Lantz, A. and R. McKeown (1977) 'Rapid growth and the impact of quality of life in rural communities: A case study', Denver Research Institute, University of Denver.

Little, Ronald L. (1977) 'Some social consequences of boom towns', *North Dakota Law Review* **53**: 401–425.

Little, Ronald L. and Richard S. Krannich (1989) 'A model for assessing the social impacts of natural resource utilization on resource-dependent communities', *Impact Assessment Bulletin* **6** (2): 21–35.

Lovejoy, Stephen B. and Richard S. Krannich (1982) 'Rural industrial development and domestic dependency relations: Toward an integrated perspective', *Rural Sociology* **47**(3): 475–495.

Moen, E., E. Boulding, J. Lillydahl and R. Palms (eds) (1981) *Women and the Social Costs of Economic Development: Two Colorado Case Studies*, Boulder: Westview Press.

Murdock, S.H. and F.L Leistritz (1982) *Energy Development in the Western United States: Impact on Rural Areas*, New York: Praeger.

Murdock, S.H. and E. Schriner (1979) 'Community service satisfaction and stages of community development: An examination of evidence from impacted communities', *Journal of the Community Development Society* 10(1): 109–124.

Murdock, S.H., F.L. Leistritz and R.R. Hamm (1986) 'The state of socioeconomic impact analysis in the United States of America: Limitations and opportunities for alternative futures', *Journal of Environmental Management* 23: 99–117.

Nelson, Lowry (1952) *The Mormon Village*, Salt Lake City: University of Utah Press.

Seyfrit, C.L. and N.C. Sadler-Hammer (1988) 'Social impact of rapid energy development on rural youth: A statewide comparison', *Society and Natural Resources* 1(1): 57–67.

Summers, G., S. Evans, F. Clemente, E. Beck and J. Minkoff (1976) *Industrial Invasion of Nonmetropolitan America*, New York: Praeger.

Thompson, James G. (1979) 'The Gillette Syndrome,: Myth or reality?', *Wyoming Issues* 2 (Spring): 30–35.

Weber, Bruce and Robert Howell (eds) (1982) *Coping with Rapid Growth in Rural Communities*, Boulder, CO: Westview Press.

Weisz, R. (1979) 'Stress and mental health in a boom town', pp. 31–47 in J.A. Davenport and J. Davenport (eds), *Boom Towns and Human Services*, Laramie, WY: University of Wyoming Press.

Wilkinson, K. and M. Camasso (1984) 'Juvenile delinquency and energy development in a traditional setting', unpublished manuscript, Department of Rural Sociology, Pennsylvania State University.

Wilkinson, K., R. Reynolds, J. Thompson and L. Ostresh (1983) 'Divorce and recent net migration into the Old West', *Journal of Marriage and the Family* 45 (May): 437–445.

—— (1984) 'Violent crime in the western energy development region', *Sociological Perspectives* 27 (April): 241–256.

Wilkinson, K., J. Thompson, R. Reynolds, Jr., and L. Ostresh (1980) 'Social disruption and rapid community growth: An examination of the 'boom town' hypothesis', presented at the annual meeting of the Rural Sociological Society, Ithaca, NY, August.

—— (1982) 'Local social disruption and western energy development: A critical review', *Pacific Sociological Review* 25(3): 275–296.

11

Counterurbanization and the planning of British rural settlements: the integration of local housing needs

Ken Sherwood and Gareth Lewis

Introduction

The dominant feature in the redistribution of population in most advanced economics during the past two decades has been the turnaround in the fortunes of the countryside at the expense of major cities and metropolitan areas (Champion, 1989; Nam *et al.*, 1990). It is generally agreed that this process, often referred to as counterurbanization, first became evident in the USA in the early 1970s since when similar patterns have been identified elsewhere; (Fielding, 1982; Hugo, 1988; Kontuly and Bierens, 1990). While there are indications from the 1990 US census that this movement may have been only a *temporary reversal* of the long-term trend of rural depopulation (Chapter 9), however, within the United Kingdom, the evidence suggested that counterurbanization was well underway in the hinterland of the major cities in the 1960s, from where it spread into more intermediate locales and, during the 1970s, to the remoter countryside (Jones *et al.*, 1986; Perry *et al.*, 1986). This continued to hold validity during the 1980s. Indeed, during the early 1980s the population of the non-metropolitan counties continued to grow twice as fast (2.8 per cent per annum) as the national average (1.3 per cent), whilst that of the metropolitan counties continued to decline (–1.0 per cent) (OPCS, 1988). Between 1987 and 1989 the evidence suggests not only that this trend is continuing but also that the rural growth regions of the 1970s, a semi-circular belt about 100–190 km distance from London, continue to be among the fastest growing areas. Beyond this belt growth is much more uneven, though currently it is particularly evident in the West Country and West Wales (OPCS, 1990).

The impact of counterurbanization upon the rural economy and society has been most noticeable within the housing market. The inmigration of middle class households, including those in retirement, has sharpened social divisions within rural communities and reduced markedly the housing options for lower income households, particularly those with 'local' connections (Shucksmith, 1990a). Restrictions on the volume of new housing provision in the countryside, articulated in County Structure Plans committed to policies of restraint, have contributed to accelerating costs for land and to higher prices for housing, whilst the size of the rented sector has declined either through private landlords selling properties at inflated prices or through the government's 'right to buy' policy for tenants in public, council housing (Shucksmith, 1991).

Progessively during the 1980s the government has shifted the role of the local authority from that of house builder to enabler (Nicholson, 1989) and has steered funding for publicly subsidized housing schemes to the Housing Corporation (a government body) for distribution to housing associations. Indeed, the diverse, small-scale and charitable, non-profit making characteristics of the housing association movement are now seen as being particularly appropriate in offering the desired flexibility to cater for the multiplicity of housing needs in a locality (Chope, 1990). However, because such needs have been based upon indicators which have given a high profile to urban areas, minimal amounts of new housing have gone to the countryside: indeed, as late as 1987, less than 0.8 per cent of funding was directed to village housing schemes. As a result housing associations have had little impact thus far in stimulating alternative rented provision in rural areas.

This chapter will examine the consequences of the decline in the provision of rented housing, through an examination of local housing needs policy. Following a discussion of central government policy, we turn to a case study of housing needs in Northamptonshire.

Housing need

The consequence within the rural housing market of a diminishing supply of rented housing and of affordable houses for sale has been most succinctly described by McGhie:

> Agricultural wages are about £122 per week [compared to a median male wage of £235]. Shop assistants, garage attendants and lots of others are at about the same level. There is a desperate shortage of housing to suit those incomes. For instance we helped one couple that had one child and expected another. They had split up to live with their respective parents because neither family could house all three of them. The stories of similar cases are endless. Sometimes we feel it is quite hopeless (McGhie, 1991: 51).

The depth of this view has been amplified in recent years by a number of major reports which, although adopting rather different perspectives, have focused upon definitions and measurements of need together with their implications, at a national and/or local level, for the provision of low cost (social) housing (Barnett and Lowe, 1990). For example Bramley (1989) in an analysis of housing needs in the non-metropolitan districts of England

and Wales revealed a close association between those people on waiting lists for council housing and the conventionally recognized needs categories – sharing, concealed and overcrowded households and the elderly. However, in their prioritization of waiting lists local councils are guided by statutory definitions dating back to the slum clearance programmes of post-1945 housing policies. The utility of this context for the late 1980s/early 1990s is questionable, since certain large groups currently in need of housing are given low priority, notably the elderly and single persons (Spicher, 1987). Furthermore, although a recent study estimated 153,000 names on waiting lists in rural England (Clark, 1990), these are at best an imperfect measure of need since they are no more than queues of people seeking houses, with numbers dependent upon an individual's perception of the value of registering. Indeed, a study by NACRT (a charity which encourages the provision of rented houses in villages) stated that in certain rural areas 'the housing problem is almost impossible to define. Waiting lists in these areas are negligible, because it is apparent to would-be applicants that there is little or no chance of a local authority property becoming available' (NACRT, 1987).

An alternative approach to exploring the depth of the housing need issue has been to relate household incomes in an area to local house prices. For example, the report *Homes We Can Afford* (ACC, 1989) illustrated the growing marginalization of low-income households within the rural housing market by providing case studies from different parts of England. Thus, between 1974 and 1985 house prices in the Windermere area of the Lake District National Park increased by 35 per cent more than the national average: in 1986 the average annual income of a working family was below £8,000, yet the cheapest house was priced at £30,000. In Dorset between 1981 and 1987 house prices increased between 89 per cent and 100 per cent, (average earnings increased by 55 per cent), whilst in the Chiltern Hills of Buckinghamshire former council houses, brought under the 'right to buy legislation' of the early 1980s were being resold for about £100,000. Bramley *et al.* (1987, 1990) have demonstrated the effects of these processes by estimating, at a regional, county and local authority level, the number of households unable to buy (Figure 11.1). Outside London, the evidence suggests that the greatest need exists in the counties of lowland England, particularly in the east and south-east, where about one third of all households have an income too small to enable them to get on to the first rung of the housing ladder – and this number has doubled over the past five years. It is little wonder, therefore, that it has been estimated that between 116,000 and 189,000 properties will be required over the next five years to solve the housing 'needs' of rural dwellers in England (Clark, 1990).

So pervasive has this issue of housing need become that few would disagree with the widely acclaimed Church of England report, *Faith in the Countryside* (ACORA, 1990) that affordable housing is *the* central issue facing the countryside in the 1990s (NHF, 1989; RICS, 1990; RSRU, 1990). It is against this background that attention has now switched to the response

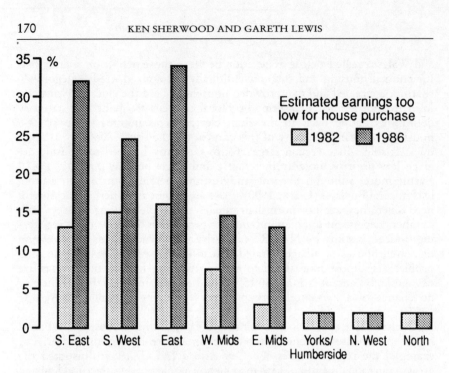

Figure 11.1 Housing affordability in the standard regions of England,
1982–86 (after Bramley)

of central and local government and to the creation of enabling policies and
initiatives within which such needs could be met.

The policy response of central government

By the late 1980s, while the Department of Environment (DoE) had recognized that 'there are real unmet needs for low cost housing in rural areas for
local people' (DoE, 1988a, para. 5) it had also highlighted a potential conflict
with other 'local' opinion, that concerned with preventing further housing
development outside existing urban areas. It was clear, therefore, that any
central directives were likely to steer a cautious path, encouraging low-cost
housing schemes which met community needs, yet which were sufficiently
small-scale and sympathetic in design, location and materials as to complement 'the local vernacular (housing) . . . the countryside and the environment (DoE, 1988a, para. 16). In this sense the evident purpose of central
policy was to be integrative and conservative; to initiate adjustments in the
system which, through clarification and guidance, would create a framework
within which very modest amounts of specifically targeted housing could be
provided, yet without disrupting established policy (Shucksmith, 1990b).
Three particular initiatives can be identified.

First, it had become evident that government funding for housing purposes, either through Housing Investment Programme (HIP) allocations to local authorities or through the Housing Corporation, had been distorted by the choice of 'needs indicators' which consistently had channelled the vast proportion of state subsidy into urban rather than rural areas. Given the fact that local authorities were no longer to be seen as house builders, and that HIP funds should be directed into housing repairs and renovation, the Housing Corporation was given a prominent role in the 'rented' sector, allocating funds to housing associations for building purposes (NFHA, 1989). Furthermore, the funding guidelines at the national level were revised in order to target low-cost housing activity in smaller and more isolated rural settlements. In association with the Rural Housing Trust, formerly the National Agricultural Centre Rural Trust (NACRT), it is intended that newly created rural housing associations would increase the number of approvals from 185 in 1987–88 to 1850 by 1992–93, and this would be in addition to £50 million of local authority credit approvals (out of a total of £2 billion) specifically set aside for a new programme of low-cost rural housing through council sponsorship of housing association schemes (Hansard, 1990). Underpinning this approach was an intention to use housing associations to meet 'the acute need in many villages, for 4 or 5 . . . rented houses or low cost ownership units that do enable people that were born and brought up in the village and need to stay there to do just that' (HC: 1990; para. 589).

Second, it was fundamental to the retention of low-cost housing for local households that the advantages available to first time occupants be passed on to subsequent occupiers. This, however, created a major dilemma since the 1980 and 1985 Housing Acts had specifically stated that households living in dwellings funded by public subsidy (e.g. council houses and/or some housing association schemes) had the right to 'staircase' to outright ownership. Clearly once this had been achieved the dwelling could be offered for sale on the open market (unless an area had been defined as 'rural' under section 19 of the 1980 Act) and lost, therefore, to that local, low-income element of the population for whom it was initially provided. By contrast, where rented housing had been provided from private funding, clauses could be inserted preventing the ownership of the property extending beyond a certain share of the total equity: this meant that the dwelling always retained a rented element which, through keeping the price down, could pass on the affordable advantage to subsequent occupants. However, whilst the shared-equity issue on publicly funded housing schemes remains, the prospect of sustaining long-term low-cost housing in rural areas is bleak. For this reason the DoE has compromised and in May 1991 indicated that 'in future, public subsidy for housing association and other private shared ownership schemes in settlements of less than 3,000 population will not be conditional on the shared owner having the right to staircase to full ownership' (DoE, 1991, para. 21). In order to avoid locking in shared owners to their existing properties, and so encourage them to move to full ownership on the open market (thus freeing the property for others) it was suggested that the limit on staircasing be set at a minimum of 80 per cent of the total equity – somewhat higher than the 60 per cent which has been widely accepted hitherto.

The third initiative concerns a clarification of planning policy relating to housing need (Greenwood, 1989). A basic tenet of the British planning system has been its concern with the use to which land is put and not with the user(s) of that land. Exceptions have been created in rural areas where housing can be specifically targeted at an identified need for farming or forestry, but other attempts to incorporate specific populations into the housing policies of County Structure Plans have rarely gone beyond bland, well intentioned but non-achievable statements of intent, because of this basic principle.

From the 1970s several planning authorities have tried to circumvent this problem by using section 52 of the Town and County Planning Act (1971) in order to enter into voluntary agreements with developers and/or landowners on the size and occupancy characteristics of any land released for housing. This is only so long, however, as it is exceptional to land already allocated for housing, and agreement has been reached prior to permission being sought. Despite early doubts about its legal status (Nott and Morgan, 1984), and its widely publicized problems in the Lake District (Shucksmith, 1981), many local authorities have been able successfully to defend section 52 agreements when appeals have been made to the Secretary of State (Constable, 1988; Croft, 1988).

Given this sympathetic viewpoint it is not surprising that the DoE has stepped in to provide greater clarification for local planning authorities, initially as a written reply to a question from an MP (Hansard, 1989), later by a Guidance Note (DoE, 1989), and, most recently, by a policy Circular (DoE, 1991). In essence this initiative has sustained the basic premiss of the planning system but recognized that 'a community's need for affordable housing is a material planning consideration which may properly be taken into account in formulating local plan policies' (DoE, 1991, para. 1). This could be achieved in two ways. First, a mix of house types and sizes, in 'new villages' or in existing settlements, could be included within the general needs provision of a County Structure Plan (DoE, 1988b). Second, a local planning authority could release small sites, within or adjacent to existing villages, 'which would not otherwise be allocated for housing' (DoE, 1991, para. 8). Such 'exceptional' sites were specifically for low-cost, local needs housing, with each planning authority responsible for the provision of guidance, in the Local Plan, on the type of need and kind of development and for justifying 'the adoption of low cost housing policies . . . with clear evidence of local need' (DoE, 1991, para. 12). The 1991 circular indicated the categories of need most likely to feature in a 'local needs' policy: existing residents needing separate accommodation; people working in the community (or unable to take up the offer of a job due to the lack of affordable housing); and non-residents with long-standing links with the community.

It also reinforced the central role of housing associations in the provision of housing for rent or shared ownership, although local authorities could also promote schemes in partnership with private developers on land in the authority's ownership; these would also qualify for the 80 per cent restriction on staircasing.

In summary it seems likely that there may be a considerable mismatch between the generation of policy statements on low-cost, local housing schemes and actual outcomes in terms of new housing provision. Underpinning these initiatives is a unequivocal directive that the 'basis of the policy is essentially one of permitting very limited exceptions to established policies of restraint, not the creation of a new form of development plan application' (DoE, 1991, para. 15). Nevertheless, it is equally evident that these initiatives, emphasizing as they do the primacy of each local planning authority in the determination of local needs, have stimulated substantial activity at the local level, both in the creation of county-wide Structure Plans and in their expansion in District based Local Plans. In order to examine these responses in more detail, attention will be focused upon Northamptonshire, a largely rural county which has undergone recent rapid population growth and which is located in the heart of 'shire' England (Figure 11.2).

The local context: Northamptonshire – a case study

The county of Northamptonshire lies within that belt of counties, about 100–150 km distance from London, which has experienced considerable population growth in recent years: indeed, in each decade since 1961, Northamptonshire has been amongst the ten fastest growing counties of England and Wales. This expansion has been partly the result of government policy during the 1960s which encouraged decentralization of population and economic activity to overspill towns (Daventry, Wellingborough) or New Towns (Northampton), and partly the result of an expanding commuter population seeking relatively cheap homes in a non-metropolitan setting yet within easy reach of work. A succession of strategies on the part of the County Planning Authority has endeavoured to deflect new house building for this increasing population into the urban areas and a few larger 'key' villages of each of its seven administrative Districts (NCC, 1983; NCC, 1989a). The outcome of this process, however, has been to widen the gap between urban and rural house prices, and between house prices in larger and smaller villages. A survey of house prices in the county in 1990, for example, concluded that average house prices in the rural areas (£108,080) were 54 per cent higher than in the towns whilst, in the villages houses in the smallest settlements (under 1,000 population) were on average £50,000 more expensive than those in the larger settlements (NCC, 1990a). When this is coupled to county-wide average house prices (£79,200) which are more akin to affluent South East England (£79,482) than to neighbouring

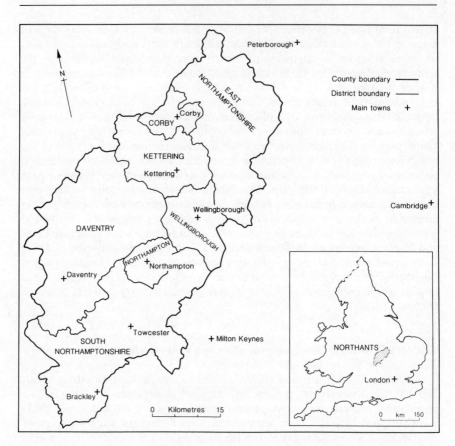

Figure 11.2   The administrative districts of Northamptonshire

counties of the East Midlands (£55,342), it is not surprising that Bramley's nationwide survey of affordable homes concluded that, in the Midlands, 'access is most difficult in Northampton and surrounding districts' (Bramley, 1990: 34).

In keeping with government policy, building for rent by the county's District Councils has been negligible during the 1980s. Thus in the District of South Northamptonshire, an overwhelming rural area of the county, only fifty-four council houses were built between 1981 and 1989 (compared to 329 between 1973 and 1980) and these were exclusively maisonettes or flats for the elderly located in five villages. During the same period 1,432 council households exercised their 'right to buy' under the 1980 Housing Act, decreasing the total stock by one third and producing a net loss of 1,378 dwellings: under the discretionary right to buy policy in operation between 1973 and 1980 only 373 houses had been sold, generating a net loss of less than fifty. Within the county's privately rented sector the pattern has been much the same, as private landlords have sold off their stock of houses at inflated prices (Bowler and Lewis, 1987) but with negligible replacement from private developers or housing associations.

Indeed, of 2,105 housing association dwellings in the county in 1989, nearly 90 per cent were in the towns, whilst in the two most rural Districts (Daventry and South Northamptonshire) they comprised less than 0.4 per cent of the total housing stock. In the District of East Northamptonshire there are plans to build forty-eight starter homes for households on the council's waiting list and with local connections – through family or work. All these houses are subject to section 52 agreements (now section 106 of the 1990 Town and County Planning Act), but these only extend to physical constraints on the size of dwelling and social constraints on the first occupants. Since these dwellings are not subject to the 1991 directive, the occupants can staircase to full ownership, and it is only the hope that the re-sale value of these small properties will be within reach of low income households that any control on future occupants can be achieved; as to the origins of such households there are no stipulations whatsoever (ENDC, 1990).

An effective 'local need' policy

The issue of retaining the benefits of low cost housing is central to the government's overall strategy on an effective 'local need' policy. As has been indicated, this was first articulated in February 1989 as a written reply from the Secretary of State for the Environment, ironically to a Northampton-shire MP. This reply, later amplified as a guidance note PPG3 to all local authorities, was made at precisely the same time as he gave approval to Northamptonshire's County Structure Plan for the period 1983–2001. This Plan developed prior to all the local need initiatives emanating from central government, and made but a lame statement on housing, indicating that it would 'take account of the range of housing needs in the locality and in particular the demand arising from smaller households' (NCC, 1989a, res. 2). With the incentive of the guidance note (and its elevation to the status of circular in May 1991), the County Planning Authority responded immediately to the DoE's expectation of 'an early review of the Plan's housing policy . . . in the light of . . . pressures for development in the County' (NCC, 1989a, para. 54) and within one year had produced a Draft Alteration Document for consultation (NCC, 1989b) and a Statement of Policy (NCC, 1990b) ready for detailed public scrutiny.

This new strategy, to cover the period 1988–2006, attempts to integrate the many government statements on housing provision in rural areas, in-cluding local need housing, into a coherent framework which will be the basis for detailed Local Plans produced by each of the county's seven District Councils. Currently these Local Plans are now being prepared, to a

Structure Plan which has not received DoE approval rather than to the one which has! In general terms the County Council guidelines, as they relate to rural housing provision, are as follows:

1. There will be an underlying policy of restraint, with the maintenance of the scale, charm and character of rural settlements of prime importance.
2. Where there are environmental constraints on housing development, District Councils may consider the creation of new well designed free-standing small scale villages; these would include a variety of housing types (including low cost housing) and, with imaginative layouts, landscaping and design could fit successfully into the rural landscape.
3. In order to help meet specific local needs for low cost housing that would not otherwise be met, local planning authorities may exceptionally consider granting planning permission on land where permission would not normally be granted. Schemes should be small scale and closely related to existing villages and be accommodated without undue harm to the environment (NCC, 1990b, 19).

By mid 1991 each District had made sufficient progress in the preparation of local need policies in their Local Plans (Table 11.1) to permit comment on the likely issues which need to be addressed if government policy is to be successful (Table 11.2).

Issues

First, implicit within these initiatives is the need to take account of the views of the village community as a basis for purposeful policies targeted on a demonstrated need. This 'bottom-up' approach to Local Plan preparation is innovative within the British planning system, and the mechanisms by which a parish or village view is obtained are complex (Lewis *et al.*, 1990). South Northamptonshire District Council has chosen to conduct a District-wide survey by a deliver and return questionnaire to each household. This has achieved a 50 per cent response rate but although it has the advantage of an immediate snapshot view and a yardstick against which to judge proposals from potential developers, it is, at best, an indicative statement rather than a precise tool (Sherwood, 1990). Those other Districts which have placed the onus upon the villagers face a different set of problems for, despite the support on questionnaire design, data gathering and processing by agencies such as the Rural Community Councils and the Rural Housing Trust, some Parish Councils may decide there is no housing problem and, therefore, no need for a survey. In other parishes, a survey may be carried out by a village organization but, without the legitimacy of the elected representatives, it is difficult to see how this can be recognized by the District planning authority. In any survey there is bound to be a range of household views and, whilst many will recognize a housing need, few wish to see this converted into actual housing development (SNDC, 1991, para.10). Finally, in all

Table 11.1 Housing need strategies in District Council Local Plans (1991). Population estimates for 1987. Housing Strategies based upon Local Plan information published by District Councils (May 1991)

District	Rural housing strategy
Northampton Population 177,200 7 parishes under 3,000 population Containing 2.9% of District total	1. No rural local plan 2. No rural housing strategy 3. All housing under general needs of County Structure Plan.
Corby Population 50,200 7 parishes under 3,000, population Containing 9.8% of District total	1. No rural local plan 2. Supports County Structure Plan for low-cost housing on 'exceptional' land. 3. Emphasises balance between growth and conservation. 4. Need throughout District for affordable housing. Hopes that 50% of all new housing will be low cost – for sale and rent.
Kettering Population 73,800 22 parishes under 3,000 population Containing 15.3% of District total	1. Rural local plan 2. 'New' settlement as one option – consultants to recommend sites 3. Emphasis on design and environment 4. Local need a key element of general housing policy and low cost housing on exceptional land
Wellingborouqh Population 65,800 14 parishes under 3,000 population Containing 28.4% of District total	1. Rural local plan 2. Strategy in preparation (mid-1991)

Table 11.1 Continued

District	Rural housing strategy
East Northamptonshire	1. Rural local plan
Population 65,300	2. Rejects concept of village hierarchy as basis for any housing strategy; prefers flexible approach to housing provision
53 parishes under 3,000 population	3. Supports local involvement in preparation of village needs. Villages to conduct their own housing surveys
Containing 37.5% of District Total	4. Has had recent experience of low cost housing schemes for locals and is a strong advocate of this policy
Daventry	1. Rural local plan
Population 62,300	2. Strong supporter of low cost, local need housing. Plan contains detailed guidance (see Table 11.2)
73 parishes under 3,000 population	3. Information pack for all Parish Councils on how to conduct local surveys of housing need and who to consult on drawing up agreements
Containing 72.3% of District Total	
South Northamptonshire	1. Rural local plan
Population 67,300	2. Supports low cost housing in general needs strategy and on 'exceptional' land
73 parishes under 3,000 population	3. Local needs to be identified by a questionnaire survey conducted by District council. Results to be made available to parishes, developers and housing associations
Containing 80.3% of District Total	4. Favours placing local needs housing in 20 specified villages

Table 11.2 Daventry District Council: Local Plan policy for local needs housing in rural areas

---

Policy HS30   *For Housing within the General Needs Policy of the County Structure Plan*

Proposals will only receive planning permission where they provide for a variety of dwelling types to cater for a range of buyers. The District Council is concerned that the needs of the whole community are considered including those for smaller and lower cost homes. This will include the needs of such groups as young married couples, expanding families on lower incomes and the elderly. Applicants (for developments) should have regard to the needs as expressed through local housing surveys and the Council's housing waiting list.

Policy HS 31   *For Small Scale Low-Cost Housing to meet local needs that cannot be accommodated under HS30. Development exceptional to the General Needs Policy.*

Proposals for affordable housing for rent or sale on sites in villages which would not receive planning permission will be considered against the following criteria.

(a)   Identification of Local Housing Need. Developers must convince the District Council that a local need exists, namely people connected with the locality (a settlement together with parishes immediately adjoining it) who cannot afford to purchase or rent at the prevailing market value and for whom a suitable type of housing is not available for example: first time buyers; households currently in socially unacceptable dwellings; households lacking separate accommodation; persons taking up employment locally; close relatives of persons currently resident in the locality; retired people who have lived locally for at least 5 of the preceding 10 years.

(b)   The proposal should have the support of the Parish Council.

(c)   The proposal must be of a size, scale and type to meet the identified need and should be available at below market prices e.g. by building on land not sold at market value.

(d)   A legal covenant should be available to retain low cost advantages to subsequent occupants. Housing Associations would be likely landlords.

(e)   The proposal should be in keeping with the form/scale and character of the village and should not occupy environmentally important open space. Normally such schemes will go to villages with a basic provision of social and community amenities.

---

surveys there are the difficulties of separating need from demand (Clark, 1990), of converting expressed need into an up-to-date register for future provision, of identifying a village view from the myriad of answers (particularly where the overall response rate has been low) and of producing a policy which falls within the definitions of local need outlined in the County or District Plan. Furthermore, as the Titchmarsh Parish Council Policy indicates (Table 11.3), an approach which meets low cost housing need but does

Table 11.3 Titchmarsh Parish Council, East Northamptonshire: Development Policy (January 1990)

1. The Council will press for a small development of starter homes in the village in cooperation with housing associations and local landowners. This development must be on a shared equity, rental or buy-back basis so that housing will retain its starter home character.

2. The Parish Council would welcome a development of 3–4 medium priced houses so that there would be a possible progression from starter to 'second' home within the village.

3. The Parish Council is of the view that the proportion of executive housing development in recent years has been excessive and would recommend that until all those properties in this category at present permitted have been completed and their residents assimilated in the village there should be no further development of this nature. This process could well take 4–5 years.

4. The Parish Council welcomes the zoning of part of the parish on the Thrapston side of the A605 main road for housing development.

not encourage mobility by providing other property types can be, at best, but a partial solution to the problem.

Second, it has already been shown that housing associations' activity in rural Northamptonshire has been minimal and that although the establishment of the Northamptonshire Rural Housing Association (November, 1990) is a step in the direction of a properly integrated county-wide approach, the issue of available land for such housing remains (Rogers and Winter, 1988). Land provided from public sources such as a local authority now can be protected from staircasing to full ownership only in villages below 3,000 population (DoE, 1991), but two of the District Local Plans have stated that low-cost housing, whether within a general needs policy or for 'local need on exceptional land' will only be considered in a few villages – usually the larger ones with an array of support services. Admittedly very few of these exceed the 3,000 population threshold but it does seem to run counter to the evidence that affordable houses are at the greatest premium in the smallest villages: moreover it questions the value of 'need' surveys in such villages when the likelihood of them receiving such housing, either under the rigid hierarchical allocations of general need housing through the Structure Plan or under the 'exceptional' policy, seems remote indeed.

Third, the desire for a specifically *rural* housing need policy in a District's Local Plan preparation seems directly related to the number of rural parishes in the District and the proportion of its population contained within them (Table 11.1). Whilst this would seem a logical outcome, the 'fate' of a village in terms of housing need would seem to rest more upon its location for administrative purposes than on the precise characteristics of its housing market. Thus there are some villages within Northampton District which will be excluded from any local plan policy – simply because this District will formulate such plans to urban issues – whilst Kettering District Council's Local Plan consideration of the 'new village' option was virtually forced upon it as the only way of accommodating the housing allocated to its rural area under the 1989 Structure Plan.

Conclusions

There is little likelihood that these enabling mechanisms will be a panacea for the rural housing issue and that any 'measured need' emanating either from national or local surveys, however they are considered, is ever going to produce other than a few housing units into a few villages (Shucksmith, 1990b). Although Clark has indicated that 'local need' surveys can double the estimates of need contained within local authority waiting lists (Clark, 1990), there seems little likelihood that this loosening of planning restrictions will create 'a giant loophole through which the nation's vast pent-up demand for homes in the country can be expected to burst' (Shoard, 1990). Rather it is clear from all government statements that the purpose of such initiatives is integrative: to provide a mix of households in the countryside which is essential to a community's well being and to the survival of local services such as shops and schools; to complement the built environment with a type and scale of development appropriate to the local vernacular style; to support wider strategies aimed at restraining large scale housing programmes and population expansion in the countryside; to provide an unambiguous framework within which localities can proceed with policies best suited to their particular circumstances. Quite how these initiatives are going to work out in practice remains to be seen since the creation of a policy framework is but the first step in a complex and often lengthy process of prioritizing households and establishing queues for specified dwelling types in particular localities, notwithstanding the provision of cheap land on which such properties will be built. Indeed it may well be that the whole issue of meeting housing need hinges not so much on the identification of 'needy' households but on the willingness of land owners to supply sites at a price which will produce affordable dwellings for their occupants. Furthermore, the success of these many initiatives may depend ultimately upon how effectively they break the link between the cost of land and the cost of housing, particularly in those parts of the country where these are at their highest and where access for local, low-income households, inevitably, is most difficult.

References

ACC (1989) *Homes we can Afford*: Report into the problems associated with rural housing, Association of County Councils.

ACORA (1990) *Faith in the Countryside*, Churchman and ACORA: Worthing and London.

Barnett, R. and S.G. Lowe (1990) 'Measuring housing need and the provision of social housing', *Housing Studies*, 5, 184–94.

Bowler, I.R. and G.J. Lewis (1987) 'The decline of private rented housing in rural areas: a case study of villages in Northamptonshire', in Lockhart, D.G. and B. Ilbery (eds) *The Future of the British Rural Landscape*, Geobooks: Norwich.

Bramley, G. and D. Paice (1987) *Housing Need in Non-Metropolitan Areas*, Association of District Councils: London.

Bramley, G. (1989) *Meeting Housing Need*, Association of District Councils: London. See also Barnett, R., J. Bradshaw and S.G. Lowe (1989) *Not Meeting Housing Need: A critique of the ADC Report 'Meeting Housing "Need"'*, University of York: York.

Bramley, G. (1990) *Bridging the Affordability Gap: A Report of Research on Access and Range of Housing Options*, Association of District Councils and House Builders Federation: London.

Champion, A.G. (ed.) (1989) *Counterurbanisation*, Arnold: London.

Chope, C. (1990) 'Social Housing in the 1990s', *Housing Review*, 39, January–February, 5–8.

Clark, D. (1989) *Affordable Housing in the Countryside: A Role for Private Developers*, ACRE: Cirencester.

Clark, D. (1990) *Affordable Housing in Villages*, ACRE: Cirencester.

Constable, M. (1988) 'Update on Section 52 Agreements and Local Needs Statements', *Village Housing*, 3.

Croft, P. (1988) 'The New Forest Experience', speech at the Housing Centre Trust Seminar, London: quoted in Shucksmith, M. (1990c) op. cit.

DOE (1988a) *Housing in Rural Areas: A Statement by the Secretary of State*, Department of the Environment: London.

DOE (1988b) *Housing and New Villages*, Department of the Environment: London.

DOE (1989) *Draft Planning Policy Guidance: Note 3, Housing*, Department of the Environment: London.

DOE (1991) *Planning and Affordable Housing, Circular 7/91*, Department of the Environment: London.

ENDC (1990) *Residential Proposals in the Rural Areas for the Provision of Starter Homes*, East Northamptonshire District Council: Thrapston.

Fielding, A.J. (1982) 'Counterurbanisation in Western Europe', *Progress in Planning*, Part 1.

Greenwood, J. (1989) *Planning for Low-cost Rural Housing*, Working Paper 112, School of Planning, Oxford Polytechnic.

Hansard (1989) *Parliamentary Debates*, Sixth Series, Vol. 146: Written Answers to Questions (Rural Housing) 3rd February, HMSO: London.

Hansard (1990) *Parliamentary Debates*, Sixth Series, Vol. 182: Oral Answers (Rural Housing) 12th December, HMSO : London.

HC (House of Commons) (1990) *Public Accounts Committee: 27th Report, Housing Associations and Housing Needs and Allocations*, HMSO: London.

Hugo, G.J. (1988) *Australia's Changing Population*, Oxford University Press: Melbourne.

Jones, H., J. Caird, W. Berry and J. Dewhurst (1986) 'Peripheral Counter-urbanisation: Findings from an integration of census and survey data in Northern Scotland' *Regional Studies*, 20, 15–26.

Kontuly, T. and Bierens H.J. (1990) 'Testing the recession theory as an explanation for the migration turnaround', *Environment and Planning A*, **22**, 253–70.

Lewis, G.J., P. McDermott and K.B. Sherwood (1990) 'The counterurbanisation process and policy response in rural England', in Lewis, G.J. and K.B. Sherwood, op.cit.

Lewis, G.J. and K.B. Sherwood (1990) (eds) *Rural Mobility and Housing*: Proceedings of the Institute of British Geographers' Rural Study Group Annual Conference, Department of Geography, University of Leicester.

McGhie, C. (1991) 'Why English villagers feel deserted', *The Independent on Sunday*, 14th April.

NACRT (1987) *Village Homes for Village People*, National Agricultural Centre Rural Housing Trust: London.

Nam, C.B., W.J. Serow and D.F. Sly (eds) (1990) *International Handbook of Internal Migration*, Greenwood Press: Westport.

NCC (1983) *County Structure Plan; Written Statement*, Northamptonshire County Council: Northampton.

NCC (1989a) *County Structure Plan; Written Statement* Northamptonshire County Council: Northampton.

NCC (1989b) *County Structure Plan; Alteration No. 1: Draft for Consultation*, Northamptonshire County Council: Northampton.

NCC (1990a) *Northamptonshire House Price Survey*, Northamptonshire County Council: Northampton.

NCC (1990b) *County Structure Plan; Alteration No. 1: Explanatory Memorandum*: Northamptonshire County Council: Northampton.

NFHA (1989) *Rural Housing: Hidden Problems and Possible Solutions*, National Federation of Housing Associations: London.

NHF (1989) *Housing Needs in the 1990s*, National Housing Forum: London.

Nicholson, G. (1989) 'UK housing policy: transferring the burden', *Land Use Policy*, **6**, 277–80.

Nott, S.M. and P.H. Morgan (1984) 'Section 52 agreements – not worth the paper they are written on?', *Estates Gazette*, **269**, 11th February, 477–8.

OPCS (1988) *Mid 1987 Estimates for England and Wales*, Office of Population Censuses and Surveys: London.

OPCS (1990) *Mid 1989 Population Estimates for England and Wales*, Office of Population Censuses and Surveys: London.

Perry, R., K. Dean and B. Brown (1986) *Counterurbanisation: Case Studies of Urban to Rural Movement*, Geo Books: Norwich.

RICS (1990) *A Place to Live: Housing in the Rural Community*, Royal Institution of Chartered Surveyors: London.

Rogers, A. and M. Winter (eds) (1988) *Who Can Afford to Live in the Countryside? Access to Housing Land*, Centre for Rural Studies, Royal Agricultural College: Cirencester.

RSRU (1990) *The Demand for Social Housing in Rural Wales*, Rural Surveys Research Unit: University College of Wales, Aberystwyth.

Sherwood, K.B. (1990) 'The Local Authority and Local Needs Housing: a case study from South Northamptonshire', Lewis, G.J. and K.B. Sherwood, op.cit.

Shoard, M. (1990) 'How are we going to keep them down in the village?' *The Times*, 25th August.

Shucksmith, M. (1981) *No Homes for Locals?*, Gower: Aldershot.

Shucksmith, M. (1990a) 'A theoretical perspective on rural housing: housing classes in rural Britain', *Sociologia Ruralis*, **30**, 210–19.

Shucksmith, M. (1990b) 'Rural Housing in the U.K.: Current policy issues', *Land Use Policy*, **7**, 283–6.

Shucksmith, M. (1990c) *House Building in Britain's Countryside*, Routledge: London.

Shucksmith, M. (1991) 'Still no homes for locals? Affordable housing and planning controls in rural areas', in Champion, A.G. and C. Watkins *People in the Countryside: Studies of Social Change in Rural Britain*, Chapman: London.

SNDC (1991) *Report of Housing Survey*, South Northamptonshire District Council: Towcester.

Spicher, P. (1987) 'Concepts of need in housing allocation', *Policy and Politics*, **15**, 17–27.

12

Rural society and environmental change: the settlement of rural Sweden

Gärd Folkesdotter

Introduction

This chapter focuses on settlement development in rural areas, including small localities during the period after the Second World War. It will concentrate on the policies of local and central government, concerning building, land use planning and the acquisition of land, and on the attitudes and actions of local landowners, relating them to the development of housing. It will also discuss the motives for settling in rural areas and the type of people who are able to do so. The county of Gävleborg and kommuns (municipalities) of Arbrå and Bollnäs are used as case study areas to exemplify the points made.

First, some contextual data about Sweden are presented. The chapter includes a short review of the period 1900–1947. Thereafter new planning and building legislation was approved, national housing policy was reformed and a new system for state housing loans and subsidies established. Although many alterations have since been made, many of the main features still exist.

Until the Second World War, the Swedish government encouraged small-scale farming, but after the war agricultural policy aimed at increasing farm sizes on supposed efficiency grounds. During the 1950s and 1960s many farms were amalgamated. The present century has also seen a growth of urban communities in Sweden. During the 1950s and 1960s, this growth was fastest in the large and medium sized urban areas and few houses were constructed in rural areas. This situation changed, however, in the 1970s, and the rural population increased in a number of counties. It appeared that the increase of new single-family houses in rural areas was neither wanted nor foreseen and a research project 'settlement development in small communities' was set up at the National Swedish Institute for Building Research, to examine the processes involved. The aim was in particular to describe and analyse the action of property owners in relation to local government planning and policy. The research project has employed a combination of methods and a wide variety of source material: plans, maps, property registers, population records, interviews with property owners, residents, local politicians, local officials and estate agents.

The Swedish case

More than half of the land area of Sweden is forest land and population density is only twenty inhabitants per km². Agriculture was the largest sector of the economy until the 1930s when it was overtaken by the industrial sector. Since then agriculture has declined and in 1986 only 4 per cent of the workforce was in agriculture and forestry. In the rural areas there are few large estates: most Swedish farms are family based employing little external labour. With some exceptions, Swedish farmers combine agriculture and forestry.

In the 1950s, 65 per cent of the population lived in an urban settlement – defined as a collection of dwellings having at least 200 residents, with the distance between dwellings not normally exceeding 200 metres. By 1960 the figure had risen to 73 per cent and by 1980 to 83 per cent. In this year 16 per cent of the population lived outside settlements with less than 200 people, 11 per cent in settlements with 200–1999 people, 17 per cent in settlements with 2,000–9,999 people, 22 per cent in settlements with 10,000–49,999 people and 33 per cent in larger settlements.

The Swedish housing stock is relatively new, with around half the dwellings having been built after the Second World War. About 45 per cent of the dwellings in Sweden are either detached or semi-detached houses. Roughly 40 per cent of all households are owner-occupiers, about 43 per cent live in rented dwellings, mainly in multi-dwelling buildings, and the remainder are occupants of co-operative building society dwellings. Around 20 per cent of all Swedes own a holiday home and another 20 per cent have the use of one. There are, however, marked regional variations: with nearly one-third in the extreme northern parts owing a holiday home, one-quarter in Stockholm and one-seventh in the south of Sweden.

The Swedish kommuns have a statutory responsibility to both provide housing and regulate development. They must draw up programmes for housing provision, plans for built-up areas, and provide a variety of services for the inhabitants. Some services, such as primary and secondary education are free of charge; others, for example, water supply and sewerage, may be charged for on a non-profit basis. Local income tax is levied at a rate decided by the kommun and grants are also received from the State. After the Second World War many kommuns were amalgamated; the number of kommuns decreased from around 2,500 in the 1950s to 284 in the 1980s. By 1990 many Swedish kommuns had around 20,000 inhabitants, the smallest with less than 3,000, the largest, Stockholm, with a population of around 672,000.

Retrospect – rural housing and rural policy from 1900 to 1947

Rural housing has, until recently, been linked to policies concerning agriculture and forestry. At the beginning of the century the government encouraged smallholding through favourable mortgages. In some areas of northern Sweden the Government also encouraged reclamation of forest land. In 1904 a special fund was created by the State so that 'less well-off working people' in rural areas, and also in the towns, could borrow money to buy land to build on. This fund existed, with several alterations, until 1957, although other forms of state mortgages were introduced after the Second World War. Some small-holdings were from the outset very small and the owner had to find alternative permanent employment. Others were supposed to be sufficiently large to support a family, though as time passed, many of these holdings turned out to be too small so supplementary incomes were required. For example, in the north of Sweden, this involved forestry work in winter.

In the 1930s new legislation was passed which allowed everyone who owned a house on leased land, and who had lived there for some years, the right to buy the site of the house. Many people took this opportunity and several crofts belonging to large farms, and houses on common land, were sold off. Since the Second World War, agricultural policy has been aimed primarily towards achieving a more efficient farm size structure and, as a result, the government has not encouraged or subsidized smallholdings.

By the 1940s most dwellings in rural areas were detached owner-occupied houses. Young, particularly single, people, however, remained within the apartment and rental market, though most became owner-occupiers on starting a family.

Development in rural areas after 1947

During the 1950s and 1960s the larger and medium sized urban communities saw a rapid expansion, with little growth in rural areas. The mechanization and rationalization of both agriculture and forestry caused a decline in rural labour, and during these decades many farms were amalgamated and the farmhouses parcelled off. There was, however, the development of some small settlements by the larger timber companies, to house their workers, and some smaller industrial enterprises chose to locate their workshops in rural zones. However, overall, these decades saw the decline of many rural settlements and the conversion of much rural housing to second and holiday homes.

The situation changed dramatically in the 1970s when the rural population started to increase in a number of counties. Housing construction began to be more frequent in rural zones and smaller urban settlements In the 1970s 4 per cent of all new single-family dwellings were in rural areas, rising threefold to 12 per cent by 1979.

Conditions varied, however, from one area to another. The proportion of new single-family dwellings built in non-urban areas was largest in the county of Gotland: between 1976 and 1980 50 per cent of new detached houses were built outside urban areas. According to data supplied by the Gävleborg County Administration, the proportion of sites in that county parcelled for permanent homes in areas not covered by detailed urban Development Plans was 42 per cent in 1980 and 48 per cent in 1981. The County Administration stated that most new settlement not covered by previous planning regulations had taken place in small localities: housing construction in purely rural areas had expanded but was still a minor proportion of all unplanned settlement.

Similar conditions applied in the county of Örebro, where between 40 per cent and 50 per cent of single-family dwellings were built outside planned areas between 1980 and 1982. The corresponding figure for the counties of Östergötland and Skaraborg between 1978 and 1981 was about 13 per cent.

Only four counties had figures below 10 per cent during the years 1976–80. Conditions also varied a great deal between kommuns within the same county. The proportion of single-family dwellings built outside planned areas was about 10 per cent in certain kommuns and 40–50 per cent or even more in others.

The settlement of rural areas

There are numerous arguments about rural settlement and its implications for different residential groups, for the kommun and for the state, both in the long and short term. Some of these opinions are related to the ideologies of different political parties, while others may be more in agreement with traditional planning attitudes. The attitudes of the political parties to building in the countryside and outside planned areas can be grouped on a right-to-left scale, with the Conservatives and Centre Party (earlier called the Farmers' Federation) most in favour of such building, while the Liberals take an intermediate position and the Socialist parties oppose it. There are, of course, great variations in attitude at the local level and even within local party political groups. It is interesting to note, however, that rural building outside planned areas was hardly discussed or made a subject of party political standpoints, legislative proposals or official comments until the end of the 1970s.

The Conservatives maintain that people must be free to choose their own residential locality and form of tenure, and that great importance must be attached to individual interest, though considerations of local government finance should not be ignored. The Socialist parties wish to encourage the construction of multi-family dwellings in the larger urban areas and maintain that scattered dwelling, especially in the form of detached houses, implies the ongoing privatization of housing. They also express fears that rural building is accentuating segregation. In addition, scattered settlement is taken to mean heavier capital costs, an increase in the use of the private car and thus high energy consumption. Multi-family dwellings are, by comparison, regarded as the superior dwelling form, conducive to community participation, and involving least environmental impact. It is also common for apprehension to be expressed about the difficulties and cost involved in providing municipal services for scattered settlements. The Centre Party argues that building development in the countryside and in small urban areas can underpin existing infrastructure and that residents there can often utilize existing services. However, the Centre Party also argues that arable land should not be built on, and that agricultural interests must be taken into consideration.

Attitudes to rural building can be said to agree quite well with the basic ideological attitudes and electoral followings of the various political parties. The non-socialist parties put more emphasis on the individual and his or her freedom of choice, while the Socialist parties pay more attention to community participation, solidarity and the need for services. The Centre Party has a powerful following among the rural population, while the Social Democrats and VP (Left Party) often derive their support from larger, industrialized localities. With the exception of the Conservatives, however, parties are increasingly taking on board environmental concerns.

The opinions of planners and officials are often greatly influenced by the explicit and implicit principle of building legislation, whereby land must be subjected to planning before built on. Within this group there are also fears that environmental considerations may be prejudiced. Nature conservation and recreation areas may be disrupted by additional building development, which may be unsuitably designed and positioned. The inappropriate siting of new housing accommodation can also cause inconvenience to agriculture and forestry. Indeed planners in Sweden have, generally, taken the view that scattered settlement is a bad thing. Many have been influenced by the planner, Uno Ahrén, who wrote in 1947 that settlements should be of at least 1,000 inhabitants. Ahrén underlined that scattered development offered no natural collective connection, no social community of interest and also argued in terms of the need to economize nature, woods, land and shores, taking the view that scattered development had already caused irreparable damage in occupying areas of natural beauty. As these ideas were strongly supported among Swedish planners they tended to be incorporated into building and planning legislation and its supplementary regulations: environmental protection thus being inherent in the very ideology many planners adhere to.

Other concerns include access to work for rural residents and the supply of energy and of transport infrastructure and services. Representatives of the national authorities also fear that the state and kommuns may lose money on State-mortgage houses in rural areas which cannot be sold at a high enough price to cover the mortgage costs. Some officials and politicians have also regarded the growth of rural building during the 1970s as endangering the possibilities of building ready-planned housing areas and service centres in the central locality. In places where the Municipal Housing Cooperative has empty apartments, continuing production of single-family dwellings in the countryside can aggravate the problem. If the kommun succeeds in restraining rural building, it may be in danger of losing population to a neighbouring kommun which is better disposed to this type of development. Or again, there may be an increase in the number of holiday homes converted into permanent dwellings.

The rural population

Type of households settling in rural areas

It has, above all, been young families with children who have settled in rural areas, many having had previous experience of living in such areas. The majority of migrants living in both newly built dwellings and holiday homes converted to permanent dwellings have low to medium incomes and have retained the jobs they had prior to relocation, with many still being employed in a central locality. However, there was substantial regional variability (Folkesdotter 1986).

Household motives for settling rural areas

There is unanimity concerning the principal motives which induce house-holds to settle in the country: these are primarily improved environmental and dwelling conditions. Several surveys indicate that working conditions are of minor importance as a motive for migration, though those employed in agriculture and forestry are more likely to migrate for employment reasons.

Motives for relocation can be divided into pull factors (those attracting households to rural areas) and push factors (those repelling households from their previous homes and housing localities) although where the individual household is concerned, a combination of factors may well be involved (Folkesdotter 1986).

PUSH FACTORS

Dissatisfaction with the previous home, its immediate surroundings and negative residential experiences are very common motives. A survey in the Gothenburg region suggested that negative residential experiences helped to bring about migration within a broad majority of the households concerned. The majority based their decision to relocate on social conditions ranging from simple lack of satisfaction to more intensively perceived disadvantages. Among those cited were, for example, joy riding in lifts, moped traffic on footpaths, loud music, clogs on stairs, rules forbidding children to ride bicycles or play ball games, neighbours with drink problems, wild parties, thefts of toys and bicycles, a general rise in criminal behaviour, police intervention and so on. Other frequently expressed viewpoints were a desire to get away from noise, soot and air pollution (Folkesdotter 1986).

PULL FACTORS

Some pull factors could be described as inverted push factors. Play amenities for children are considered better in the country, the dwelling environment is superior to that in towns, and so on. The most common reasons given for wanting to live in the country were 'wanting to live close to nature', 'good for the children', 'no neighbours crowding you', 'a much freer life than in town', 'close to friends and relatives', and 'returning to where I came from'. Proximity to nature was an important motive in all surveys. In more sparsely populated areas outside the metropolitan regions, returning to one's native community was the most important motive, while in the Gothenburg region this was of minor importance

As previously mentioned, several surveys (Stahre and Wretblad, 1972; Forsström and Olsson, 1982; Nyström, 1982; Matsson, 1979 among others) indicated that working conditions are of minor importance compared to housing and environmental factors as a motive for relocation. For agricultural households, though, this was the most important motive. Persons employed in agriculture or forestry tended to move more often for reasons of employment and less often for housing and environmental reasons, compared with other migrants. Indeed working conditions, however, were the most important cause of relocation for between a quarter and one-third of migrants in the Nyköping and Växjö-Tingsryd areas (Stahre and Wretblad, 1972). Occupational factors played a limited part in migration to the sparsely populated areas of the Gothenburg region, with only 11 per cent of relocations being thus induced. (Forsström and Olsson, 1982) In a survey of Arvidsjaur nearly half the interviewees had some form of combined employment, often connected with forestry or agriculture (Nyström, 1982).

Economic motives do not appear to have played a very important part in inducing people to settle in the country. However, in some reports it was observed that households which are able to build on land belonging to parents or other relatives can derive economic and other advantages from doing so.

Jerkbrant and Malbert (1979) point out that most of the people settling in a recreational area they studied in the Gothenburg region deliberately opted for a lower standard of living in return for other values. Where most of them are concerned, a new single-family/terraced house in the municipal expansion areas is economically and emotionally inconceivable. The alternative has often been a flat in some outlying areas the same distance away from the centre of Gothenburg.

The various studies also refer to motives of the 'peace and quiet' and 'no neighbours crowding you' variety. According to one survey report (Stahre and Wretblad, 1972) about one-third of those interviewed wanted 'fewer people around them', and very few of them felt that they were living too far away from their neighbours. In both the areas investigated by the authors, the medium distance from the nearest neighbour is 80 m; at distances of less than 100 m, one-fifth of the respondents felt that their neighbours were too close.

In conclusion, both the author's survey and other Swedish work has stressed environmental concerns as the main factors leading to inmigration into rural zones in recent years.

The classification of motives for relocation clearly has difficulties. As has been pointed out in a number of surveys, a balance often has to be struck between the various motives of the household and of its individual members. It may also be that respondents prefer to plead proximity to nature and consideration for the children rather than, say, financial motives; and of course, one cannot exclude the possibility of an element of *post facto* rationalization.

The tendency in this material, however, agrees well with other studies of the dwelling environment preferred by Swedes. In general there appears massive support in favour of the traditional provincial idyll, with people bundled together in nuclear families, living in freehold detached houses.

The state and its measures

The state has in many ways – directly and indirectly – affected development and settlement. In general policies at the national and regional level concerning rural housing and planning have been restrictive, following more or less the aims of the Building Act. With the three factors of land, labour and capital in mind, this chapter will now concentrate on policies concerning acquisition of land, building and planning, and in broad terms describe some instruments provided and/or used by the state – namely building and planning legislation, regulation of building and construction workforce, state housing loans, housing provision programmes and compulsory acquisition legislation.

The building and planning legislation has to a large degree been handled at the local level by the kommuns, though the state at the regional level has had some power. Since the Second World War the power and the responsibility of the kommuns have increased and the new planning and building legislation of 1987 is another step in this direction. The regulation of building and construction workforce has mainly taken place at the regional level (with some major decisions at the national level). Financing through state housing loans has been handled at the regional level after the local government has itself considered the applications. During the period more of the responsibility has been laid at the local level. The use of compulsory acquisition legislation has mainly been in the hands of the kommuns. Looking very broadly at the three factors of land, labour and capital, the state has (through

County Boards) controlled the labour, the kommuns have managed the land and the capital has been controlled by the state, although the kommuns have had their say.

Building and planning legislation

The Building Act of 1947 and the new Planning and Building Act of 1987 state that both private and public interests should be properly considered. As there are no precise definitions of private and public interests the terms are open to a variety of interpretations. However, private interests can be linked to how the property-owners wished to use land, while public interests relate to state management through the different authorities. Public interests may be, for instance, public economy, sanitation, traffic needs, fire safety, recreation, environmental protection and safeguarding historical buildings.

COMPULSORY ACQUISITION LEGISLATION

The Compulsory Acquisition Act 1972 and its predecessors state that property not belonging to the state may be compulsorily purchased, for instance to make it possible for kommuns to acquire land needed for the future development of built-up areas. Compulsory acquisition in built-up areas may only take place if the land in question will be affected by development or construction in the near future.

Since 1967 the kommuns have also had the right to take over property sold to others at the original purchase price. Special loans were given to the kommuns in order to facilitate land acquisition. It is also worth mentioning that such loans are not given if the price of the land is too high. There are several rules and regulations, the underlying aims of which are largely to stimulate the kommuns to have an active land policy.

REGULATION OF BUILDING AND CONSTRUCTION WORK-FORCE

The regulation has aimed at a stable employment in the building trade, levelling out booms and depressions, and variations between seasons. When it comes to the pattern of housing development, this regulation has not been an important factor outside larger metropolitan areas.

HOUSING PROVISION PROGRAMS

Since 1947 central government has had power to force the kommuns to develop housing provision programmes. Initially only those with more than 10,000 inhabitants were so compelled. The system was revised in 1967 and since 1974 all kommuns have had to draw up 5-year programmes. The programmes were used by the County Housing Boards as a basis for building quotas and state housing loans. The National Housing Board as a rule established the framework for the counties concerning the number of dwellings available for loans and the County Board – in collaboration with the County Housing Board and the County Labour Board – distributed the quotas among the kommuns.

STATE HOUSING LOANS SYSTEM

During the period 1945 to 1984 most new dwellings were financed with state housing loans. A general rule for obtaining a loan is that the dwelling will be a first home. Especially in rural areas such financing has been the only option for most people, as private financing has been expensive and difficult to obtain.

A state housing loan provides direct state financing of usually 30 per cent of approved construction costs for new multi-dwelling buildings and usually 25 per cent for new single-family houses; access to mortgage institutions for financing 70 per cent of approved costs; and a substantial subsidy of interest payments.

The kommun and its measures

The different local government policies concerning rural housing can be divided crudely into two groups. The Green Party, the Left Party and the Centre Party are more 'green' than the Conservatives and Social Democrats, which are both considered 'grey concrete' parties. Those kommuns which are pro-rural development have plans and land available for development of dwellings in different built-up areas. The inhabitants largely live in sparsely populated areas and the kommun has the opinion that it is possible to develop these areas with small-scale enterprises and a combination of different jobs. With regard also to the positive social effects of housing development in rural areas the kommun in principle looks positively at new permanent dwellings outside urban areas. This policy is most likely to be found in kommuns with a large rural population and a non-socialist majority.

A basic social goal of the more green parties grouping is to locate new dwellings near work places, services, public transport and recreation facilities in order to provide good possibilities for everyone to work and to take part in the social life. The Kommun has the guideline that 85–90 per cent of the new dwellings should be built in the central urban area and the major part of the remaining 10–15 per cent in other urban areas – mainly for people who for specific reasons have to live in the countryside. This policy is evident at the national and regional level, and is more in accord with the views of the socialist parties and kommuns with a large urban population.

Case study: the kommuns of Arbrå and Bollnäs

During the studied period 1952–1981 Arbrå was a kommun of its own until the merger in 1974, when five kommuns – Alfta, Arbrå, Bollnäs, Hanebo and Rengsjö – were amalgamated into the present kommun of Bollnäs. However, even before the merger, these kommuns had formed a bloc and cooperated in making housing provision programmes and in comprehensive planning. The area studied in the research project is shown stippled within a solid black line in Figure 12.1.

Bollnäs had around 17,300 inhabitants before the merger and Arbrå 5,100. Bollnäs had a socialist majority both before and after the merger. Arbrå had a non-socialist majority. Until the end of 1961, there was in Arbrå kommun a locality with limited municipal rights, mainly identical with the urban area of Arbrå (see Figure 12.1). This locality had a Building Committee and a local council of its own, with a socialist majority.

Planning and development in Arbrå kommun 1952–1962

The Building Committee was not very restrictive. Building permits were (with some exceptions) not needed in large parts of the kommun and the committee rarely denied building permission. There were detailed local plans for the urban area of Arbrå, for three smaller localities and a village. Rules for unplanned development were approved for an area along the river Ljusnan and a decree, based on the Shore Act, was promulgated for an area east of the river. In 1962 a detailed local plan was drawn up for an area of holiday homes. During the decade the kommun bought land in the urban areas of Vallsta and Arbrå. Sites for detached houses were mainly sold to builders by private landowners and there was a large demand. Around 152 detached houses were built, 88 in the urban area of Arbrå where the population increased by nearly 30 per cent, though the population in the whole kommun decreased.

Planning and development in Arbrå kommun 1963–1973

During the 1960s activity was very high. On request from the Building Committee, the County Board promulgated rules for unplanned settlement covering the whole kommun, thus giving the Committee more power to control the development. In 1966 new decrees based on the Shore Act were promulgated for larger areas. More land was purchased in Vallsta for housing and in the urban area of Arbrå for housing, schools and industrial enterprises.

During the 1960s and the beginning of the 1970s development in the urban area of Arbrå was considerable. Several multi-dwelling houses and most of the single-family houses were built there, and also a school and an indoor

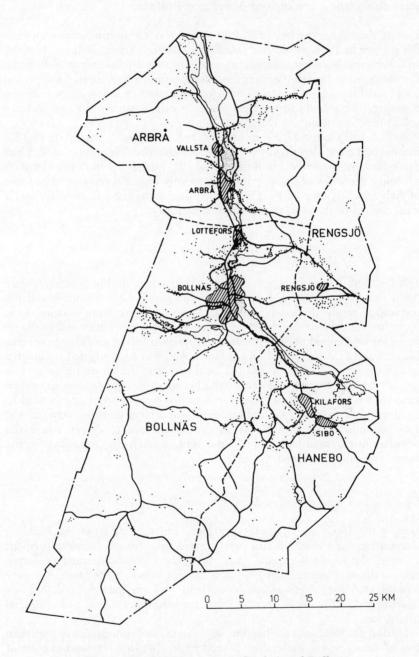

Figure 12.1   The kommuns of Arbrå and Bollnäs

swimming pool. Many holiday homes were built outside the urban area of Arbrå but few permanent homes. The development in the Arbrå urban area may depend on the expansion of an engineering company and the subsequent need for housing. The coming merger was also considered a reason for the building boom. The population in the Arbrå urban area increased, while the population in the kommun as a whole decreased.

Planning and development in the kommun of Bollnäs and the district of Arbrå 1974–1981

In the 1960s the settlement policy in Bollnäs seems to have been more restrictive than in Arbrå concerning unplanned settlement. In sparsely populated areas no permanent homes and no detailed local plans were thought necessary (except plans for holiday homes) and state loans to houses in such an area were not generally granted. After the merger no detailed local plans were made for Arbrå but at the end of the 1970s some plans were approved. A comprehensive plan for the whole kommun was made and approved in 1977 (revised 1980) and some guidelines were worked out for a number of small localities, among others Vallsta. According to these guidelines there is considered unlikely to be a demand for flats in multi-dwelling houses in these localities, but planning includes single-family houses. The housing provision programmes indicate a relatively large number of dwellings in the beginning of the 1970s, mostly multi-dwelling houses in the largest localities. Building outside areas with detailed local plans was not mentioned in the programmes until 1978 – being at that time a large part of the construction it could hardly be ignored. But the suggested development in the programme this year was, as earlier, mainly in the larger urban areas.

At the time of the merger, in 1974, public land ownership was reported as 'sufficient' in Hanebo, 'unsatisfactory' in Arbrå and Rengsjö and 'miserable' in Bollnäs. Around 250 dwellings per year were built in 1965–74, (in the kommuns Bollnäs, Arbrå, Hanebo and Rengsjö together) but only around 185 per year in 1975–82. During the latter period building permits were given for 285 single-family dwellings in areas with detailed local plans and no less than 338 outside such areas. However, during the years 1975–80 the population in rural areas and small localities increased, possibly an effect of the development outside areas with detailed local plans.

The views of the landowners

An officer, working with land acquisition in Arbrå in 1955–64 gave the following reasons for landowners to sell land to the municipality. They would typically be landowners who were positive to the development of the community; they were likely to be outside the locality or the proposed site was occupied by old buildings, needing large capital investment, and thirdly they valued the additional income thus raised.

He also remarked that those who owned only a few sites kept these in reserve for relatives and friends. His opinion is largely in accordance with findings from interviews in the investigation area. Some of the landowners in this area had land that could be parcelled off for sites. Most thought some development was good; they did not want the vicinity to 'die': many found it important that young families could settle in the area. However, in relation to their own land, property-owners were unwilling to sell, especially land close to their own house. In those cases when lots had been parcelled off, as a rule a son or a daughter had received them. The decisions not to sell land can of course depend on the fact that it is economically favourable to own land, and that farmers have interests in keeping arable land and forest land. But other reasons may exist as well. People do not want to live too close to neighbours. It is not regarded as fair to sell off land that belongs to the farm and the family. These kinds of feelings seem to have a long tradition in Scandinavia and old laws carefully regulated the ways that inherited land could be sold. One of these medieval laws stated:

> If a man wants to sell inherited land, he shall offer it to his nearest relatives . . . If they do not want to buy, and do not allow him to sell, he may lease out the land for no more than three years board and lodging, until he asks them a second time. If they still do not want to buy . . . he may then sell to anyone.

Most landowners interviewed seemed not to calculate what they could gain on selling land; the idea of selling was unfamiliar to them. An old farmer, now retired, said his son criticized him for selling arable land to the kommun. The old farmer's excuse was that it had made it possible to build flats for people wanting to live in Vallsta.

The emergence of scattered development

The chapter will now discuss the three 'actors' – the state, the kommun and the owners of property – and the pattern of housing development in Bollnäs. The interest of the state in settlement policy favours development in urban areas and wishes to avoid scattered development. There is clearly a heavy environmental interest component in this. The landowners are more in favour of scattered development. The kommun has been under pressure from both the state and the inhabitants, many of whom wanted a dwelling in the area where they were brought up and may thus also press for scattered development.

During the period 1952–1962 the state was influential through state housing loans and also through the building and planning legislation. The loans were as a rule given without trouble; some years there were delays but no refusals from the County Housing Board. The kommun had no town architect and many decisions had to be approved by the County Board and the County Architect. The property owners in large parts of Arbrå kommun had the right to build without a building permit, and they did. However, the difference between their intentions and the local government policy does not seem to have been large.

More power was given to the kommun when legislation was changed in 1959. In the period 1963–1973 local government strengthened its control over housing development with the help of the legislation and a town architect was engaged – a condition for the local government's handling of certain issues. The coming merger with Bollnäs seems to have joined the local government's forces in an attempt to build as much as possible before 1974. The decisions among local politicians to concentrate development in the urban area of Arbrå seem to have been unanimous, but people living elsewhere in the kommun may have been reluctant to see such concentration taking place.

During nearly the whole period 1963–1973 the managing of building quotas played an important role. The building quotas for the whole county of Gävleborg did not vary very much from one year to another during the period, but some of the kommuns increased their share and others decreased. Some kommuns complained, asking for a larger share. The combined building quotas for Bollnäs, Arbrå, Hanebo and Rengsjö were fairly stable from 1966 to 1973 – around 250 dwellings per year. Eighty-two per cent of the quotas for Bollnäs and 53 per cent of the quotas for Arbrå were used for multi-storey dwellings blocks; Bollnäs kommun, in particular, seems to have prioritized this kind of development. Both Arbrå and Bollnäs favoured development in the large urban areas and scattered development was held back.

The years 1974–82 saw a significant change. In the beginning of the 1970s the planning legislation was changed, aiming at a stronger control of settlement development. The ambition of Bollnäs kommun was – as earlier – to concentrate housing development in the larger urban areas. However, the development in rural areas without detailed local plans showed a remarkable increase in the 1970s, neither wanted nor foreseen by politicians and administrators but in accordance with property-owners' intentions (see Figure 12.2).

A probable explanation for this increase can be linked to the phenomenon of vacant flats. Around 1972 some municipal housing companies had problems with vacant flats and new flat construction was cut down. In Bollnäs less than half of the building quota was used in 1974, and, consequently, there were resources for loans to detached houses in rural areas. The delegation of power in 1975 was combined with a greater responsibility for the kommuns to pay for the losses that might occur. However, this increased responsibility does not seem to have caused a decrease in new state housing loans for houses in rural areas, outside areas with detailed local plans. The change in planning legislation in 1977 was aimed at facilitating development in rural areas, but interviewed officers do not believe this alteration played a

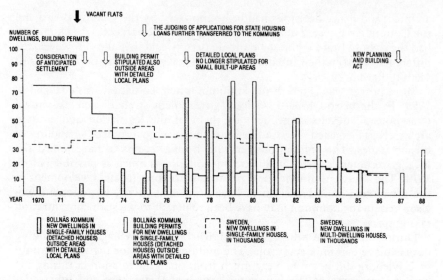

Figure 12.2 Housing development in rural areas, 1970–88.

major role, saying that the kommuns could already approve such development and also prevent development after 1977 if they wanted to.

The instruments and the will to use them

The means available for the kommuns were thus strengthened but their development control less successful. Were these instruments not useful in the new situation or was the will to use them not there? Kommuns with a socialist majority tended to encourage the construction of multi-dwelling houses and were as a rule more reluctant to permit scattered development than others (Folkesdotter 1986), and Bollnäs had such a policy.

Scattered development was easy to hold back as long as the quotas were mainly used for multi-dwelling blocks. But later, faced with people wanting to build a new detached house in a rural area, the local politicians hesitated to use the planning legislation or the rules for state housing loans to stop them. Psychologically it is not easy to prevent people building a house near their parents. The policy and the housing provision programmes were, after many discussions, altered at the beginning of the 1980s, towards a more realistic line with regard to the demands from the inhabitants. A larger proportion of new dwellings were planned to be built in small localities, outside urban areas and in single-family houses.

In the late 1980s, the number of building permits in Bollnäs kommun for new dwellings outside areas with detailed local plans declined, but then increased again, though not reaching the high level of the mid-1970s. The peak around 1979 was perhaps the result of demand having been held back for a long time.

The new planning and building legislation will not help the kommuns to hold back scattered development better than the old legislation; on the contrary the kommun has to show that the proposed building is not acceptable, to say nothing about willingness to use the legislation.

Socialist parties in Sweden have – at least since the 1940s – had full, or high employment as their most important objective, much more important than development control. In a situation when construction was cut down (vacant flats), both central and local government had an interest in keeping up employment in the building sector. In this perspective it seems logical that the state has kept control of labour – building and construction work-force – at the regional and central levels, but delegated the less important development control to the kommuns. However, the result has been the potential for increased scattered settlement – at odds with the socialist view of environmental protection.

The future

As discussed in Chapter 6, agriculture policy is changing; Sweden now has a considerable surplus of grain and other products that must be reduced. The number of the population directly working in agriculture and forestry has heavily decreased. Djurfeldt (1990) for example has argued that one-man farms are perhaps on the verge of outnumbering family farms; the proportion of spare-time and part-time farming has grown since the mid-1960s and today constitutes the majority of Swedish farms.

It is already obvious that most people living in rural areas are depending on other kinds of income than farming and forestry and it is possible that recreation and tourism will be more important in the future. In addition, the current non-socialist government (in power from 1991) has said that the housing sector will be less regulated, less subsidized and more market orientated.

Clearly, despite the greening of the Swedish people and its institutions, the combination of social, economic and political factors operating at the development level is threatening the greening of Swedish rural policy.

References

Bjerén, Gunilla (1981) 'Female and male in a Swedish region: Old roles under new conditions', *Antropologiska studier*, 30–31, pp. 56–85.

Björnberg, Ulla *et al.* (1980) *Livsformer i en region. En jämförande analys av familjeoch samhällsliv i 1970-talets Sverige*, Kungälv.

Djurfeldt, Göran (1981) 'What happened to the agrarian bourgeoisie and rural proletariat under monopoly capitalism?' *Acta Sociologica*, 24(3): 167–191.

Djurfeldt, Göran (1990) 'Fler enmansgårdar och deltidsbruk? Produktionsformer i svenskt lantbruk', *Sociologisk Forskning* 1990 (2): 2–21 (Abstract in English).

Floderus, Åsel (1989) 'The decentralization of physical planning in Sweden', in Read, Eric (ed.) *Britain and Sweden: Current Issues in Local Government*. The National Swedish Institute for Building Research, Research report SB:18, Gävle, Sweden, pp. 51–53.

Forsström, Åke, Olsson, Ragnar (1982) Boende i glesbygd, Bosättnings-förändringar i Bohuslän ur ett nationellt perspektiv, BFR-rapport R 100. (In Swedish). (Living in rural areas. Settlement changes in Bohuslän viewed in a national perspective.)

Folkesdotter, Gärd (1986) *Housing construction and rural settlement, a descriptive bibliography*, The National Swedish Institute for Building Research, Bulletin M85:23, Gävle.

Folkesdotter, Gärd (1987) 'Research and policy for rural housing in Sweden', in MacGregor, B.D., Robertson, D.S. Shucksmith, M. (eds) *Rural housing in Scotland, recent research and policy*, Aberdeen, pp. 167–182.

Folkesdotter, Gärd (1989) 'Public policy, landowners' actions and the pattern of physical development', in Reade, Eric (ed.) *Britain and Sweden: Current Issues in Local Government*, The National Swedish Institute for Building Research, research report SB:18, Gävle, Sweden, pp. 72–81, (distributor Almqvist & Wiksell International, Box 45150, S-104 30 Stockholm, Sweden).

Hanssen, Börje (1977, 1952) *Österlen: allmoge, köpstadsfolk och kultursammanhang i slutet av 1700-talet i sydöstra Skåne*, Stockholm, Gidlunds.

Jerkbrant, Conny, Malbert, Björn (1979) Fritidshus blir helårsbostad, Om mål och medel i samband med permanentning, BFR-rapport T 21. (In Swedish) (Holiday homes into permanent homes. Means and ends in connection with permanent habitation.)

Källtorp, Ove (1978) *Transformation of social structure in peripheral village communities*, Umeå (dissertation).

Marklund, Staffan (1975) *Living conditions and social policy in rural change*, Umeå (dissertation).

Matsson, Ing-Britt (1979) Nybebyggelse i glesbygd i Eskilstuna kommun. (In Swedish). (New building in rural areas. A pilot project on housing localization in rural areas of the Municipality of Eskilstuna.)

Nyström, Majvor (1982) Bosättning i byar och mindre orter i Arvidsjaur kommun under 1970-talet. (In Swedish). (Settlement in villages and small localities in the Municipality of Arvidsjaur during the 1970s.)

Rundblad, Bengt (1951) *Forestville*, Uppsala University.

Seyler, Hans (1983) *Hur bonden blev lönearbetare: industrisamhället och den svenska bondeklassens omvandling*, Uppsala (dissertation) (Summary in English).

Stahre, Ulf, Wretblad, Leif (1972) Flyttning till landsbygden, en studie i två regioner. (In Swedish). (Migration to the countryside. A study of two regions.)

Author Index

Subject Index

formal social ties 156, 159
Friends of the Earth 36, 43–4
friendship ties 156

Gavelborg 185, 188, 199
GIS (Geographical Information
　Systems) 137–8
Gillette, Wyoming, 152, 158–9,
'Gillette Syndrome' 152
global warming 8, 35, 68, 76
Gothenburg 190–1
Gotland 188
Great Depression 106–07
Great Grain Robbery 68
green 7, 53
　Green Party 20–21, 35, 42, 194
　Green Peace 36
　green movement 5, 6, 44
　(see also environmental movement)
　Green politics 35–9
greenhouse gases 8, 35, 68, 73, 77
greening 4, 7, 8, 10–13, 21, 23–4, 28, 37,
　44, 104
Green Peace 36
growth 154–5, 156–9, 167
Gulf War 56–9
　(see also Kuwait)

health 152
heavy metals 84, 95–6
Hindhead Common 3–4, 10–11
home 156
　mobile homes 156
Homes We Can Afford 169
housing 172, 185
　council housing
　(see Local Authority housing)
　holiday homes 186–7
　(see second homes)
　housing association 168, 171, 173,
　175
　housing market 167–8
　housing needs 168–9, 172, 175
　(see also local needs housing)
　housing policy 170–73, 185
　house prices 173
　housing stock 186
　Local Authority Housing 169, 171,
　174–5
　local housing schemes 173

low cost housing 170–3, 175
　rented housing 168, 171 , 186
　Rural Housing Trust 176
　starter homes 175
Housing Board (Sweden)
　County 193
　National 193
Housing Corporation (UK)168
Housing Investment Programme (UK)
　171

idyll 4, 6–7, 27, 37–8
　rural idyll 4, 6, 7, 27, 37–8
impact assistance 159
impact mitigation programmes 10, 151,
　159–63
indicators 168
　(see also social indicators)
informal social ties 156, 159
Iraq 56–9
　(see also Gulf War)
Ixhuatepec 43

kommunes 186, 188–200
Kuwait 43, 57–8
　(see also Gulf War)

Lake District 172
　(see also Windemere)
Lancaster County 140–7
land use 8, 67, 74–8
　land use control 139
　land use planning 135–6, 139–40,
　146–48, 185
leaching 82–4, 87–9, 90, 95
Left Party (Sweden) 194
Liberal Democrats (UK) 35
life satisfaction 159
　(see also community satisfaction)
lifestyles 162
Local Authority 32
　housing 169, 171, 174–5
Local Authority Planning (UK) 176
local needs housing 172, 175–181
Local Plans (UK) 175–82
　(see also plans)
lowland heath 3

MAFF (UK) 69, 71, 77
Major, John 44